LIFE SCIENCE LIBRARY

ENERGY

TIME
LIFE
BOOKS
®

LIFE SCIENCE LIBRARY

CONSULTING EDITORS
René Dubos
Henry Margenau
C. P. Snow

ENERGY

by Mitchell Wilson
and the Editors of **TIME-LIFE BOOKS**

TIME-LIFE BOOKS   NEW YORK

ABOUT THIS BOOK

Two KINDS OF STUFF fundamentally make up the universe: matter and energy. This volume explains the role that energy plays in the universe, describes the basic types of energy—including heat, light and electricity —and recounts how matter is transformed into energy by stars and by man-made nuclear devices.

Chapters of text in this book alternate with picture essays. The essays illustrate or complement the chapters, although each can be read independently. Thus Chapter 5 discusses chemical energy; Essay 5 describes how oil, a prime source of such energy, is obtained and put to use. Chapter 6 recounts the discovery of electricity, while the following essay tells how to build a miniature electric motor with paper clips, thumbtacks, two nails and a few feet of wire.

THE AUTHOR

MITCHELL WILSON is a writer of nonfiction and of novels, both of which reflect his earlier training as a physicist. As a student he did research on cosmic-ray mesons at Columbia University and wrote suspense stories as a hobby. After working several years as a research physicist, he turned to full-time writing. His pictorial history, *American Science and Invention*, is a classic work on U.S. technological development. His novels include *Live with Lightning* and *Meeting at a Far Meridian*.

THE CONSULTING EDITORS

RENÉ DUBOS, a member and professor of The Rockefeller University, is a distinguished microbiologist and experimental pathologist who was awarded the Arches of Science Award in 1966 and the Pulitzer Prize in 1969 for his book *So Human an Animal: How We Are Shaped by Surroundings and Events*. He is also the author of *Mirage of Health* and *Man Adapting* and coauthor of *Health and Disease* in this series.

HENRY MARGENAU is Eugene Higgins Professor of Physics and Natural Philosophy Emeritus at Yale, and an authority in spectroscopy and nuclear physics. He wrote *Open Vistas, The Nature of Physical Reality*, and is coauthor of *The Scientist* in this series.

C. P. SNOW has won an international audience for his novels, including *The New Men, The Affair* and *Corridors of Power*, which explore the effects of science on today's society.

ON THE COVER

The glowing candle and the sun (symbolized on the back cover) are both sources of heat and light, two of the six forms of energy that power the universe. But the sun pours forth six trillion quadrillion (6 followed by 27 zeros) calories of heat per minute to a candle's 1,600, and shines as if each square inch of its "surface" were covered with 300,000 candles.

CONTENTS

TIME-LIFE BOOKS

EDITOR
Maitland A. Edey
EXECUTIVE EDITOR
Jerry Korn
TEXT DIRECTOR   ART DIRECTOR
Martin Mann   Sheldon Cotler
CHIEF OF RESEARCH
Beatrice T. Dobie
PICTURE EDITOR
Robert G. Mason
Assistant Text Directors:
Ogden Tanner, Diana Hirsh
Assistant Art Director: Arnold C. Holeywell
Assistant Chief of Research: Martha T. Goolrick
Assistant Picture Editor: Melvin L. Scott

PUBLISHER
Walter C. Rohrer
General Manager: John D. McSweeney
Business Manager: John Steven Maxwell
Production Manager: Louis Bronzo

Sales Director: Joan D. Manley
Promotion Director: Beatrice K. Tolleris

LIFE SCIENCE LIBRARY

SERIES EDITOR: Martin Mann
Editorial staff for *Energy:*
Editor: George McCue
Assistants to the Editor: Simone Daro Gossner,
Harvey B. Loomis, John MacDonald
Designer: Arnold C. Holeywell
Associate Designer: Edwin Taylor
Staff Writers: Tom Alexander, James Cox,
Stephen Espie, Paul Trachtman
Chief Researcher: Sheila Osmundsen
Researchers: David Beckwith, Tim Carr,
Valentin Y.L. Chu, Joan C. Coates,
Beatrice M. Combs, Mollie Cooper,
Eleanor W. Engelmann, Elizabeth Evans,
Owen Fang, John L. Hochmann, Mary-Jo Kline,
Leonard Lipton, Robert R. McLaughlin,
Victor H. Waldrop
EDITORIAL PRODUCTION
Production Editor: Douglas B. Graham
Color Director: Robert L. Young
Assistant: James J. Cox
Copy Staff: Rosalind Stubenberg,
Suzanne Seixas, Florence Keith
Picture Department: Dolores A. Littles,
Barbara Simon
Traffic: Arthur A. Goldberger
Art Assistants: W. Lee Einhorn,
Charles Mikolaycak

The text for this book was written by Mitchell Wilson, the picture essays by the editorial staff. The following individuals and departments of Time Inc. were helpful in producing the book: Editorial Production, Robert W. Boyd Jr., Margaret T. Fischer; Editorial Reference, Peter Draz; Picture Collection, Doris O'Neil; Photographic Laboratory, George Karas; TIME-LIFE News Service, Murray J. Gart. Reprints staff: Paula Arno (editor), Alice Kantor (assistant editor).

INTRODUCTION

ENERGY has always been the key to man's greatest goals and to his dreams of a better world. It is sometimes said that the caveman started along the path to civilization after he had utilized the energy in fire for heat and light, and the energy in his body, through the club and the bow, for food and survival. In the centuries since then, man's quest for material well-being has been tied largely to the harnessing of various forms of energy—in coal, in petroleum, in electricity. In modern times, man has developed increasingly complex and effective means of tapping energy for more difficult goals. Today, the quest for the moon is made possible by the harnessing of chemical energy for the rockets at Cape Kennedy; tomorrow the exploration of the planets will depend on harnessing the energy in the nucleus of the atom.

But what, precisely, *is* energy? It is not something you can always detect with the senses. If a physicist wanted to describe an apple to someone who had never seen one, he might simply put a piece of the fruit on a table and let it be felt, smelled, tasted. But energy cannot simply be put on a table, for, as the text and the pictures in this book clearly reveal, energy can appear in many forms. It can appear as the energy of motion, or kinetic energy. It can appear in the form of heat and light. It can appear on an atomic or molecular scale as chemical energy. It can appear in the flow of electrical current. On a nuclear scale it can appear in one of the most fearsome forms—as nuclear energy. It can even appear in the form of an apple, as it did (so the story goes) to Sir Isaac Newton, who was led to the discovery of gravitation when he was struck by an apple that had fallen from a tree. The apple in falling released potential energy.

If the mastery of energy accounts for the rise of civilization, it may also lead to mankind's downfall. With ever-increasing energy at our command, we are able not only to better our daily lives but, unfortunately, to wage war on a more efficient and grander scale as well. Nuclear energy, whose promise is so bright for the peaceful future, could well be the source of the world's destruction. If we and our children, and our children's children, are to avoid this, it is imperative that we understand ourselves and our surroundings. There is no better starting place than to investigate the nature of energy.

GLENN T. SEABORG
Chairman, Atomic Energy Commission

1

The Prime Mover
of the
Universe

IN THE LANGUAGE with which we label the world around us, we confidently take for granted the meaning of "energy." In daily life, the word is highly evocative. It suggests motion, vitality, strength. We think of a "man with energy" as a man to admire. We are told that food with "high energy content" ought to be part of our daily diet. Petroleum companies splash the countryside with billboards advertising "high energy fuel." The word has charged the modern world with a new attitude toward life. Yet what does "energy" really mean? In its popular sense, it offers the promise of achievement: the energetic man is one who lives with verve; the energetic gasoline speeds our car farther and faster. Energy—to people who covet it—is tantamount to power.

Indeed, modern man has no difficulty in picturing energy and matter as the two faces of the universe. Matter and energy, the two go dancing off together to form our cosmos—matter the substance, energy the mover of the substance. But this dualism is a very sophisticated idea, and the concept of energy itself is a relative newcomer in the edifice of knowledge. Unseen and untouched, energy can only be imagined in the mind of man. How it came to be conceived in all its complexity and how it came to be put to work in our everyday lives constitute one of the greatest detective stories in the history of science.

Matter has always been a much easier notion for man to grasp. Matter is stuff; it has weight and occupies space; it can be seen, smelled, felt. It is one thing to see a stone hurtling toward you and to feel the bruise when it hits. But how much more difficult it is to imagine that there is an intangible quality in that moving stone that seems to vanish as soon as it reaches the ground again. Yet it was in thinking about moving objects that man first began to evolve his concept of energy—a concept that would ultimately regard energy as the all-embracing power of the universe.

The ancient Greeks, who wondered about all things, were certain that heavy bodies fell to the ground because they were motivated by some inner desire to "seek their places"; but this notion never led them into any important scientific examination of falling bodies. Aristotle postulated an "Unmoved Mover" slaving endlessly to keep the planets in motion, and for centuries after his time it was always assumed that every motion required a continual force to maintain it. Arrows and cannon balls, once fired, were kept in horizontal motion by the aid of the air that pressed in behind them to speed them to their destructive end. For Aristotle believed that a flying object compressed the air it moved through, causing that air to rush to the rear of the object and supply it with extra force.

These ideas were to be destroyed by that dedicated foe of erroneous Aristotelian ideas, Galileo Galilei. In fact, the true study of energy—

THE JOY OF ENERGY
Arms and legs flailing, the seven exuberant children on the opposite page (count the heads carefully) are the embodiment of energy as they noisily swoop on the cooling waters of New York's Long Island Sound. Energy appears in countless forms everywhere around us all the time, but nowhere does it seem so obviously abundant as in the tireless animation of a child.

indeed of all of modern physical science—was begun in the fertile mind of this 16th Century Italian genius. Galileo, the legend goes, made his first recorded observation of physical phenomena in 1583 at the age of 19, when he was distracted from his prayers in the cathedral at Pisa by the rhythmic swinging of a lamp suspended on a long chain. He noticed that while the arc of movement back and forth grew steadily shorter and shorter, the time the lamp took to go from one side to the other remained *constant*. The pocket watch not having been invented, Galileo simply counted the number of his own pulse beats during each swing.

Using string and various simple weights, Galileo went on to make several crude pendulums, and carefully studied their action. He noted that each time a pendulum swings upward it goes very nearly as high as the point from which it had previously swung downward. Thus, Galileo could state with assurance that "in general every momentum acquired by fall through an arc [of a pendulum] is equal to that which can lift the same body through the same arc."

A feeling for falling

Fascinated by the promises he found in falling bodies, Galileo attacked another generally accepted theory of the Aristotelians, who had arbitrarily stated that bodies will fall at speeds dependent upon their weights. According to the possibly apocryphal story, never written down in his own lifetime, Galileo pushed a 100-pound iron cannon ball and a one-pound ball off the top level of the 180-foot tower of Pisa. Supposedly they fell together and together hit the ground. Whether the event ever occurred is unimportant. The fact is that Galileo definitely did perform more careful experiments from which he deduced that all falling bodies fall at exactly the same rate if the effects of air resistance are discounted. Galileo's results were to stimulate many others in the study of "mechanics," the science that led to man's present understanding of energy.

The investigation began to take shape with mathematicians. In the 17th Century, men like René Descartes, Isaac Newton and Gottfried Wilhelm von Leibniz sought to refine the familiar idea of force, which we today commonly call push or pull. Observing that force acted on objects in a way that put the objects into motion, they initially tried to define force in terms of the amount of motion it produced. They faced questions like these: How could one *measure* the effect of a force? How could one *compare* the effects of two different forces?

Leibniz, in his attempt to work out some yardstick for the measurement of force, turned to Galileo's experiments with falling bodies. The Italian had found that all objects fall at the same speed no matter how big or how heavy they may be. However, Leibniz realized that an object weighing a ton would do a lot more damage when it hit the ground than

ENERGY AT THE PLAYGROUND

A child on a playground swing illustrates the difference between potential and kinetic energy. At A, that point of momentary motionlessness just before the downward plunge, she has only potential energy. As she starts down she develops kinetic energy. Halfway through the cycle, at B, her energy becomes completely kinetic, then gradually changes back to potential as the swing rises again. Because of friction the cycle does not continue indefinitely—pumping is a requisite of the ride.

one weighing an ounce, even if they both arrived at the same time. Here was a way to measure force: simply figure out a way to measure how big an impact an object will make. It is perfectly obvious, Leibniz said, that the impact depends on two things: how much the object weighs and how far it falls. This is a common-sense observation; everyone knows that a brick dropped from a foot does a lot less damage than one dropped from a hundred feet.

But suppose you are not interested in the force created by a *falling* object. Suppose the object you are interested in is *rising* into the air, like a thrown ball, or *rolling* along the level, like a bowling ball. Where does height fit into such a measurement? Leibniz realized that it was not really the height that was important. It was how fast an object was falling—which, of course, also happens to be directly related to the height from which it falls. The farther it falls, the faster it goes. Leibniz modified his formula to say that the measurement of force depended on the weight of an object *and* how fast it was going when it was stopped.

Leibniz went on to invent a name for the impact. He called it the *vis viva*, meaning living force. It was the quality within the object which enabled it to do damage to yet another object. The formula that Leibniz used to measure *vis viva* is the same one that modern physicists use to measure "kinetic energy," the energy of motion. What Leibniz had done, although he did not know it, was to work out a mathematical description of kinetic energy.

At the same time Leibniz was studying the properties of moving bodies in Germany, the Dutch mathematician Christian Huygens was pursuing another related line of inquiry. Huygens spent tedious hours studying what happened when two moving objects collided. In 1699, the results of his meticulous observations were published, declaring that in a collision such as might take place between two perfectly hard billiard balls, the sum of the *vis viva* in each of the balls is the same before and after impact. One ball might be slowed by the collision but the other would be speeded up. Therefore the sum of the two *vis vivas* would always be the same.

An old law amended

Today, by substituting the phrase "kinetic energy" for *vis viva*, we can see that Huygens' observation means that the kinetic energy is conserved when two objects collide: i.e., while it may be *changed*, none of it is *lost*. Here in Huygens' 17th Century observation is the beginning of a fundamental concept of modern physics: the Law of the Conservation of Energy, formulated in the late 1840s, which states simply that energy in the universe can neither be created nor destroyed. In the last 100 years, this law has been extended from its original application in the

CONSERVING ENERGY, WHATEVER THE GAME

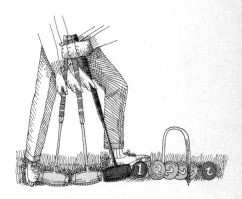

A PAIR OF ENERGETIC SPORTS

Energy can be changed in form, but cannot be created or destroyed; this is the basic law of the conservation of energy. For example, the croquet player, using his foot, positions his ball, 1, against an opponent's ball, 2, and then swings his mallet and transmits energy through ball 1 to ball 2, which rockets off. The pool shark's cue has the same effect on the cue ball and the stacked balls. In each case, measurements would show that the total energy of the moving croquet or pool balls equals that imparted by the cue stick or mallet, allowing for some heat energy loss to friction.

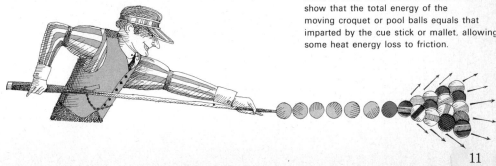

study of kinetic energy to cover all the other forms in which energy manifests itself. Only in recent years—with the discovery that matter could be actually turned into energy and energy back into matter—has the law had to be amended. But for all forms of energy in everyday life, it is as precise and as applicable today as it was in 1699.

Near the beginning of the 19th Century, after the concept of *vis viva* had been accepted for more than 100 years, a subtle idea suddenly occurred to a French military strategist named L.N.M. Carnot (whose son, Sadi, was later to make an equally vital contribution to the study of heat energy). Carnot realized that a weight raised to an elevated position possessed energy simply because it was in a position to fall and thereby generate kinetic energy. Carnot called this capacity "latent" *vis viva*, an accurate precursor of another modern notion—kinetic energy's best-known partner, "potential energy."

Carnot identified latent *vis viva* in 1803. Four years later, in 1807, the word "energy" first entered the technical vocabulary of science. A word which in Greek originally meant "work," "energy" was proposed to describe many of the same phenomena originally attributed to *vis viva*. The suggestion was made by a remarkable English physician and physicist, Thomas Young, who at the age of 19 had begun the study of medicine, and at 28 had been named Professor of Natural Philosophy in the Royal Institution of London. Young was described as "one of the most clear-sighted men who have ever lived," his admirer adding that it was Young's misfortune to have been "too greatly superior in sagacity to his contemporaries." One of his ideas, which lay unnoticed in the archives of science for decades, was the perceptive definition of energy as the ability to do work. It lies at the heart of any understanding of energy.

A job of definition

In general, as it is now commonly understood, "work" means the application of effort to accomplish a task; in the broadest terms, any physical exertion can be described as work. When a strong man in the circus stands in the center of a spotlight and, to the roll of drums, lifts a bar bell weighing a quarter of a ton, he is—for all the fanfare—simply performing work. Yet something as seemingly negligible as the attraction of a common household pin to a tiny magnet is evidence of physical effort—the magnet is also performing work.

In the precise meaning, work implies the application of some kind of force, and the scientific concept embodies the idea in the most specific form possible: work is defined as "the application of a force through a distance." It is a force of a given number of pounds, ounces or tons, which is lifting, pushing or pulling an object through a given number of inches, feet or miles. In a sense, work is *realized* energy which may be applied in limitless ways, for work covers such disparate activities as the building of the ancient pyramids, the creation of atomic nuclei and the formation of the stars. The rate at which work is performed is called "power" and machines of all kinds, therefore, are realistically described in terms of their "power-output"—the relation between power and work being similar to that between speed and distance.

Energy—realized in work—manifests itself in many guises, not all of them equally apparent to the layman. The many names they bear today are a far cry from the relatively simple notion of *mechanical* energy as Thomas Young first defined it more than 150 years ago. Now we speak of at least five other major forms of energy—*heat* and *light* together with *chemical, electrical* and *nuclear* energy. Intricately interrelated, all of them are involved in that familiar work horse of energy, the steam-driven railroad train.

Mechanical energy, in the form of moving pistons, drives the wheels of the locomotive. Part of that driving motion powers generators under each car which create *electrical energy* that gives *heat* and *light* to the passengers. Surplus electricity is fed back into storage batteries where it is converted into *chemical energy.* When the train stops, the storage batteries then reverse the process and take over the light and heating job. The mechanical energy of the locomotive is supplied by the heat of the steam and that heat in turn is furnished by the chemical energy of coal. Coal itself is the fossilized remains of plants that lived millions of years ago and drew their sustenance from the light of the sun. And the sun, scientists have now discovered, derives its power from *nuclear energy* released by atomic reactions going on in its interior.

Depending upon their particular orientation, physicists sometimes classify forms of energy into different groupings from the six that are described in the foregoing example of the railroad train. The groups may be as few as four or as many as 20, and they may bear different names. Nevertheless, for the purposes of this book, energy will be considered according to the six major forms which most closely follow traditional usage.

Of the six, *mechanical energy* is perhaps the most familiar. It is, as this chapter has revealed, simply the energy of a moving object. It is the moving force behind all machinery. The churning pistons of a steam engine or a gasoline engine have mechanical energy. They do work by making wheels go around. It also appears in very simple guises. A hammer on its smashing descent toward a nail has mechanical energy and it will drive a nail a distance into the wood. Even a rock flying through the air has mechanical energy. The work it does may be destructive, but it almost certainly will move something—if only a little dirt—before it comes to rest.

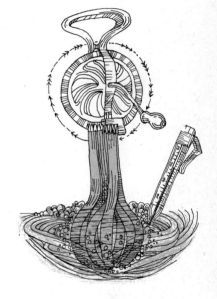

HEATING AN EGG BY BEATING
With only muscles and an eggbeater, a housewife simulates the experiments by which James Joule determined the mechanical equivalent of heat. Best known of his devices was a falling weight which turned a paddlewheel in water, heating the liquid by friction. By this and other experiments, he found that 772 foot-pounds of work raised the temperature of one pound of water 1° F. The housewife cannot verify today's accurate figure, 778 foot-pounds, but she can whip up a perceptible increase in the egg's temperature.

The physicist generally thinks of two distinct aspects of mechanical energy. When an object is actually moving, he would say it has *kinetic energy*. The phrase comes from *kinema*, the Greek word for "motion," which has also inspired our modern word "cinema" (that is, *motion* pictures) and "kinescope" (a motion picture made of a television program).

When an automobile rolls down a hill it obviously has kinetic energy. But what about the same car parked at the top of the hill with its brakes on? The physicist recognizes that such a car would have mechanical energy stored up in it by virtue of its position on the hill. If the brakes were released, it would roll down and might do a great deal of undesirable work—damage, that is—at the bottom of the hill. Thus, when mechanical energy is stored, it is called *potential energy*. In classical physics, kinetic and potential energy are the two faces of mechanical energy. However, in modern terminology, with its greater number of forms of energy, potential is often used to describe *any* kind of latent or stored energy.

Putting gravity to work

Potential energy is often created by gravity. Any object that is lifted from the ground contains it. As soon as the object is freed from restraints, gravity will pull it down and work will result from its descent. The water that is stored behind a dam is such a reservoir of potential energy. As it runs through the dam, it passes through turbines and turns electric generators. But not all potential energy depends upon gravity. The wound spring in a clock, the taut string of an archer's bow, the stretched strand of a rubber band all contain stored energy and will do work when they are released.

Heat is the second of the six major energy forms. If the pistons of a steam engine make the wheels go around, it is the heat of the steam generated by a furnace filled with burning coal that makes the pistons move. Similarly, it is the heat of exploding gases in the cylinder blocks that make a gasoline engine operate.

Light, or more properly *radiant energy*, is the puniest of the energy forms we witness, the hardest one for us to perceive at work. Yet it floods the universe in such quantities, pouring from all the stars such as our sun, that its cumulative effects are awesome. Here on earth, all green plants find their sustenance in the energy of light, and of course all animal life, including man, ultimately depends on plants for food. In addition to light, radio waves, X-rays, infrared and ultraviolet waves are all invisible forms of radiant energy which man has put to work. Gamma radiation, a product of fallout and other radioactivity, is a form of radiant energy whose work is so deadly that man is forced to take extraordinary precautions to shield himself against it.

HOW BIG IS AN ERG?

Scientists use the erg to measure the energy levels of various phenomena *(below)*. Technically, it is the energy expended when a force of one dyne is exerted through a distance of one centimeter. A dyne is the force necessary to accelerate a gram one centimeter per second per second. An erg, therefore, is very small. A 50-cent piece slipping from a man's pocket, for example, develops one million ergs of energy by the time it falls three feet to the ground.

A WORK SCALE: CRICKETS, QUAKES AND COSMIC CHAOS

Each of the events on the scale at right involves a certain amount of energy, measurable in ergs *(above)*. The arrows show approximate values. To read these values on the logarithmic scale used here, add as many zeros to the numeral as are indicated by the small, raised figures. For example, 10^2 equals 100 ergs (one plus two zeros) and 10^{10} equals 10 billion ergs. A minus sign denotes a fraction, so that 10^{-2} is 1/100 of an erg. Energies of 10^{64} ergs—far transcending this scale—are emitted by celestial objects called quasars.

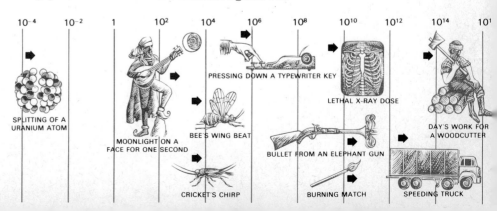

10^{-4} 10^{-2} 1 10^2 10^4 10^6 10^8 10^{10} 10^{12} 10^{14} 10^1

PRESSING DOWN A TYPEWRITER KEY

LETHAL X-RAY DOSE

SPLITTING OF A URANIUM ATOM

BEE'S WING BEAT

DAY'S WORK FOR A WOODCUTTER

MOONLIGHT ON A FACE FOR ONE SECOND

BULLET FROM AN ELEPHANT GUN

CRICKET'S CHIRP

BURNING MATCH

SPEEDING TRUCK

Chemical energy is the energy of food and fuels or, more precisely, the energy tied up in chemical molecules. With three good meals a day, a man can do a lot of work. And the energy of coal, wood, oil and gas—released in the form of heat—can run engines and keep us warm.

Electrical energy is the energy associated with magnets, electric currents and combinations of the two. Electricity manages to do its work with less fuss than any of the other forms of energy. Enough current to turn a five-horsepower motor or to heat a five-room house can, for example, spew endlessly out of a copper wire half as thick as a lead pencil.

Nuclear energy is the latest and the most dangerous of the energy forms which man has identified. As its name suggests, it is the energy from the nucleus of the atom, from the forces that hold that tiniest speck of matter together. Its first use was as an agent of destruction. Responsible for the uncontrolled explosions of A-bombs and H-bombs, it can release heat and mechanical energy capable of burning and pulverizing the earth for miles around. However, it is possible to release this energy slowly as heat which can be harnessed, like the energy from ordinary coal to generate steam, for peaceful purposes.

These brief definitions are reminders of the complex interrelationships of the various energy forms. The railroad train mentioned earlier is but one of many examples familiar to everyone. Consider the complexity of yet another. The water of lakes and oceans is evaporated into the atmosphere by heat produced by the radiant energy of the sun. The vapor collects as clouds, then falls as rain high in the mountains. Flowing downhill it turns the generators of an electric plant and the resulting current may flow through a wire to light a bulb, heat a house or charge a chemical storage battery.

A totally changeable nature

This interchangeability among its various forms is one of the most important properties of energy. Physicists can imagine *no* exception to the statement that any form of energy can ultimately be converted into any other. Sometimes the conversions seem a little awkward and roundabout. For example, we do not ordinarily try to change mechanical into heat energy directly. Yet it can be done—the friction of two sticks rubbing together is enough to start a fire. Similarly man's attempts to convert heat directly into electricity have so far proved impractical. Instead heat is used to run a turbine, and the mechanical energy of the turbine spins an electric generator. Because the intervening mechanical step is inefficient, engineers are seeking breakthroughs in technology that will convert heat *directly* into electricity on a large scale. Devices to do this already exist but only on a laboratory scale. Light offers another thorny problem in conversion. Although a limitless amount of radiant

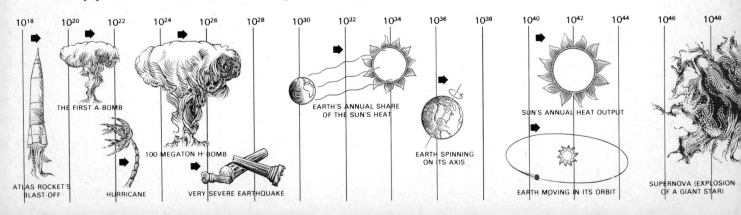

10^{18} 10^{20} 10^{22} 10^{24} 10^{26} 10^{28} 10^{30} 10^{32} 10^{34} 10^{36} 10^{38} 10^{40} 10^{42} 10^{44} 10^{46} 10^{48}

THE FIRST A-BOMB

100-MEGATON H-BOMB

EARTH'S ANNUAL SHARE OF THE SUN'S HEAT

SUN'S ANNUAL HEAT OUTPUT

EARTH SPINNING ON ITS AXIS

ATLAS ROCKET'S BLAST-OFF

HURRICANE

VERY SEVERE EARTHQUAKE

EARTH MOVING IN ITS ORBIT

SUPERNOVA (EXPLOSION OF A GIANT STAR)

energy falls on earth every day and is wasted, man has no truly efficient way to capture this energy for work. Only the green plants of the earth are able to do it on any large scale—although promising man-made devices to utilize solar energy are now coming into use.

Perhaps the most difficult of all the transformations is that from any other form of energy to nuclear energy. It does occur, but generally the nuclear physicist is the only one who witnesses the transformations. For example, in a frequently performed laboratory experiment, light can be observed turning back into the substance of the atom. That one transformation is enough to satisfy a physicist. All other forms of energy can be turned into light and all of them conceivably could eventually be put into a nuclear form.

Today's engineers deal with these complex energy transformations as if by second nature. They can tell to a few calories or watts just how much energy they will need to do a job and the form of energy that will do it best and cheapest. Yet this familiarity with energy is based on less than 200 years of experience—virtually all of it gained since Thomas Young first defined the word in 1807.

The remaining chapters of this book will in part recall how the six forms of energy were identified through the years. The narratives begin in Chapter 2 with the story of heat, a masterpiece of sleuthing, and end with man's current search for new sources of energy.

Energy in Nature: Beautiful and Boundless

Man lives in an ocean of energy. Around him at all times nature is doing work, expending energy in such endless quantities that man can tap only a fraction of it. The falling water of rivers could yield enough hydroelectric power to meet 80 per cent of man's total energy consumption, though he uses it for only 1 or 2 per cent. If the winds were tethered, they could turn out twice as much electricity as water power now does. The tides' surge, if put to use, could provide half our energy needs. The most colossal dynamo of all is the sun, an unimaginably vast powerhouse which directly or indirectly affects everything on earth. If all the world's fuels were gathered in one place and burned at a rate to match the sun's fierce output, they would be consumed in four days. On the following pages are examples of nature's raw power; the final photographic essay in this book *(pages 176-191)* shows some of the ways man hopes to apply this power to future needs.

CELESTIAL POWER PLANT
The sun, seen here just before setting, is an atomic furnace that turns mass into energy. Every second it converts 657 million tons of hydrogen into 653 million tons of helium. The missing four million tons of mass are discharged into space as energy. The earth receives only one two-billionths of this. But in one year this would be enough to melt 114 feet of ice over its entire surface.

WIND
**Blowing Hot or Cold,
a Capricious Bearer
of Mixed Blessings**

The earth's atmosphere acts as a giant heat engine. The sun's rays, stronger near the equator than in the polar regions, cause tropical air to warm and rise while cooler polar air moves in to replace it. This flow is constantly disturbed by the rotation of the earth and local atmospheric conditions. The result is wind. These interacting forces can create a gentle zephyr or can spawn the blasts of an Arctic gale or the appalling, concentrated fury of a 500-mile-an-hour tornado like the one above. Though unpredictable and fickle, wind has nevertheless always been an important

source of energy to man. For centuries it has moved sailing ships, pumped water and milled grain. In the future, windmills may be an important source of electrical power. Even modern airplanes get a boost from the wind: in the jet stream that blows a steady 200 mph—30,000 feet up.

A DUST CLOUD OF DESTRUCTION
A tornado, one of the most destructive forces known, touches earth at Scotts Bluff, Nebraska. Winds in tornadoes, whirling about a partial vacuum, can lift a whole building or drive a blade of grass into a tree. About 150 a year hit the U.S., mostly in the South and Midwest.

PONDEROUS ICE POWER
With inexorable power, the Athabaska glacier in Alberta, Canada, seven miles long and three quarters of a mile wide, grinds a channel as it crawls between Mount Athabaska, left, and Mount Kitchener. Most glaciers travel only a few feet or even inches a day, though movements up to 150 feet per day have been recorded.

ROARING WATER POWER
The Zambesi River flows at the rate of 25 million gallons a minute over Africa's Victoria Falls. This mile-wide cataract on the border between Northern and Southern Rhodesia is 355 feet high, as compared with Niagara's 167 feet. Twenty-five million gallons of water falling 355 feet is equivalent to two million horsepower.

WATER

**Flowing and Grinding,
a Force That
Shapes the Earth**

About a third of the sun's energy reaching the earth goes into a project of staggering proportions of immense consequence to man. Every year it evaporates and lifts 100,000 cubic miles of moisture from the seas, rivers, lakes and streams. For example, the Mediterranean Sea loses more water through evaporation than is replaced by all its tributaries, and a strong flow from the Atlantic is needed to fill the void. Much of the moisture falls in the ocean, but a third hits the land as rain, snow, sleet, hail and dew. This helps form the rivers, streams and glaciers that have reshaped the earth and provided man with a valuable source of power. The overwhelming strength of moving water is shown by the estimate that three billion tons of rock are carried into the ocean every year by the earth's streams. Hydropower is the source of one fifth of the electricity produced in the U.S., and at that we are using less than 30 per cent of the hydroelectric potential of 80 million horsepower. As for glaciers, the terrain of the whole northern half of the U.S. bears witness to their monumental grinding power, as do the peaks of the Alps or the fjords of Norway. The scars left by the scourge of the ice ages are the features of the land today.

THE SEA

An Endless Supply
of Surging Power
and Unseen Treasure

A magnificent reservoir of energy churns in the oceans that cover 70.8 per cent of the earth. Most obvious, of course, is the rolling, heaving power of wind and tide. Waves, piled up by the wind, remorselessly gouge, rip and smash the shoreline, tearing it away here and building it up there. The tide, in its daily comings and goings, keeps countless billions of gallons of water in constant movement. Not only the vast oceans but also the continents themselves respond to the gravitational pull of the moon and the sun. The rise and fall of land and sea tides actually affects the shape of the earth.

But there is a great deal more energy in the ocean than meets the eye. Locked in sea water's molecules is an elemental source of prodigious energy: deuterium, the heavy hydrogen atom. The controlled fusion of deuterium—a goal which science is now pursuing—would convert the sea into a source which could supply energy at our present demand for a billion years. Still another indirect source of energy is the sea's vegetation. Some day microscopic algae, 100 pounds of it to an acre, may provide an endless if somewhat bizarre source of food for an overpopulated world.

SHAPERS OF THE SHORE
Waves surging in from the North Atlantic carve the rocky profile of Cape Wrath on Scotland's northwest coast. In heavy storms, engineers estimate, the force of breakers here is as high as three tons to a square foot. Wind and wave have sculptured the twin spires on Cathedral Rock offshore. Though storm-driven waves are mere surface movements compared to the tide, they are still powerful enough to hurl boulders into the air and smash houses to kindling.

A TOWER OF STEAM
Castle Geyser spouts in Yellowstone Park *(left)*, not far from famous Old Faithful. There have been no volcanoes in the area for thousands of years, but a great amount of earth heat is released in the park's 200 geysers—enough, it is estimated, to melt three tons of ice a second.

A MOUNTAIN OF FIRE
Molten lava bursts from Kapoho rift on the island of Hawaii during a spectacular 36-day eruption in 1960. Some jets of liquid magma being forced from the earth's depths were sent 1,700 feet in the air. So much lava poured out that the remaining pool may take a century to cool.

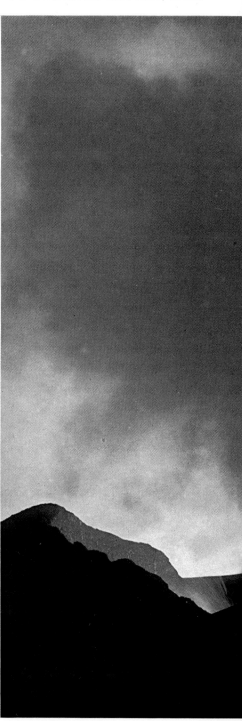

EARTH HEAT

Violent Eruptions That Tell of the Earth's Great Underground Caldron

Less than 40 miles under the earth's face begins a layer containing molten rock and gases, called magma, which seethes at temperatures up to 3,300°F. This molten mass is caused by tremendous subsurface pressures and heat, created by the energetic decay of radioactive substances. Occasionally this magma finds a fissure in the earth's crust and explodes in a volcanic eruption. In some areas hot gases from cooling magma heat underground water to such a point that it spouts up in geysers.

Some volcanologists point to evidence that in the last few billion years volcanoes may have produced all the gases in the atmosphere, all the water in the oceans and much of the land we live on. Only 500 volcanoes are known to have been active in recorded time, but some of their eruptions have dwarfed nuclear blasts. When Krakatoa exploded in the Pacific in 1883, a mountain vanished, walls cracked 100 miles away, tidal waves killed 36,000 people, and the sound was heard 3,000 miles.

LIGHTNING

Dazzling Flashes
That Recharge
a Leaking Planet

The earth is like a huge battery that always needs recharging. Wherever there are no clouds, electricity leaks from the negatively charged earth toward the positively charged upper atmosphere. This leakage is restored to the earth by thunderclouds, which pick up and store the lost electricity. In building up its own negative electric charge, a cloud induces a positive charge on the earth's surface beneath it. The attraction between opposite charges forces electrons from the cloud toward the earth, and lightning is formed, just as a spark bridges the points of a spark plug.

About 100 times every second the earth is struck by lightning, which streams down in belts 1,000 to 9,000 feet long. A single bolt may develop 3,750 million kilowatts, more than the combined peak capacity of every electricity plant in the U.S. But because the bolt lasts only a fraction of a second, its energy is worth only $7.50 at average home rates. About 75 per cent of the energy in lightning is dissipated as heat that raises the temperature of air in a lightning channel to about 27,000°F. This forces the air to expand quickly, like the gases in an explosion. The movement creates sound waves that can be heard as thunder for distances up to 18 miles.

GIANT SPARKS IN THE NIGHT
Night lightning crackles over New York, reflecting brightly off the clouds. These bolts did not all flash at once, but were recorded in a multiple exposure over several minutes. Since lightning heads for the nearest conductor, lightning rods protect buildings by taking the charge straight to the ground. Skyscrapers naturally attract lightning—New York's Empire State Building gets hit about 20 times a year—but steel frames protect them in the same way.

2

Getting Warm on the Trail of Heat

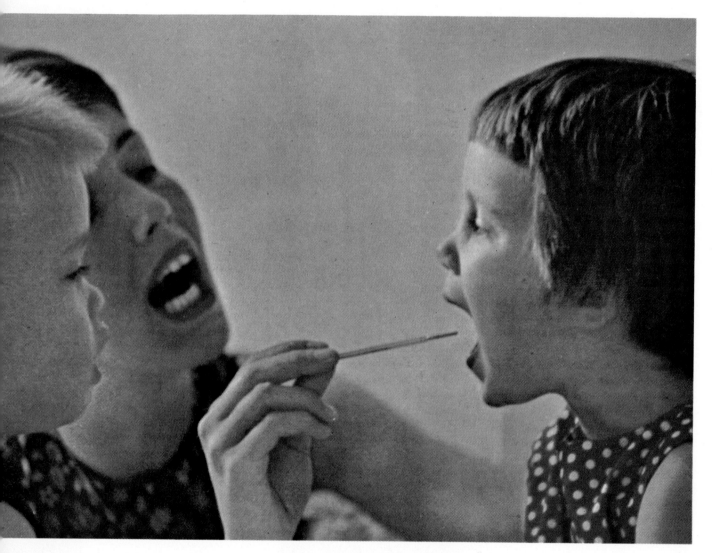

TAKING TEMPERATURE'S MEASURE
Finding out if a little girl has a fever is only one way in which the thermometer has served man since its invention by Galileo more than 350 years ago. In providing a yardstick for measuring heat's intensity, it made possible the 19th Century scientists' exploration and eventual understanding of the complex nature of heat.

"ABOUT TEN YEARS AGO," Daniel Gabriel Fahrenheit wrote in 1724, "I read in the 'History of Sciences' . . . that the celebrated [Guillaume] Amontons, using a thermometer of his own invention, had discovered that water boils at a fixed degree of heat. I was at once inflamed with a great desire to make for myself a thermometer of the same sort, so that I might with my own eyes perceive this beautiful phenomenon of nature and be convinced of the truth of the experiment."

To the comfort of everyone who worries about weather, Fahrenheit not only set out to duplicate the Amontons device, but his effort at improvement gave mankind the first reliable thermometer and made possible the systematic study of that form of energy known as heat.

Improbable as it seems in this day of dime store thermometers and hourly temperature reports, as recently as the 18th Century no way of accurately measuring degrees of hot and cold existed. No one could ever be sure of how much hotter one day was than another except by the use of his senses. A doctor, for example, had to gauge the extent of his patient's fever by feeling his forehead—just as good cooks used their experience with fires to judge the temperatures of ovens. Scientists, unable to thrive in the world of guesses, had been more frustrated than anyone else because, until Fahrenheit solved their problem, they had no satisfactory instrument with which to penetrate the mysteries of heat.

Primitive efforts to measure variations between hot and cold began at the turn of the 17th Century, when Galileo Galilei devised the thermoscope shown on the following page. "Galilei took a glass vessel about the size of a hen's egg, fitted to a tube the width of a straw and about two spans long," a student reported; "he heated the glass bulb in his hands and turned the glass upside down so that the tube [could be] dipped in water contained in another vessel. As soon as the bulb cooled down the water rose in the tube to the height of a span above the level in the vessel. This instrument he used to investigate degrees of heat and cold."

Little is known about Galileo's scale of measurement beyond a mention in his *Dialogues* of six, nine and 10 degrees of heat, but his device gave others a basis on which to build. Some investigators found that air pressure, changing with altitude and weather conditions, so affected the height of the gauge that it was seldom a dependable measure of temperature. Trying to avoid such inaccuracy, a French physician named Jean Rey inverted Galileo's arrangement by filling the bulb with water and the stem with air, then noting the expansion of the liquid as a gauge of temperature. The hands of a fever patient, Rey said, caused the water in the tube to fluctuate as a reflection of body heat.

Rey's instrument was inaccurate because evaporation of water from the open top of the stem affected the height of the water. A Tuscan grand duke, Ferdinand II, in an effort to construct a better device, led members

THE FIRST STEP TOWARD
TRACKING DOWN TEMPERATURE

A STAMP OF GENIUS
Issued in 1942, this Italian stamp commemorates the 300th anniversary of Galileo's death. It shows the inventor of the thermoscope *(below)* when he was studying at Arcetri, where he was forced to live in seclusion after being attacked by the Inquisition for his heretical scientific views.

BULB

GLASS TUBE

WATER

GALILEO'S BREAKTHROUGH
In 1593, according to one of his students, Galileo built his thermoscope, a device which, by registering changes in temperature, was the first thermometer of modern times. The original instrument is no longer in existence; this picture is from a model in the Museo de Storia della Scienza in Florence.

of his Accademia del Cimento in a series of experiments in their famous Florentine laboratories. Using spirits of wine—a crude alcohol—in place of water, they sealed the end of the tube and marked off degrees with beads of glass. Yet even the intense dedication of the academicians fell short of the mark.

What all the early instruments lacked was a clear scale of measurement with a high and low point based on some natural phenomena that always took place at the same temperature at constant atmospheric pressure. The Florentines had chosen the cold of winter and the heat of summer as their low and high points. By cold of winter they said they meant the temperature of snow or ice in the severest frost. For the heat of summer they used the temperature of a cow or a deer. Another early thermometrist took two equally shaky standards—the temperature of air during freezing as his low and the melting point of butter as his high.

It remained for Fahrenheit to choose a high and low, which if not perfect, at least were within a few degrees of being invariant. He picked for his low the temperature of a "freezing" mixture of ice, water and salt. For a high he settled on the body temperature of a healthy man, to which he arbitrarily assigned the number 96 (a conveniently divisible figure) instead of 98.6° as we measure it today. Using mercury as the expansive fluid he determined that pure ice melted at 32° and, in extending this new scale upwards, he could then calculate that water boiled at 212°. "Perhaps imperfect in many ways," Fahrenheit said modestly, "the result answered my prayer; and with great pleasure of mind I observed the truth of the thing."

A scale turned upside down

Fahrenheit had established standards of hot and cold which others were to improve. In 1730 R.A.F. de Réaumur proposed a scale still occasionally used in Europe which divides the interval between boiling and freezing into 80 degrees. Twelve years later Anders Celsius of Sweden suggested taking zero as the boiling point and 100° as freezing—a scale that was soon turned upside down with the boiling point at 100° and freezing at 0°. In making life less complicated for scientists everywhere, these refinements, which resulted in the scale now called the Centigrade, or Celsius, scale, also provided a simple measuring device for average citizens everywhere except the United States and some British Commonwealth nations, the only countries in the world which still cling to the more cumbersome Fahrenheit scale.

There is still one more temperature scale which is widely used by scientists, who have realized that if cold is simply the absence of heat, it follows that there ought to be a point when there is absolutely no heat. This understanding brought about the development in 1848 of the Kelvin scale, named in honor of the great English physicist, Lord Kelvin. The zero on the Kelvin scale is the equivalent of −459.7° F. and is the most frigid temperature conceivable in the universe.

The British chemist Sir Humphry Davy once cited the development of a new instrument as the most important impetus to the advancement of scientific theory, and there is little doubt that the thermometer has helped to open more new paths for scientific pioneers than any other tool. In this vanguard was a Scots chemist named Joseph Black, who was to become a mentor of James Watt, indirectly leading him to devise his steam engine. In experiments with Fahrenheit's thermometer, Black's first and most fundamental discovery was that heat and temperature are not the same thing. Viewed from the 20th Century, this discovery may seem less than world-shaking, yet none of Black's contemporaries had been able to establish a sharp distinction between the two.

Cooking an iron disk

In effect, Black showed what happens when an iron disk is set on one burner of a stove while a pan of water of equal size is placed on another. When for a period of 10 minutes the same amount of heat is given off by each burner, the iron becomes too hot to touch and the water remains lukewarm—equal heat has resulted in unequal temperatures. Black concluded that heat is obviously an amount of something, while temperature is the degree of hotness.

Black tested his theory on a number of substances and found that each one required a different amount of heat to raise its temperature one degree. He called this property of substances "the capacity for heat." Later scientists arbitrarily assigned the figure "one" as a measurement of the capacity for heat of water, and now the ability of other materials to soak up heat is compared to that figure and called "specific heat." This value is not a constant but varies somewhat with the temperature. Iron at room temperature has a specific heat of .107, which means it takes only about one tenth as much heat to raise the temperature of iron one degree as would be required to raise the same amount of water one degree. Strangely enough, the specific heat of nearly all the gases, metals and solids so far tested has proved to be less than that of water. Only two liquids have higher specific heat—ammonia at 1.125 and ether, which achieves a specific heat of 1.041 only after its temperature has been increased to 356° F. This means that water, compared with almost every other substance, is slow to show an increase or decrease in temperature.

Although the ability of water to retain heat is no surprise to anyone who ever has taken a hot-water bottle to bed and basked in its lingering warmth, few people appreciate the incomparably greater phenomenon by which the relatively high specific heat of water moderates the tem-

BIRTH OF THE BAROMETER
Evangelista Torricelli, a disciple of Galileo, invented the mercury barometer but died in 1647 before proving its value. A year later a Frenchman, Florin Périer, experimented with the device (above) on the slopes of Puy-de-Dôme in France's Auvergne Mountains. Taking measurements as he climbed, Périer saw that the column of mercury fell with increasing altitude, thus proving the barometer to be a yardstick of atmospheric pressure.

perature of the earth and makes most of it habitable. Because 73 per cent of the global surface is covered with water, tremendous quantities of heat from the sun are absorbed by the world's oceans and inland waters in the summer and slowly fed back to the atmosphere in winter. The moderating effect is felt in any part of the world where the temperatures vary throughout the year, but it is particularly noticeable along the coasts. Off Coney Island, for instance, the Atlantic Ocean seldom gets hotter than 70°F. in August, or colder than 55°F. in January. Coney Island itself thus tends to have moderate temperatures—cooler in summer and similarly warmer in winter than they might otherwise be. The lush orchards around the Great Lakes depend on this principle; trees and vines stay alive through the winter, while only a few miles north or south all but the hardiest plants are killed by the bitter northern cold.

The quest for what is hot

In his pioneering study of heat, Joseph Black used the thermometer to probe many phenomena that had previously defied understanding. To his predecessors it had seemed logical—as indeed it does today that a kettle of water kept on a stove would get hotter and hotter, and that in coming to a boil it should continue to increase in temperature until all the water boiled away. Dunking his new thermometer in his own hot pot, Black established what really happens: water ceases to get hotter after it has reached 212°F., but it still boils away.

Black also established that a mixture of ice and water remains at the same temperature—though heat may be lost or added—until it is transformed entirely into ice or into water. Thus he made it clear why deep snowbanks along a country road can withstand the sun even after the rest of the snowfall has long since melted away, as well as why the temperature of an iced drink stays at the melting point of ice as long as the smallest piece of ice remains.

In observing ice melting into water and water vaporizing into steam, Black recognized that heat was necessary for these changes in the physical state of water. His conclusion was that water in the form of ice stays solid at 32°F. because it lacks a sufficient amount of heat to change itself into a liquid. He further concluded that water never becomes hotter than 212°F. because at that temperature it completely utilizes all the heat that is available in the process of changing itself from a liquid into a gas. In the other process, when water changes from a liquid to a solid, Black hypothesized the presence of what he called "latent heat." In order for water to freeze, he reasoned, the latent heat has to be withdrawn—the phenomenon that is taking place when hot air is thrown out by a refrigerator in the process of cooling.

"My conjecture, when put into form, was to this purpose," Black

TAKING AN EARLY TEMPERATURE
Sanctorius, a 17th Century professor of medicine at Padua, was inspired by Galileo's thermoscope *(page 30)* and adapted it to make the first medical thermometer. As the patient breathed on the bulb *(above),* the air inside warmed up, expanded, and pushed the water down in the tube. Sanctorius measured variations in his patients' body heat on a rude scale using the heat of a candle flame and the cold of snow as its high and low extremes.

wrote. "I imagined that, during boiling, heat is absorbed by the water, and enters into the composition of the vapour produced from it, in the same manner as it is absorbed by ice in melting, and enters into the composition of the produced water."

Joseph Black was only one of the many talented European scientists who contributed to the growing knowledge about heat. In 1787 a Parisian physicist, Jacques Charles, established that all gases held at constant pressure will expand in proportion to the amount of heat applied. A similar conclusion was reached independently in 1802 by another French-man, Joseph Louis Gay-Lussac, and the resultant law of gas behavior is sometimes credited to one of them, sometimes to the other.

Since a hot gas expands, it becomes less dense and lighter than a cool-er one; therefore it tends to rise. This effect is familiar to anyone in a heated room who has ever felt cold air on his feet while the air around his head was perfectly comfortable. This is why hot air in going up a chimney creates a draft of cold air which rushes in to take its place. For the same reason, smoke rises from towering stacks instead of falling to the ground. Even more important, the expansion of gas is the under-lying principle of steam and gasoline engines.

The process is a simple one. When a hot gas like steam is introduced into a piston chamber its heat is so great that its pressure pushes the piston backward in the chamber, and this movement is harnessed to force a crankshaft to revolve, causing wheels to turn. The same energy of motion is produced when gasoline is exploded by spark plugs in auto-mobile piston chambers. Hot gases thus fired expand to push the pistons outward, empowering a car to move at any desired speed. Such devices, because they convert heat energy into mechanical energy, are called "heat engines."

Heat and the pendulum

Study of expansivity also showed that most liquids and solids—as well as all gases—expand with increased temperature, and that the amount of expansion for each degree of temperature increase depends upon the substance. For instance, because the thermal expansion of metal or plas-tic is larger than that of glass, housewives often run hot water over the metal covers of foods packed in jars, or on the plastic tops of nail polish bottles. This act of heating the covers causes the metal or plastic to ex-pand, loosening the grip on the container. By the same token, heat tends to make the metal pendulums of clocks grow longer and therefore grandfather clocks, unless corrected, will lose time in warm weather.

Expansion is of great technological importance because it frequently forces engineers to provide necessary allowances for many structural materials. A mile of railroad track expands as much as a full yard in

WHEN IS A THREE-MINUTE EGG NOT A THREE-MINUTE EGG?

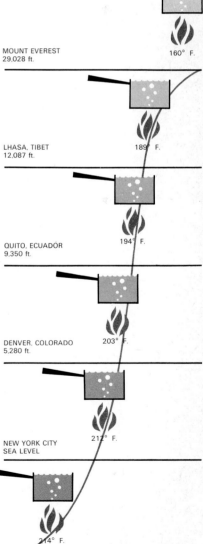

MOUNT EVEREST
29,028 ft.   160° F.

LHASA, TIBET
12,087 ft.   189° F.

QUITO, ECUADOR
9,350 ft.   194° F.

DENVER, COLORADO
5,280 ft.   203° F.

NEW YORK CITY
SEA LEVEL   212° F.

BOILING POINT

DEAD SEA
−1,292 ft.   214° F.

LOW PRESSURE IN A HIGH POT
Water boils when, during heating, the pressure of its escaping molecules equals that of the atmosphere. The higher one goes, the lower the atmospheric pressure —and the lower the temperature, therefore, at which water boils (right). Since this means they are receiving less heat even though the water is "at a boil," foods take longer to cook in high places. A three-minute egg on Everest is almost raw.

length in summer heat, and the cracks between sections of rail allow for this. So too a 1,000-foot metal bridge may change its length by seven or eight inches. Though few New Yorkers worry about it, summer heat causes the cables of the Brooklyn Bridge to sag—at the same time the roadbed is expanding—so that the road tends to buckle. The problem has been licked, however, by prescient engineers, who devised a telescopic center joint which allows for a play of about one foot.

Three strange phenomena—specific heat, latent heat, and the orderly expansion of heated gases and other substances—had been discovered in quick succession after the invention of the thermometer. To explain them scientists turned to an old concept which was later to be known as the theory of the caloric. The basis of this was the belief that heat was an invisible fluid called caloric and that when any substance was heated caloric flowed into it and when it cooled off caloric flowed out. After Black's discoveries, this basic idea was so refined and developed that it accounted conveniently for all the phenomena of heat known at the time.

Here were its essential postulates as set down in 1779:

Caloric is an elastic fluid whose particles repel one another.

Caloric particles are strongly attracted by the particles of other matter, and different kinds of matter attract caloric with different strength.

Caloric is indestructible and uncreatable.

Caloric can be either sensible or latent (i.e., either felt or stored), and in the latter state is combined "chemically" with particles of matter to change a solid to a liquid or a liquid to a vapor.

Caloric does not have weight.

Calorists caper on Easy Street

How well this theory worked is easy to see. That caloric particles were attracted by particles of other matter explained why things get hot. That they repelled each other explained why most things seemed to expand when full of caloric. Since different forms of matter can attract caloric with different strengths, different substances can absorb different quantities of heat, i.e., they have different specific heats. Latent heat was explained as the caloric combining chemically with the particles of matter and producing a new state of matter. Under this theory water was simply ice combined with caloric; steam was water combined with still more caloric. The necessity of including the statement that caloric was without weight came along only after opponents of the theory pointed out that if caloric actually existed, then an object should weigh more when it was hot than when it was cold. Try as they might, no difference could be detected, so the calorists simply revised their theory to say that caloric was weightless.

The theory offered in opposition to the caloric was never so pat and it

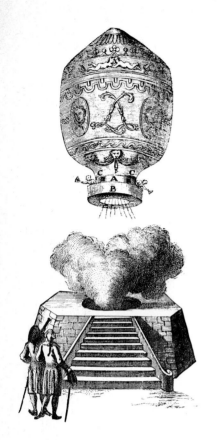

GOING UP IN SMOKE

This ornate balloon carried Pilâtre de Rozier and the Marquis d'Arlandes over Paris on November 21, 1783, in man's first flight. The balloon got its "lift" from the smoke of a wool-straw-coal fire, utilizing the principle that heated air, by expanding, weighs less than cold air. Once aloft, the balloon provided its own hot air—and a fire hazard—with a blaze in a brazier, A, which the aeronauts tended through portholes, C, from their gallery, B.

17TH CENTURY JET JALOPY

This four-wheeled carriage, powered by a jet of steam from a backward-pointing nozzle connected to a round boiler, was proposed as a practical illustration of Sir Isaac Newton's third law of motion, that action and reaction are equal in magnitude and opposite in direction. The machine was never built, but modern scientists say it could have worked if equipped with a nozzle narrow enough to develop sufficient pressure and with wheel ball bearings to keep friction low.

was long in evolving. As early as 1620 Sir Francis Bacon had said roundly, "Heat itself, its essence and quiddity, is motion and nothing else." The famous English physicist Robert Boyle expressed the same view, and his friend Robert Hooke had described heat as being "nothing else but a very brisk and vehement agitation of the parts of a body." In the 18th Century, John Locke had joined this growing chorus, and a half century or so later, at the height of caloric enthusiasm, the mode-of-motion view was adopted by a turncoat American, the redoubtable Benjamin Thompson, who had abandoned the colonies for England and then had joined the service of the Elector of Bavaria, rising rapidly to become a counsellor with the title of Count Rumford.

In a series of accurate experiments, Rumford showed that there was no change in the weight of liquid when heat was either subtracted or added. He determined, for example, that water neither gained nor lost any weight when it changed to or from its states of being liquid or solid. But though he was concerned with the weight effect of heat, his major contribution was the demonstration that motion which produced friction was the source of heat.

The count and the cannon

While supervising the boring of brass cannon for the Bavarian army, Rumford's attention was arrested by the very large amounts of heat produced during the boring. He knew that calorists attributed such heat to the squeezing out of caloric from any substance—in this case from the brass in the action of the drill. He asserted that if this theory were correct, there should be less caloric in the shavings than in the same weight of solid brass, because a great deal of heat had been evolved in the conversion. "But no such change had taken place," Rumford said. There had been no diminishment of specific heat in the hollowing process that had turned the cannon's center into a pile of shavings. He pointed out that "the portion of water into which the [hot] chips were put was not, to all appearances, heated either less or more than the other portion in which the slips of [equally hot solid] metal were put."

"What is Heat?" Rumford asked in a treatise he wrote about his experiments. "Is there any such thing as an *igneous fluid?* Is there *anything* that can with propriety be called *caloric?*"

His answer was negative. He contrived a water-filled box to fit around the tip of a cannon barrel and a blunt steel borer rammed into it. As the cannon slowly turned against the drill, friction heated up the brass, which in turn warmed the water around it. After two and a half hours of boring, the water boiled. Rumford later reported the astonishment of the bystanders at seeing water boil "without any fire."

He said that since the heat appeared to be inexhaustible, it "cannot

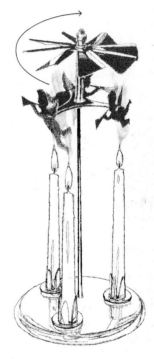

THREE CANDLE POWER

The Christmas decoration above shows one way in which heat accomplishes work. Heated by the candles, air expands and becomes less dense as its molecules get excited and move more rapidly. The air rises on convection currents, so called because they convey heat or cold from place to place. The moving, heated air pushes against the paddles of the device, which are slanted off the horizontal, and makes them rotate in the direction of the arrow.

possibly be *a material substance:* and it appears to me to be extremely difficult, if not quite impossible, to form any idea of any thing, capable of being excited and communicated, in the manner the Heat was excited and communicated in these Experiments, except it be MOTION." Motion, Rumford concluded, was the source of the heat.

Ice times ice equals heat

Rumford's cannon-boring observations were confirmed in independent experiments performed by Humphry Davy, who was to gain great fame as a lecturer in chemistry at the Royal Institution in London. Using machinery he devised, Davy produced friction between two metals in a vacuum and melted wax in the process, although the temperature of the wax was below freezing. He also is reputed to have melted ice on a bitter winter day by rubbing two pieces of ice together to demonstrate that the heat required to melt the ice was created by motion. Though his use of ice to create frictional heat may seem striking proof that heat is motion and not caloric, almost half a century was to elapse before the nature of heat was reinvestigated by J. Robert Mayer in Germany and James Prescott Joule in England.

It is to these two men that we are chiefly indebted for the ideas which lead to the modern concept of heat; and it is to their inspired thinking that we owe the modern scientific doctrine of the conservation of energy. Until that time, the concept of energy conservation was limited to purely mechanical transformations involving moving objects.

As an obscure German physician, Mayer for a time practiced medicine on the island of Java, where he observed that blood in the veins of his Javanese patients exhibited a bright red color usually found only in the highly oxygenated blood of the arteries. Reflecting on this in 1840, he concluded that in hot climates the body will require less oxidation to maintain body temperature than would be required in a cooler climate. This led him to his great hunch—that the energy of the world is constant. In his 1842 paper, "Remarks on the Forces of Inorganic Nature," he gave the general outline of his new theory, asserting that "force [the then prevailing term for energy] once in existence cannot be annihilated; it can only change its form."

Utilizing available experimental data on the heat required to maintain the temperature of expanding air, Mayer was able to contribute a very good estimate of how much mechanical work is equivalent to a given amount of heat even though he was lacking in both scientific education and opportunities for experimental work. Joule, on the other hand, contributed to the mechanical theory of heat and the concept of the conservation of energy on the basis of data assembled through careful scientific investigations.

COMPARING SPECIFIC HEATS

The specific heat of a substance is the heat needed to raise a certain volume of the substance a specific number of degrees in temperature. It is usually expressed in calories per gram per degree centigrade, as in the table below. Specific heat varies somewhat with the starting temperature of a material— the values below are those that apply at 60°F. The higher a material's specific heat the longer it takes to heat up, the more heat it holds and the longer it takes to cool down.

GOLD, LEAD, PLATINUM	0.03
TIN	0.05
SILVER	0.06
COPPER, BRONZE, BRASS	0.09
STEEL	0.11
GLASS	0.20
OXYGEN (GAS)	0.22
SUGAR	0.27
LEATHER	0.36
WOOD	0.42
RUBBER	0.45
BUTANE GAS (LIQUEFIED)	0.55
PARAFFIN	0.69
WATER	1.00
AMMONIA	1.12

Both Mayer and Joule had asserted that heat could be transformed into mechanical work, and mechanical work could be transformed into heat. Each independently had insisted that there exists a principle of nature which cannot, under any circumstances, be destroyed, but which can, under varying circumstances, be transformed. With heat and mechanical work as representative of this principle, both Mayer and Joule had calculated, from different data, the exact amount of work required to create an increment of heat.

Joule performed one experiment after another. He converted electrical and mechanical energy into heat in a variety of ways, such as electrical heating, mechanical stirring and the compression of gases. In one such experiment Joule devised an insulated container in which paddlewheels churned water. As a driving mechanism, he used slowly falling weights, like those of a grandfather clock, to calculate the potential energy expended in causing the paddles to turn. He arrived at his mechanical equivalent of heat by calculating how many pounds had to fall through how many feet to raise the temperature of a given volume of water a given number of degrees. After more than thirty years of trial and error, his final answer of 772 foot-pounds was remarkably close to the 778 foot-pounds of work we now know it takes to raise the temperature of one pound of water one degree Fahrenheit.

A happy balance for Mayer and Joule

Although in the United States and Britain Joule is generally credited with the discovery of the true nature of heat, in Europe the honor is frequently given to Mayer. But about 20 years after their work, John Tyndall, who later was to become superintendent of the Royal Institution, compared the two very fairly:

"Withdrawn from mechanical appliances, Mayer fell back upon reflection, selecting with marvelous sagacity, from existing physical data, the single result on which could be founded a calculation of the mechanical equivalent of heat. In the midst of mechanical appliances, Joule resorted to experiment, and laid the broad and firm foundation which has secured for the mechanical theory the acceptance it now enjoys. A great portion of Joule's time was occupied in actual manipulation; freed from this, Mayer had time to follow the theory into its most abstruse and impressive applications. With their places reversed . . . Joule might have become Mayer and Mayer might have become Joule."

Man has long known that work can be transformed into heat in an astonishing number of ways. It is produced when one rubs one's hands together on a cold winter day; a Boy Scout can make things hot when he rubs sticks together in an effort to light a fire. Even Plato, 24 centuries ago, had discovered that "heat and fire, which generate and sus-

THREE WAYS TO GET WARM: HOW HEAT GETS AROUND

HEAT BY CONDUCTION
The simplest method of heat transfer is by direct contact, or conduction. The rubber hot water bottle passes on warmth to comfort the distressed lady's aching stomach.

HEAT BY RADIATION
Although much heat escapes up the chimney, this gentleman can warm his backside by radiation—invisible infrared rays given off by the fire, coals and hot fireplace stones.

HEAT BY CONVECTION
The orange lines show convection currents, which are made up of warm, expanding air rising from the floor register to thaw out this shivering ice skater.

tain other things," as he said, "are themselves begotten by impact and friction." But it took Joule, building on foundations laid by Rumford and Davy, to demonstrate, experimentally, the ideas of Mayer and thereby make the theory of equivalence unimpeachable. Joule had cited Davy's melting of ice in below freezing surroundings as a good attack on the caloric theory. It not only countered possible arguments of the calorists that the heat was supplied by the surrounding atmosphere, but it also supported the doctrine of the immateriality of heat because the capacity of ice for heat is less than that of water, and therefore the ice could not have supplied the required caloric for melting. It was therefore with good reason that Davy drew the inference that "the immediate cause of the phenomena of heat is motion." By the latter half of the 19th Century, it had been established beyond much doubt that heat is not a separate substance or fluid, but is kinetic energy and occurs in a great variety of ways as a result of the motion of small particles of ordinary matter.

Once heat was shown to be a form of motion and thus a form of energy, it was subsequently realized that the expenditure of a fixed amount of work always gave rise to the production of the same amount of heat. The equivalence of work and heat has been embodied in the First Law of Thermodynamics—a significant advance in the direction of a unified description of our universe.

Men and Milestones of Measurement

In a world where the flick of a switch or the turn of a knob can make hard work easy, scientific units like horsepower and calorie, volt and watt, have become household words. But it was only about 150 years ago that scientists began measuring such things as the power of steam and, later, the voltage of an electric current. Such 18th and 19th Century inventions as the thermometer and the steam engine, the battery and the electric circuit, had created a sudden need for new measures. The pages that follow turn back to the origins of modern measurements, picturing the now quaint machines and instruments that were, in their day, milestones of man's progress. Pioneers like Volta, Watt and Fahrenheit—for whom new measures were named—personified a scientific spirit summed up by the great physicist Lord Kelvin: "When you can measure what you are speaking about and express it in numbers, you know something about it."

A MEASURED ASCENT
In 1804 the great French chemist Joseph Louis Gay-Lussac and a colleague ascended to 13,120 feet in a balloon (opposite), taking measurements of the gases in the upper air. Besides a full complement of barometers, thermometers and devices to measure electricity and magnetism, they also took along frogs, insects and birds in order to study their behavior at high altitudes.

RÉAUMUR'S OFFBEAT READINGS

Fahrenheit's mercury thermometers were first adopted by the Dutch and English. In France, however, R.A.F. de Réaumur (above), a naturalist and mathematician unfamiliar with Fahrenheit's work, considered mercury unsuitable because its slight reactions to temperature change were hard to measure. He built the unwieldy alcohol thermometers shown above, dividing the scale from the freezing to boiling points of water into 80 degrees. Réaumur's instruments were hopelessly inaccurate, but his 80-degree scale was perfected and is still used in Germany.

TEMPERATURE BY TURNS

The spiral thermometer shown above, made about 1657 by a Florentine glassblower, was so sensitive that a warm breath on the lower bulb would send alcohol rising through its coils.

HOT AND COLD FROG

Instead of a glass tube, the "frog thermometer" of the 1600s (below) had six hollow balls of different weights floating in alcohol. As the temperature rose, one ball after another sank.

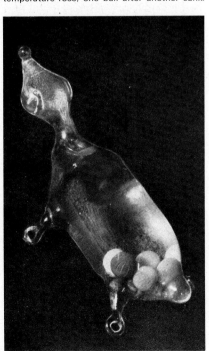

A Host of Gadgets for Gauging Hot and Cold

Galileo built the first temperature-measuring device about 1592, but it was more than 125 years before the German physicist Daniel Gabriel Fahrenheit came up with the first accurate one. In between the two came thermometers of all shapes and sizes. With a few exceptions (below, left), they were glass tubes in which liquids rose or fell as temperature changed.

The early instrument makers had their troubles: they did not agree on whether water, mercury or alcohol worked best; and their crude thermometers rarely recorded the same temperature in the same place. Furthermore, everyone seemed to have a different degree scale. By the 18th Century there were some 19 different scales in use, based on such "norms" as the melting point of butter and the coolness of earth in a Paris cellar.

The three in common use today—Fahrenheit, centigrade and Réaumur (below and opposite)—all use mercury and take the boiling and freezing points of water as the standards of reference. But the last word in thermal scales is that devised by Lord Kelvin, with which the ultimate extremes of cold and heat are measured.

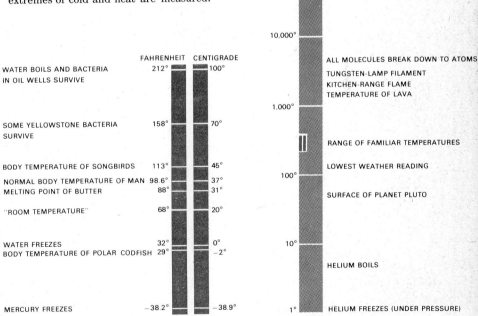

	FAHRENHEIT	CENTIGRADE
WATER BOILS AND BACTERIA IN OIL WELLS SURVIVE	212°	100°
SOME YELLOWSTONE BACTERIA SURVIVE	158°	70°
BODY TEMPERATURE OF SONGBIRDS	113°	45°
NORMAL BODY TEMPERATURE OF MAN	98.6°	37°
MELTING POINT OF BUTTER	88°	31°
"ROOM TEMPERATURE"	68°	20°
WATER FREEZES	32°	0°
BODY TEMPERATURE OF POLAR CODFISH	29°	−2°
MERCURY FREEZES	−38.2°	−38.9°

Kelvin scale:

- 10,000,000,000° — INTERIOR OF HOTTEST STARS
- 1,000,000,000°
- 100,000,000° — HYDROGEN BOMB
- 10,000,000° — SUN'S INTERIOR
- 1,000,000° — SUN'S CORONA
- — ATOMIC BOMB
- 100,000°
- 10,000°
- — ALL MOLECULES BREAK DOWN TO ATOMS
- — TUNGSTEN-LAMP FILAMENT
- — KITCHEN-RANGE FLAME
- — TEMPERATURE OF LAVA
- 1,000°
- — RANGE OF FAMILIAR TEMPERATURES
- — LOWEST WEATHER READING
- 100° — SURFACE OF PLANET PLUTO
- 10°
- — HELIUM BOILS
- 1° — HELIUM FREEZES (UNDER PRESSURE)

A DIFFERENCE OF DEGREE

Above are the Fahrenheit and centigrade scales shown side by side with the equivalent temperatures of various familiar phenomena, such as the boiling point of water: 100° on the centigrade scale and 212° on the Fahrenheit scale. Fahrenheit is the standard scale in most English-speaking countries; centigrade—officially labelled Celsius after its Swedish inventor—is in use almost everywhere else in the world.

SCALED FOR THE ULTIMATE

Lord Kelvin's absolute temperature scale is shown above. Knowing that a gas when cooled one degree from 0° to −1° C. loses 1/273 of its pressure. Kelvin reasoned that at −273° C. gas ought to have no pressure, and he called −273° C. absolute zero—a temperature which can never be reached. The orange bar on the Kelvin scale represents the familiar temperatures shown at left in degrees Fahrenheit and centigrade.

The Comforts of a Rumford Stove.

Counting Calories to Measure Heat

With the improvement of thermometers in the late 18th Century, scientists turned to experiments on the nature of heat. The Scotsman Joseph Black pointed out that temperature was a measure of heat's intensity, but not of the total amount of heat contained in an object. Scientists came to think of heat itself as a weightless fluid, named caloric, which passed unseen into and out of material bodies. Even the great French chemist Antoine Lavoisier thought of an object getting hot in terms of its soaking up caloric. Lavoisier took as his unit of heat measure the amount of heat that would raise the temperatures of a unit of water by one degree—which was the forerunner of today's calorie *(diagram opposite).*

The caloric theory, though it satisfied most scientists, was challenged by the remarkable Count Rumford, born Benjamin Thompson of Woburn, Massachusetts. Count Rumford held to an older idea—that heat somehow came from an inner motion of substances (now known to be the movement of molecules or atoms). In a famous experiment with a cannon boring machine *(opposite, top),* he showed that heat could not be a material substance because it could be produced in limitless amounts from friction alone. It was some 50 years before Rumford's evidence was fully accepted, but in the meantime he developed a stove and cooking utensils *(left)*—and ended up by marrying the widow of Lavoisier.

A COUNT AND HIS KITCHENWARE
This caricature published in 1800 shows Count Rumford warming himself before a Rumford stove, over which sit two cooking pots of his design. Rumford, a Tory, had to leave America during the Revolution, but he did well in Europe and became a Bavarian Count. He took his name from the New Hampshire town of Rumford (later called Concord) where he had once lived.

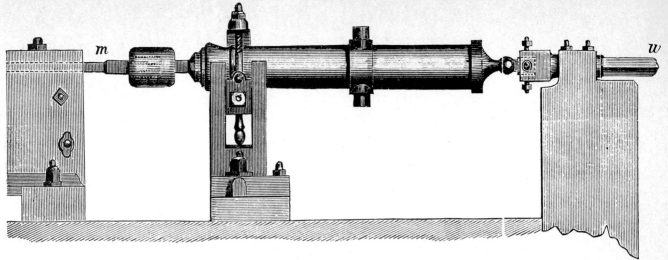

TURNING OUT HEAT

In 1798 at a Munich munitions factory, Count Rumford set up the apparatus shown in the engraving above: a steel boring rod (m) is fitted snugly into a fat cylinder which is in turn joined to a rotating cannon barrel (w). The turning cylinder was fitted with a water-filled jacket (not shown). Heat from the friction between the cylinder and borer made the water boil. Since the water boiled as long as the cylinder turned, Rumford argued that the heat supply was inexhaustible and therefore heat could not be a material substance stored in the cylinder.

PREREVOLUTION PORTRAIT

Antoine Lavoisier and his wife are shown in his laboratory in this portrait by the French painter Jacques Louis David. Though Lavoisier had reservations about the caloric theory, it was he who with three colleagues named heat *calorique*. Lavoisier was killed in the French Revolution but his wife kept his famous name even when she later married Count Rumford.

MEASURE FOR WEIGHT-WATCHERS

Today's unit of heat measure, the calorie, is the quantity of heat that raises the temperature of a gram of water by one degree (specifically, from 14.5° C. to 15.5° C., as illustrated above). The "large calorie" known to all weight-watchers is a thousand times larger than this—one calorie of food provides the body with heat that could raise 1000 grams of water 1° C.

Hitching Up Steam for Horsepower

Nowadays horsepower is something we associate with high-speed automobiles, but the term itself was coined in the late 1700s by the Scottish inventor James Watt to measure the power of his new steam engines. He estimated how many pounds a horse could lift off the ground one foot in one minute, and came up with the unit he called a horsepower *(opposite, top)*.

Watt did not invent the steam engine. When he was still a child, an inefficient steam engine was already in fairly wide use, pumping water out of English mines. This, the Newcomen engine, was itself an improvement on two earlier contrivances, the Savery and the Papin engines, which were very primitive attempts to set steam to work. Newcomen had combined the best features of these machines, but his device was still so inefficient that, as one critic complained, it took an iron mine to

manufacture it and a coal mine to run it.

Watt's interest in steam power stirred when he was asked to repair a Newcomen engine. He repaired it—and then went on to redesign it, inventing almost every possible improvement in the device. Watt made his steam engine turn a wheel as well as operate a pump and his new models, one of which is shown opposite, made the steam engine practical and efficient for the first time. In 1774 he went into partnership with an English businessman and at a factory near Birmingham, England, constructed steam engines until his retirement in 1800. These engines turned steam into a universal source of power and, some have said, brought on the industrial revolution. Although steam engines have been greatly refined and are now used in ways Watt never dreamed of, his basic principles still stand unchanged.

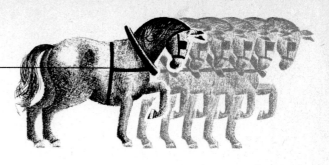

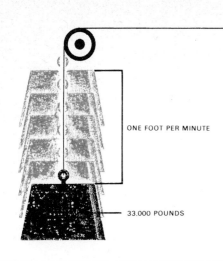

ONE FOOT PER MINUTE

33,000 POUNDS

THE MEASURE OF A HORSE

The originator of the steam engine, Thomas Savery, had noted that his engine could do the work of two horses, but it was James Watt who established the horsepower as a unit of measure. He determined that a horse, pulling for one minute, could lift some 32,400 pounds to a height of one foot. Later, to make it easier to calculate the power of his engines, Watt rounded this off and set the standard unit at 33,000 pounds raised one foot per minute, as shown here. In today's scientific shorthand this is expressed as "550 foot-pounds per second."

THE VOLT
A Unit
of Pressure

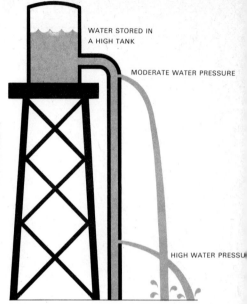

WATER STORED IN
A HIGH TANK

MODERATE WATER PRESSURE

HIGH WATER PRESSU

ELECTRICITY PILED HIGH

Volta's battery *(above)*, called a "Voltaic pile," consisted of two stacks of paired zinc and silver disks packed between layers of brine-soaked pasteboard. When the columns were connected at the top, current flowed between them, arising from chemical reaction of the paired metals.

THE FORCE OF CURRENT

In honor of Alessandro Volta, who sometimes judged a battery by the flash he saw as he touched its wires to his eyelids, electric "force" is now measured in volts. Voltage is a measure of the electrical "pressure" with which current flows through a wire. This potential is analogous to that of water stored in a high tank, ready to pour down through a pipe. The farther water drops down a pipe, the greater will be the pressure of its spurt from a spigot *(above, right)*. Similarly, the greater the voltage of a battery, the greater will be the flow of current produced.

THE OHM
A Rule
of Resistance

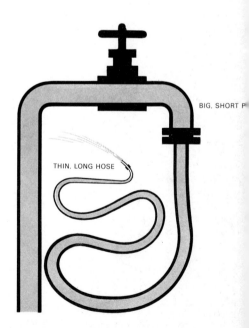

BIG, SHORT P

THIN, LONG HOSE

A BATTERY OF BOTTLES

Ohm's source of electricity was not actually a battery but a set of Leyden jars connected by brass rods *(above)*. The Leyden jar was a tinfoil-coated bottle that could store a great charge of static electricity. It could supply current for only a moment, and then had to be recharged.

THE IMPEDING OF CURRENT

George Simon Ohm, a German schoolmaster, showed that current depended on the resistance of the wire circuit it flowed through, just as water flows more easily in a short, wide pipe than through a long, thin garden hose *(above, right)*. He then went on to state Ohm's Law: that current varies in direct ratio to the voltage of the battery and in inverse ratio to the wires' resistance. Ohm's theories, published in 1826, were at first scorned and he was forced to resign his teaching post in Cologne. Later vindicated, he became a physics professor in 1849.

THE AMPERE
A Measure of Current

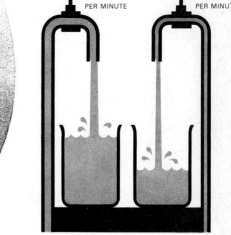

ONE GALLON PER MINUTE

HALF GALLON PER MINUTE

COMPASS FROM A CURRENT

The electric compass shown above was devised by Ampère during his studies on the magnetism produced by electricity. When a current passed through the suspended rectangular wire loop at left, the loop became magnetized and turned to align itself with the earth's magnetic field.

THE STREAM OF CURRENT

André Marie Ampère, who has been called the Newton of electricity, was the first to describe current as the flow of electricity along a wire. This flow is analogous to the surge of water through a pipe *(above, right)*. The diagram shows two pipes, one twice as big as the oth-

er: in any period of time, twice as much water comes from the wider pipe. Just as the rate of water flow is measured in gallons-per-second, current is measured in coulombs-per-second, a coulomb being a unit of electrical quantity. One coulomb-per-second is known as an ampere.

Cornerstones of Electrical Measurement

The static electricity that makes wool sweaters crackle and spark was well known by the 18th Century. But in 1791, man's idea of electricity suddenly began to change: Alessandro Volta, an Italian physics professor, put a silver spoon and a bit of tinfoil on his tongue and noticed a sour taste when he connected the two metals with a copper wire. In effect, he had tasted the first electric current. This gave him the idea for his "Voltaic pile"— man's first battery *(opposite, top)*.

André Marie Ampère, a French mathematician *(above)*, explored the magnetic nature of moving electricity and coined the name "galvanometer" for an instrument in which the electric current deflects a magnetic needle. Soon after, George Ohm used a galvanometer to show that a current's flow is affected by the wire through which it passes *(opposite)*. In honor of these men, the potential "pressure" of a current is measured in volts, its rate of flow in ampères and the resistance of its conductor in ohms *(right)*.

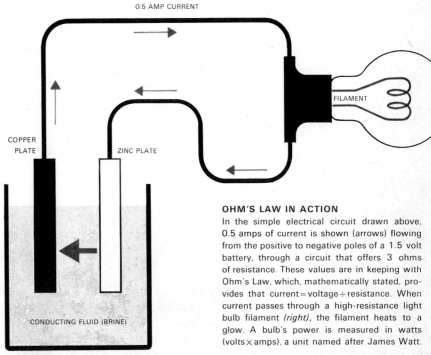

0.5 AMP CURRENT

FILAMENT

COPPER PLATE

ZINC PLATE

CONDUCTING FLUID (BRINE)

1.5 VOLT BATTERY

OHM'S LAW IN ACTION

In the simple electrical circuit drawn above, 0.5 amps of current is shown (arrows) flowing from the positive to negative poles of a 1.5 volt battery, through a circuit that offers 3 ohms of resistance. These values are in keeping with Ohm's Law, which, mathematically stated, provides that current=voltage÷resistance. When current passes through a high-resistance light bulb filament *(right)*, the filament heats to a glow. A bulb's power is measured in watts (volts×amps), a unit named after James Watt.

A CELEBRATED ENGLISHMAN
Michael Faraday, shown above in an 1863 photograph, started as an apprentice to a bookbinder. But after hearing a series of lectures on chemistry, he became a laboratory assistant at the Royal Institution, founded by Count Rumford. In time he became head of the Institution's laboratory. Faraday was so brilliant a scientist that Einstein rated him with Galileo and Newton.

AN OVERLOOKED AMERICAN
Joseph Henry *(above)* started out to be a watchmaker, turned to writing, acting and producing plays and then to teaching, becoming at 28 a teacher of mathematics at Albany Academy. He later taught at Princeton, then served as the first director of the new Smithsonian Institution.

A Horseshoe That Electrified the World

About 30 years after Volta invented the battery, two scientific papers heralded a new source of electric current. In England, Michael Faraday announced in 1832 that he had managed to "convert magnetism into electricity": he had sent a current through a coil of wires, creating a magnetic field which induced a momentary current in a second coil. In America, Joseph Henry affirmed that he had done much the same thing, using the magnet pictured on the opposite page. Actually, Henry's work preceded Faraday's, but, having failed to publish first, he would not take credit for the discovery. This momentous finding in time provided a source of current now used in the world's generators, dynamos and motors.

While Faraday was acclaimed, Henry was long overlooked. In Europe he was scorned as a mere American, while Americans thought him eccentric. But today the henry, like the farad, is an electrical unit.

MAGNET THAT MADE HISTORY
With the frowsy-looking electromagnet opposite Joseph Henry made scientific history. When he passed current from a battery through the wire coils wound about the 9½-inch-high horseshoe-shaped iron bar, the iron became magnetic. The bar in the foreground was attached to the horseshoe; it was wrapped with a second set of coils (not shown), which carried an induced current.

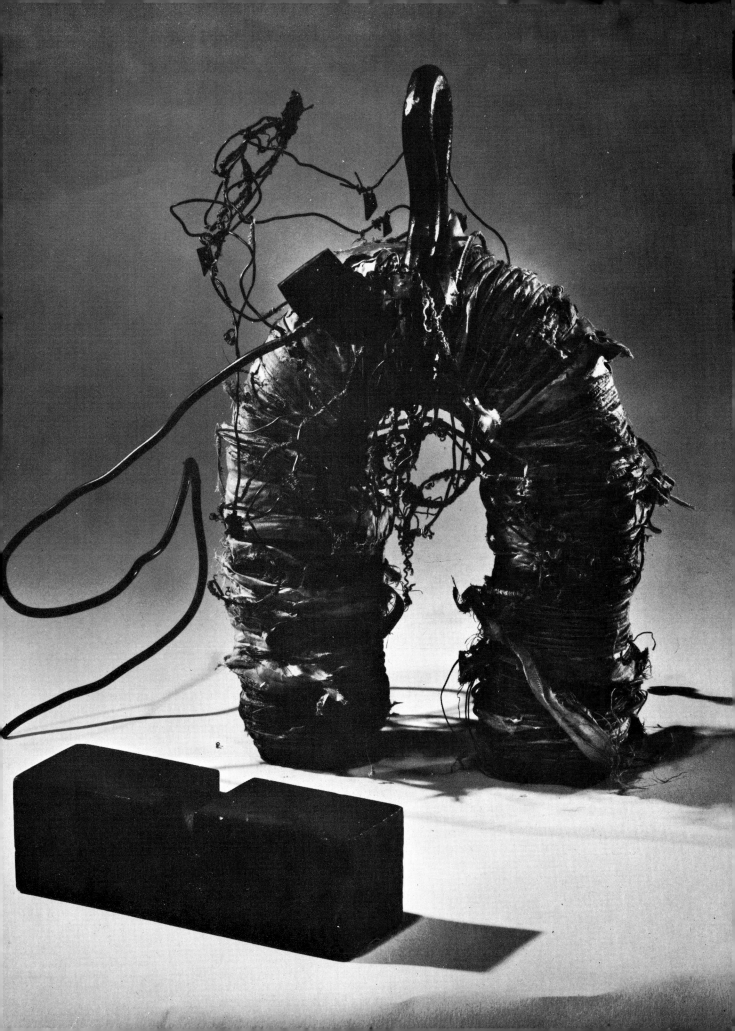

3

The Torrid Pace of Moving Molecules

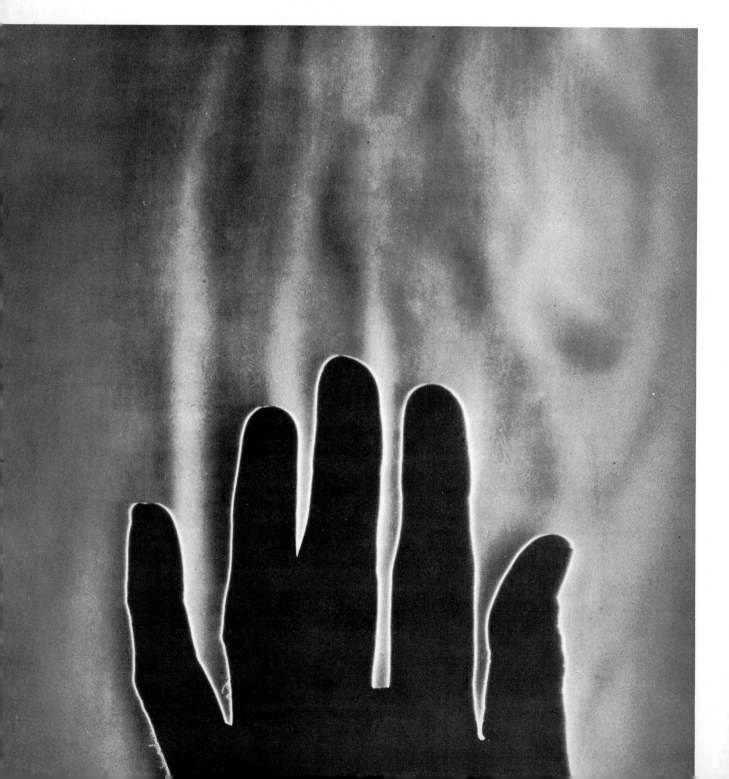

ONE DAY, billions of years from now, our bright world will fade into a gray and silent gloom. It will be not the fall of night but the death of the universe, for the inevitable extinction of light and of all the familiar features of the cosmos is a logical deduction from the new concept of heat which arose at the beginning of the 19th Century to replace the discredited caloric theory.

The work of such men as Rumford, Davy and Joule had proved that heat was a product of motion: a drill boring out a cannon muzzle; the rubbing together of two pieces of ice; a paddle wheel sloshing around in a tub of water—all generated heat. But for every one of these heat-producing motions, there is also an example of something else which gives off heat while sitting quietly: A teapot of water may be hot; so may the tires of an automobile that has just come to a halt; and even the seat of a child's pants may be warm at the end of a quick trip down a playground slide.

One could argue that such heat in nonmoving objects simply represents heat that has been stored up from some motion which has ceased a few minutes earlier. But what action is there in water being heated on a stove? And if heat has been stored in a tire or a child's britches, in what form was it hoarded if there is no such thing as caloric? The answer to both these questions depends upon a single fact: A stationary object is not really stationary. It is, instead, a mass of invisible bits of matter—atoms and molecules—vibrating or moving around at incredible speeds. Heat in any substance is a manifestation of this constant frenzy. In cold objects the molecular movements are relatively slow; in hotter objects they are faster.

The idea that our solid world may not be so solid after all is very old. Indeed the atomic theory may well be the oldest scientific hypothesis that is still acceptable today. As early as the 5th Century B.C., the Greek philosopher Democritus had speculated that the universe was put together of countless infinitesimal balls which he called *atomoi*. The Greeks never tested this idea experimentally, but the subtle proofs of science have since shown that their thinking was in the right direction.

Modern scientists have, of course, modified the hunch of the Greeks to an almost unrecognizable extent. Among other things, they have found the atom to be perhaps the most sociable entity in the universe, nearly always occurring in combination with another atom or with a whole group of other atoms. Such atomic combinations are called molecules. For example, the atom of the common gas, oxygen, usually joins with another oxygen atom to form the oxygen molecule. Indeed, oxygen made up of single atoms is a scientific curiosity and produces a dangerous poison to boot. Oxygen can also combine with carbon to form a molecule of carbon monoxide, the dangerous gas in automobile exhausts. Or it can link with

A HANDFUL OF HEAT
In this unusual photograph, air warmed by a human hand is shown rising from the fingers, much as "heat waves" shimmer above highways on hot days. Although heat is an invisible form of radiant energy, its effect on air was captured here by Schlieren photography, a complex process which uses extremely fast exposures to record different air densities as light and shadow.

CORNERSTONES
OF CHEMICAL BUILDING

HYDROGEN ATOM

OXYGEN ATOM

OXYGEN MOLECULE

WATER MOLECULE

ATOMS LIKE AND UNLIKE

The hydrogen and oxygen atoms at top are
examples of the building blocks of
chemical construction. In groups of two or
more, atoms form molecules. The molecules of
an element, such as oxygen, are composed
of *like* atoms. Those of a chemical compound
are made up of *unlike* atoms; water, for
example, has one oxygen and two hydrogens.
In both elements and compounds, atoms
join in whole numbers, never in fractions.

two atoms of hydrogen, as H_2O, to form water. In any case, no matter how many atoms combine, the unit that results is a molecule.

An average molecule is so small that you would have to go seven zeros from the decimal point to describe its diameter in inches; it would take 100 million hydrogen molecules packed along a line to measure one inch. And under ordinary conditions just one cubic inch of a gas contains 442 quintillion molecules. That is a number so large that if every man, woman and child on earth counted one molecule each second, it would take all of them 4,650 years to reach the end. If that number seems immense, consider that it takes more than 19,000 times that many: 8,540,000,000,000,-000,000,000,000 (8.54 septillion) hydrogen molecules to weigh an ounce.

It is obvious that the molecule can only make itself known by weight of sheer numbers. Yet the pioneer study of molecular behavior, published in 1738, was based on how single molecules might act. The author of this work was Daniel Bernoulli, scion of one of the famous families of science. The Bernoullis, along with such families as the Darwins and the Curies, were to science what the Bachs were to music—four generations of Bernoullis contributed brilliant work to medicine, physics and mathematics.

A collision, a bounce and a ricochet

Few of his contemporaries, however, took Daniel Bernoulli's ideas seriously and no one recognized them as the prevision of modern thinking which they turned out to be. Bernoulli in effect asked his fellow scientists to imagine a contained but completely empty space in which there is only one molecule. The lone molecule travels through this void at a high speed in straight lines, colliding with a wall, bouncing off in a new direction, ricocheting again and again within its confinement. As a result of this eternal motion, Bernoulli conceived of each wall as receiving successive isolated assaults.

While the impact of one molecule is negligible, the combined pounding of trillions upon trillions of such molecules in a container builds up a pressure against its walls. Obviously when the space in the container is reduced, the molecules will have less room to move around in and will hit the walls even more often, thus increasing the pressure. This relationship between pressure and volume had already been discovered in the 17th Century by the famous English scientist Robert Boyle. A member of that brain trust of Restoration kings and councillors, the so-called Invisible College out of which grew the Royal Society of London for Improving Natural Knowledge, Boyle had set up one of the best-equipped laboratories in Europe and had used it for a great variety of research.

With the assistance of Robert Hooke, Boyle developed the first efficient air pump and proved that the application of pressure on air, the most common of gases, reduces its volume in a simple mathematical way: When the pressure is doubled under constant temperature, the air is squeezed down to half its normal volume. Looking at Boyle's result in another way, one could say also that if air is squeezed down to half its normal volume, the pressure of its molecules is doubled. Bernoulli calculated mathematically how much pressure rapidly moving gas molecules could create. These pressures corresponded almost exactly with what Boyle had observed.

Bernoulli also went into the question of how temperature affects gases. He proved mathematically what Charles and Gay-Lussac were to determine by observation a number of decades later: Increasing the temperature causes a gas to expand in a definite mathematical proportion —double the absolute temperature of a gas under constant pressure and the gas volume doubles. He also noted that heating a gas in a tight container will cause the pressure in the container to increase.

The fact that auto tires require less inflation in summer than in winter is an example of this principle. For in warm weather the air in the tire becomes hotter and expands, thus needing less air to keep the tire pressure where it should be. This also explains why used aerosol "bombs" should not be thrown into a fire: Heat will cause even the small amount of aerosol left in the container to expand and explode the can.

Bernoulli figured that the effects of temperature on gas volume and pressure could be easily explained by assuming that heat caused the molecules in the gas to speed up. Then each molecule would hit the walls of the container more often and thus press it harder.

Actually, Bernoulli's work was at least a century ahead of its time. His theories came in the period when caloric was the most popular explanation of heat, and he went unheeded when, in his long-neglected work, *Hydrodynamica*, he turned his back on caloric by saying that "heat may be considered as an increasing internal motion of the particles." Indeed, Bernoulli's postulation was made more than 100 years prior to Joule's final statement on the equivalence of heat and motion.

The prodigy called "Dafty"

Bernoulli's work captured the imagination of one of the most brilliant scientists of the 19th Century: James Clerk Maxwell. Like many men of the period, Maxwell was a *Wunderkind*. He was born in Edinburgh in 1831 and very early showed an intense interest in the physical world around him; he would ask his father about something that caught his attention, "What's the go o' that?"

At school Maxwell was considered a gifted student, getting high honors in mathematics, English and Latin, but he was called "Dafty" by the other boys because of the somewhat foppish clothes his father selected. Yet by the time he was 17 he had so impressed his teachers that two of

GAS MOLECULES: DIFFERENT WEIGHTS BUT EQUAL NUMBERS

A COUNT'S ACCOUNTING

The stamp above commemorates the death of the Italian physicist Amedeo Avogadro, Count of Queregna. It records his discovery in 1811 that equal volumes of all gases at the same temperature and pressure contain an equal number of molecules. Each of the billions of oxygen molecules in the bottle below *(right)* weighs 16 times more than one of hydrogen *(left)*, yet the two bottles contain an equal number of molecules.

HYDROGEN   OXYGEN

BOOSTING GAS PRESSURE BY RAISING THE HEAT

CALM AND COLLECTED

THE HEAT IS ON

STEPPING UP THE PACE
What happens to the pressure of a gas if heat is added and the volume stays the same? The drawings above show that as the temperature rises, molecules gain kinetic energy. This means that they speed up and hit the walls of the container with greater frequency and force, thus raising the pressure.

his papers were read before the Royal Society of Edinburgh. They were read by his teachers because "it was not thought proper for a boy in a round jacket to mount the rostrum."

After he had graduated from Cambridge, Maxwell won a University prize for an essay on the nature of Saturn's rings. In it, he questioned various hypotheses of the time which asserted the rings were either solid, fluid or in part "aeriform," an old word meaning gaseous. Using mathematics to make his point, Maxwell argued that the rings could not be solid bands because the gravitational pull of the planet would cause them to disintegrate. He also reasoned that were the rings composed of fluid the waves created by their motion would break them up. His argument that the rings actually were made up of disconnected particles was later verified in astronomical observations.

Figuring a collision course

This examination of what he called the "flight of brickbats" led him to study the behavior of groups of colliding gas particles, and he reported "that their minute particles are in rapid motion, the velocity increasing with the temperature, [so] that the precise nature of this motion becomes a subject of rational curiosity." He extended Bernoulli's calculation by taking into account collisions of gas molecules with each other and by recognizing that all molecules probably move with a different velocity. He showed how to average these velocities properly and how to obtain the proper pressure, density and temperature relationship. "It is not necessary," Maxwell wrote, "to suppose each particle to travel to any great distance in the same straight line; for the effect in producing pressure will be the same if the particles strike against each other; so that the straight line described may be very short."

Maxwell's short, straight lines between collisions were described by his German contemporary, Rudolf Clausius, as the "mean free path," the term still in use, which means that at standard conditions of temperature and pressure, every molecule will on the average have a path of a given length: Hydrogen, for example, has an average length of path between collisions of 0.0000043 of an inch. Such distance indeed seems short, yet the diameter of an individual molecule is so minute that it is, relatively, a long distance. Were their size to be increased to that of a tennis ball, the enlarged mean free path between collisions would be slightly more than the length of a tennis court, providing ample space through which the tennis ball molecule could move at blinding speed before it might collide with one of its mates. Quintillions of them are in motion right now, colliding with each other at the rate of 15 billion collisions a second. Thus it is that a gas expands when the container is removed. The molecules continue to travel until deflected by collisions with other molecules or with other containing walls. The particles move randomly in every possible direction.

When the gas is enclosed within a stationary container, movement in one direction is matched by equal molecular movement in the opposite direction. On the other hand, when the gas begins to flow—for instance, air in the form of a wind blowing across a field or natural gas moving through a pipeline—the speed of the forward movement of the entire gaseous mass is still simply a drift, superimposed on the far higher velocities with which the separate molecules dart about erratically *within* the streaming mass of gas. Molecules in such clouds of gas have no appreciable effects on one another except during collisions.

100 millionths of an inch

Two kinds of electric forces operate between molecules: an attractive force which, like gravity, is effective over a limited range (a few times the molecule's diameter), and a highly repulsive force which operates over a much shorter range. In the solid state, the forces between molecules determine the structure. At an intermediate point (about 100 millionths of an inch from the center of the molecule), these two forces cancel each other out. Only at this hypothetical point of zero force would it be possible for a molecule to remain at rest—the forces acting on it in equilibrium. Were a second molecule moved slightly closer, the repulsive force would drive it away. Were it moved slightly away, the attractive force would bring it back. The two opposing forces establish the point of equilibrium and cause molecules to vibrate slightly toward and away from each other, as if held by invisible springs.

A small bar of iron *looks* solid and motionless, but the component atoms of the iron are entirely separate, suspended in space. Unceasingly each of the individual atoms is vibrating toward and away from each one of its neighbors. As they hang in space, the atoms form the intersections of a regular latticework. In iron, the lattice is composed of tiny cubes with an atom at each corner and one in the middle. Other substances have lattices with sides forming triangles, parallelograms, hexagons and other forms. These different lattices give each element its peculiar internal structure. When an object is broken, it normally separates along the lines of the lattice.

An increase in temperature speeds up the average velocity of molecular vibration within solids just as it does in gases. Each swinging movement of a single molecule, under the influence of heat, is wider and faster and increases the average molecular separation. In other words, a solid object expands as a whole when the temperature is increased. As the additional heat forces the vibrating movement of the tightly bound molecules to become wilder and wilder, a point is reached at

BOOSTING GAS PRESSURE BY SHRINKING THE SPACE

CALM AND COLLECTED

THE SQUEEZE IS ON

RUNNING OUT OF ROOM

What happens to the pressure of a gas at fixed temperature if its volume is cut down? Robert Boyle discovered that if the volume of a gas is halved, the pressure is doubled. The molecules, while moving at the same speed, now have only half the space and therefore push against the walls twice as much.

which some of the molecules begin to burst away from the binding forces exerted by their neighbors—they slip out of the regular lattice-work. With further heat, more and more molecules escape their captivity. As the rigid order begins to diminish, whole clusters of molecules begin to slip past each other. Finally the substance is no longer a solid, and the resultant breakdown of order reaches a stage called melting.

When internal fluidity is fully achieved, the molecules are said to be in the *liquid state*. If a man could shrink himself small enough to see this internal structure, he could tell that the molecules of liquids have more energetic motion than those of solids. In liquids, the molecules hurtle in and then out of each other's areas of influence. Thus the force of a single molecule on another can be exerted for only the briefest time. Neighbors appear and disappear in millionths of a second. Collisions take place with almost unbelievable frequency. In liquids, as in solids, the addition of heat increases the average space between molecular centers. Therefore, as with solids, the kinetic theory explains why liquids generally expand with the addition of heat.

Breaking the surface barrier

The molecular surface of a liquid acts as a sort of barrier to the outer world. For instance, a molecule below the surface, one traveling upward at a very high velocity, may pass out of the liquid into the atmosphere above. This effect is evaporation. Yet the molecule must work against the surface as well as against the pressure of air molecules to get through. Only when the temperature is high enough does the average energy of the liquid allow an appreciable escape of molecules into the atmosphere.

The fastest molecules escape as heat is added, and break through the surface. They transfer some of their kinetic energy in the form of heat to the atmosphere, which is why evaporation is a cooling process. As the heat applied to the liquid continues, more and more molecules attain speeds which enable them to escape through the surface. When enough of the molecules reach this point, there is a violent bubbling as the liquid comes to a boil.

At the boiling point, each addition of energy in the form of heat is divided among those molecules which are left behind in the liquid. Eventually their velocity is raised sufficiently so that they, too, can escape. In other words, a steadily heated liquid rises in temperature to a certain point at which the temperature becomes constant, while the liquid boils away. Kinetic theory explains this process as a matter of increasing the velocity of each molecule to the point at which its kinetic energy is sufficient to break free from the attraction of each neighboring molecule.

At this point a change of state occurs—the liquid becomes gas. And

BREAKING THE TENSION

As shown above, a liquid evaporates when some molecules, moving with enough speed and in the right direction, overcome surface tension— the attractive force which holds the surface molecules together—and escape into the air. If a liquid is heated, the kinetic energy of its molecules is increased, which makes them move faster and thus speeds up their rate of escape. Evaporation actually tends to cool the liquid, since it is mostly the faster-moving molecules that break through the surface, leaving the slower, cooler ones behind.

the heat used up in the process of the changing state is the "latent heat" of Joseph Black, discussed in Chapter 2. Black's "specific heat" can also be explained in terms of the motions of molecules. All heat that is "taken into" a substance is actually a manifestation of the motion of its component particles.

Now a question arises: how many ways can these component particles move? The answer depends on what shape they happen to have. If they are balls, they can move simply in three ways—like a ball in a tennis court that can travel up and down, from side to side or back and forth. But suppose the particles are dumbbell-shaped as many molecules are. If a dumbbell is thrown around a tennis court, it can obviously go up, down and sideways just like a ball, but it can also tumble end over end. Each kind of motion can absorb some heat energy; hence a dumbbell-shaped molecule, with its twirling motion, could take on a little more heat than a ball-shaped one which does not twirl, but this addition does not affect the thermometer. Understandably, the picture becomes even more complex if the molecule consists of three balls fastened together, like the water molecule. It would have all the motions of a ball plus those of a dumbbell plus a whole raft of complicated and fantastic gyrations which result from its three-parted shape. Since each of its individual motions would take on an equal amount of heat, its heat capacity would be higher than that of a dumbbell-shaped molecule. The difference in motion, which results from the difference in molecular structure, is therefore one factor in the variability of specific heat. There is also another factor. Specific heats are based on equal weights of substances, but because the number of molecules varies in different substances, even though the weights are equal, the number of molecules available to absorb heat is not the same.

The motive power of heat

A practical approach to the study of heat and motion was made by Nicolas Leonard Sadi Carnot, son of the French revolutionary general. The younger Carnot published in 1824 a single paper called "Reflections on the Motive Power of Heat." Though it attracted little immediate attention and was apparently forgotten, it was resurrected after 25 years and recognized for its extraordinary creative thinking.

In the paper's introduction, Carnot pointed out that the clanking, wheezing steam engines of his day had become of vital importance to the world's fast-developing industrialization. He noted that their efficiency had been improved by various changes in design and proposed to find out how far this improvement could continue.

"The question has often been raised," he wrote, "whether the motive power of heat is unbounded, whether the possible improvements in

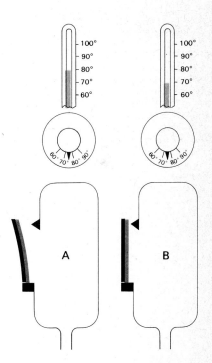

CUTTING DOWN THE FUEL BILL
A thermostat makes use of the fact that different substances have different coefficients of expansion—i.e., they expand and contract different amounts during temperature changes. Each thermostat has a bar made of two different metals. The metal next to the electric contact has the higher coefficient, so that when the heat rises above a set point, it expands more and bends the bar away from the contact to turn off the furnace (A). If the temperature falls too low, the bar bends back to the contact (B).

steam engines have . . . a limit which the nature of things will not allow to be passed by any means whatever, or whether, on the contrary, these improvements may be carried on indefinitely."

In addressing this problem, Carnot took a careful look at steam engines, asking what really happens in them. He observed that their action is a cyclical process that first adds heat to water, turning it to steam. The steam expands in the cylinder and does mechanical work by pushing the piston. Then it goes to a cold condenser, where it turns to water again and is returned to the boiler.

Reasoning that existing steam engines were inefficient mainly because of the leakage of steam and the friction of the piston, Carnot imagined an ideal heat engine with no thermal or mechanical defects. He conceived it merely as a cylinder fitted with a leakproof, frictionless piston, having the piston head and the side walls of the cylinder perfectly insulated. The heat necessary to produce steam was allowed to pass freely through the bottom of the cylinder. One full cycle of this ideal engine would therefore include heating the water to steam, letting the piston rise under the steam pressure and returning the piston to its original position by converting the steam into its former state as water. In the course of studying the cooling cycle, Carnot at last realized that some heat loss was inevitable in the operation of any steam engine. Once the piston was raised by the steam, it would be impossible to get it back down without taking the steam out of the piston chamber and condensing it. In this condensation, essentially a cooling process, some heat must necessarily be dissipated to its surroundings.

Flowing downhill to work

Here was indeed a fundamental principle of steam engines: Not all the heat received can be turned into mechanical work because some of it is lost in the condensation of the steam. Carnot had found that heat must flow "downhill," that is, change from high to low temperatures to do work. As a matter of fact, for most of his life, Carnot was a believer in caloric and he actually thought of it as a fluid moving through his engine and doing work in the same way as water turns a mill wheel. It was only at the end of his life that he conceived of heat as a product of motion.

Carnot's discovery that heat must move in a definite direction points to one of the basic laws of physics: the Second Law of Thermodynamics. The law was first formulated by the German physicist Rudolf Clausius, who stated, "It is impossible for a self-acting machine, unaided by any external agency, to convey heat from one body to another at a higher temperature." Lord Kelvin stated the same law in somewhat different words: "It is impossible, by means of inanimate material agency, to derive mechanical effect from any portion of matter by cooling it below the

A HOT IDEA MAN
The son of Napoleon's minister of interior, Sadi Carnot was more interested in devising a better steam engine than in improving the efficiency of armies. Inquiring into the theoretical basis of such engines, he made an important observation: heat does work only when it flows from a hot place to a cooler place. This is called Carnot's principle. The French engineer also determined that the greater the temperature difference the more work heat would do.

temperature of the coldest of the surrounding objects." The essence of the law is this: Heat will not flow, of its own accord, from a cold place to a hot one.

When one stops to think about the Second Law, it turns out to be a fact of everyday life. For example, suppose a toaster is sitting on the table in an ordinary kitchen where the air temperature is 65°F. If all the heat in the room were to "flow" into the toaster it would heat it to a cherry red. Yet that never happens. A toaster gets hot only if it has been plugged into an electric socket, when it then takes a fraction of a kilowatt-hour and about one-twentieth-of-a-cent's worth of electrical energy to heat it up. On the other hand, the same hot toaster when unplugged will cool down immediately without the slightest use of energy.

This one way flow of heat, as stated by the Second Law, carries with it the doom of the universe. Harking back to the analogy of heat and water, we can say that heat, like water, must flow downhill to do work. Without hills there would be no water power and, similarly, without hills of temperature (i.e., places where it is hotter than others) heat can do no work. Just as there is erosion on earth which tends to flatten out mountains, so there is a process of heat erosion in the universe which tends to level out temperature. This insidious leveler is heat loss.

Heat and a cricket's chirp

Some of the heat of an engine like Carnot's is lost—is dissipated in its surroundings. The heat generated by a cricket's muscles to create his chirp vanishes like his small sound in the night. The heat that accompanies a feather's fall diminishes and is quickly gone. Most of this lost heat is irretrievable—it is never again capable of doing work.

The conclusion of this losing game causes us to face a day when all the energy in the universe has been converted to heat and all of this heat has been evenly distributed throughout the universe. This does not mean that the universe necessarily will grow very cold. It could, instead, become either lukewarm or white hot. The point is that it will be the *same* temperature everywhere. And this, at last, means that *no more work can be done.*

To describe this leveling out of heat, Clausius coined the word "entropy"—from the Greek word for "change"—as the measure of just how level the energy of the universe is. And maximum entropy is the term for that homogeneous state when everything will be at the same temperature.

Words like "flow" and "downhill" smack of the caloric theory, and entropy, certainly, is most easily understood in such terms. But just as molecular motions are at the bottom of all other heat phenomena, they also explain entropy. When the molecules of steam are released into the piston chamber of an engine, they are, so to speak, all headed in one

PUTTING HEAT THROUGH ITS PACES

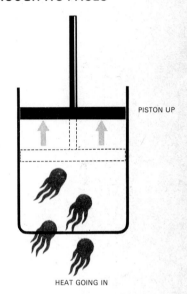

PISTON UP

HEAT GOING IN

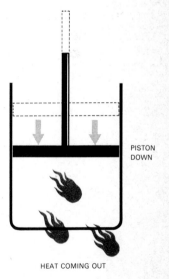

PISTON DOWN

HEAT COMING OUT

THE PENALTY OF WORK

Shown simplified above are two stages in the working of a steam engine. First, steam enters the cylinder, expands, and its heat energy is partly converted into mechanical energy to raise the piston. In the second stage, the remaining heat is drawn out of the cylinder so that the piston can repeat the cycle. Less heat is withdrawn than was put in because some went into the work done and some inevitably was lost to friction.

direction. This does not mean that every molecule is headed the same way, but simply that the sweeping direction of all the molecules is one way. There is an orderly movement of molecules, and it is this concerted push that moves the piston. But as soon as the same steam is released from the engine into the surroundings, this orderly motion disappears. The steam molecules slam into the molecules in the air and into each other, then they gradually fan out into space as they become less and less energetic.

Carnot said that heat must flow from hot to cold to do work. And one might add that *molecules must be moving in some orderly way* to do work. For while maximum entropy is the point where all temperature is the same, it is also defined as the point at which molecular motion is completely random. In either case no work would be possible—and in either case the universe would be dead.

When will maximum entropy occur? Scientists differ in their predictions. Several billions of years is one guess. And in any event, man as he now exists certainly is in no danger. More and more he is learning how to use new energy resources; he is learning how to convert the very substance of the universe into useful energy. Above all, through great advances in physics, he is learning to be more optimistic in his thinking. For, as the following picture essay indicates, some men feel that maximum entropy and its shadow of doom may not happen after all.

Heat, the Inevitable Tax on Usefulness

Every move we make, every thought we think, every revolution of an automobile wheel, every puff of wind saps away a little of the store of energy useful to man. Nature's energy can never be destroyed; it is only converted from one form to another. But every time a conversion takes place, some of the energy is lost as useless heat that diffuses out through the universe, persisting forever, but forever irretrievable. The discovery in the last century of the inevitability of this loss of available energy stamped the final label of "futile" on the centuries-long, tantalizing quest for perpetual motion machines and also led to the realization that all natural processes always tend to go in only one direction. The yardstick of energy's gradual degeneration to a useless condition is called "entropy." It carries implications of vast philosophical significance, for it predicts that the whole universe is moving slowly toward an inexorable death.

A NEVER-ENDING CYCLE AT WORK
Arrows in the diagram opposite show how different forms of energy can be changed into one another. For example, a chemical reaction such as burning can yield both heat and light. Heat, in turn, makes steam, and mechanical energy from a steam engine can be used to generate electricity. At the same time, sunlight helps create thunderstorms. In each step, however, some heat is lost.

THE INTERCHANGEABLE GUISES OF ENERGY

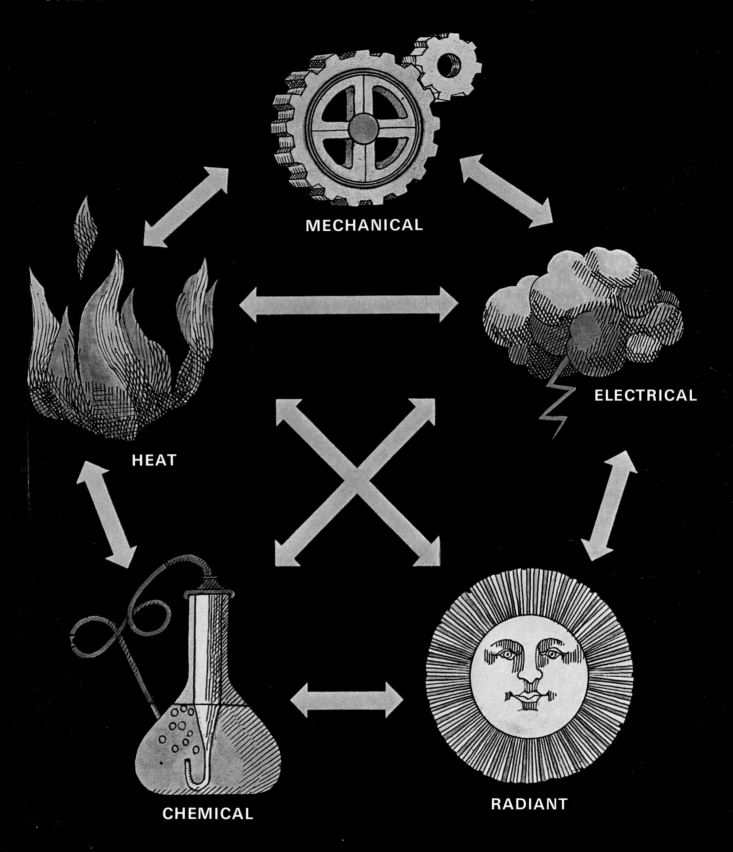

MECHANICAL

HEAT

ELECTRICAL

CHEMICAL

RADIANT

A LESSON FROM LEONARDO
In this perpetual motion device proposed by Leonardo da Vinci, the bulbs on the arms were to be partly filled with mercury, whose shifting weight was supposed to make the wheel turn with a gear mechanism. But after studying many such schemes, Leonardo wrote, "O speculators about perpetual motion, how many vain chimeras have you created in the quest? Go and take your places with the seekers after gold."

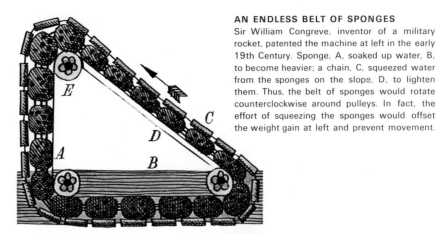

Ingenious Machines in Vain Pursuit of Perpetual Motion

Sooner or later every boy who spends much time with electric motors and generators comes up with a brilliant idea: why not hook the shaft of the motor to the shaft of the generator? This way, he argues breathlessly, the motor can drive the generator which will generate power to drive the motor. Eventually, patient explanation or bitter experience teaches the boy that his neat scheme will not work, but he all too often sets about trying to devise other, better machines that will run by themselves, using just gravity, perhaps, or magnetism.

The young inventor does not know it, but he is simply repeating painful steps taken by brilliant minds over the centuries in the absorbing search for perpetual motion. It is safe to say that no machine of the sort has ever worked, despite testimony to the contrary, and despite the clever reasoning that conceived many devices, such as those on these pages. Leonardo da Vinci concluded that most such schemes were bound to fail *(opposite)*. The French Academy of Sciences in 1775 finally closed its doors to any more perpetual motion plans with the statement, "This sort of research . . . has ruined more than one family, and in many cases mechanics who might have rendered great services have consumed their fortune, their time and their genius on it."

Neither the academy nor Leonardo knew the basic laws that deny the possibility of perpetual motion. This knowledge was to come only with a much more complete understanding of the nature of one of energy's most elusive forms, heat.

A CYCLE POWERED BY MAGNETISM

One of the simpler but more intriguing devices is this one, in which a large round lodestone, or magnet, A, was meant to pull an iron ball, C, up the incline, F. Arriving at the hole, E, the ball was to drop through, run down the trough, G, and out a trap door, D, ready to be drawn up again. The idea's defect is that a magnet strong enough to pull the ball up the plane would be too strong to let it drop through the hole again.

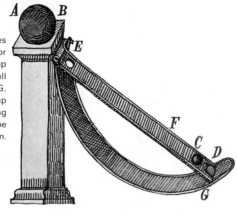

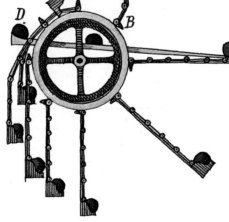

A WHEEL THAT NEVER STOPS

This English version of the overbalanced wheel had long hinged arms, A, that fell out straight to receive a ball rolling down a trough to C. Leverage of the arm was to unbalance the wheel, which would rotate and carry the arm to the bottom. The arm would then ascend, fold and deposit its ball at D. Actually, however, the wheel is balanced, since the arms and balls at left offset the leverage on the right.

A SELF-TURNING SCREW

A 16th Century "self-running" water wheel made use of the Archimedes screw, a tube, B, containing a spiral cylinder *(bottom)* that will raise water when rotated. The water flows from the top into bowls, E, F, G, and onto paddles, H, I, K, attached to the cylinder to keep it turning. One difficulty is that part of the energy of the falling water is spent overcoming resistance of the bearings in which the cylinder turns.

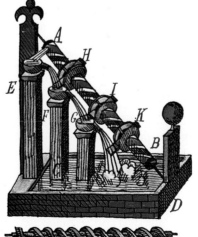

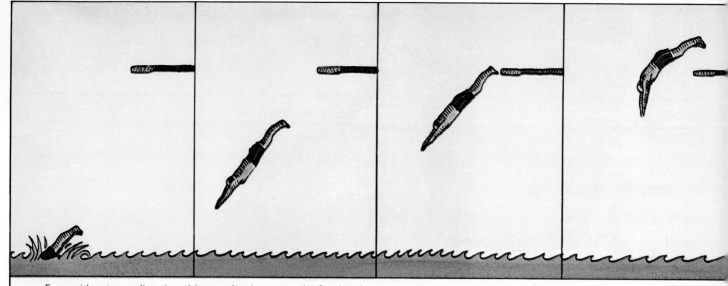

Even with a trampoline rigged just under the water, the fanciest fancy diver, having jumped from his board, could not perform this trick of

Nature's Obstinate Progress down a One-way Street

No one would expect any of the reactions pictured on these pages to happen backwards, at least not of their own accord. The diver will not return to the board; the little girl will not slip back up her slide, and the steam will not squeeze itself back into the teakettle's spout. These are all examples of what scientists term "irreversible processes."

But suppose the diver hits a trampoline just under the water of the pool. And the little girl bounces off a spring at the bottom of her slide. And the steam is somehow put to work compressing itself back into the kettle. Then could the actions be reversed? The answer is, as perpetual motion inventors have always discovered: not quite, not without getting new energy. All of them might come within a gnat's eyelash of reversal, but they would inevitably fall a little short.

The friction of the diver through air and water, and that of the little girl's bottom against the slide both generate heat. The steam molecules lose some of their energy to their surroundings as heat. A little of this heat energy eventually leaks away into space. Even if trampoline, spring and compressor were 100 per cent efficient, this tiny amount of heat loss is enough to make complete reversibility impossible.

VICTIMS OF THE HEAT

Energy lost in the form of heat makes all these activities irreversible. Expanding smoke, steam and air all cool, dissipating heat energy to the atmosphere. Friction with air and hose saps the energy of flowing water; air friction will keep the arrow from rebounding into the bow, even if it strikes a perfectly elastic target. Friction of a sliding child decreases her energy of motion.

ESCAPING SMOKE

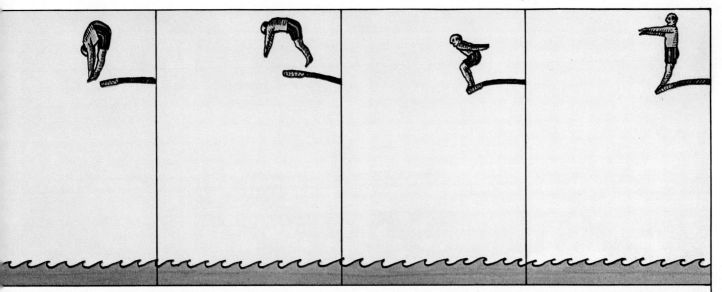

rebounding all the way to his starting place without somehow shoving himself backwards to make up for energy lost from friction with the air.

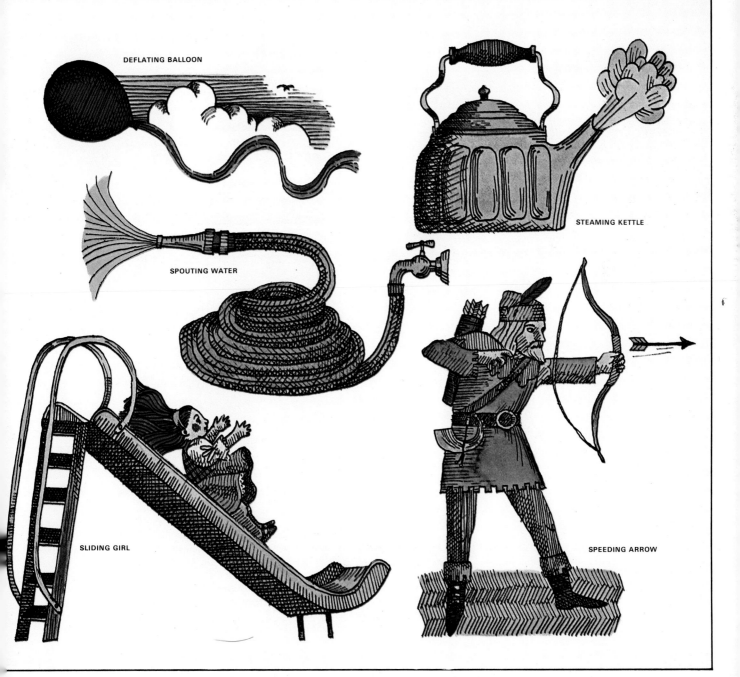

DEFLATING BALLOON

STEAMING KETTLE

SPOUTING WATER

SLIDING GIRL

SPEEDING ARROW

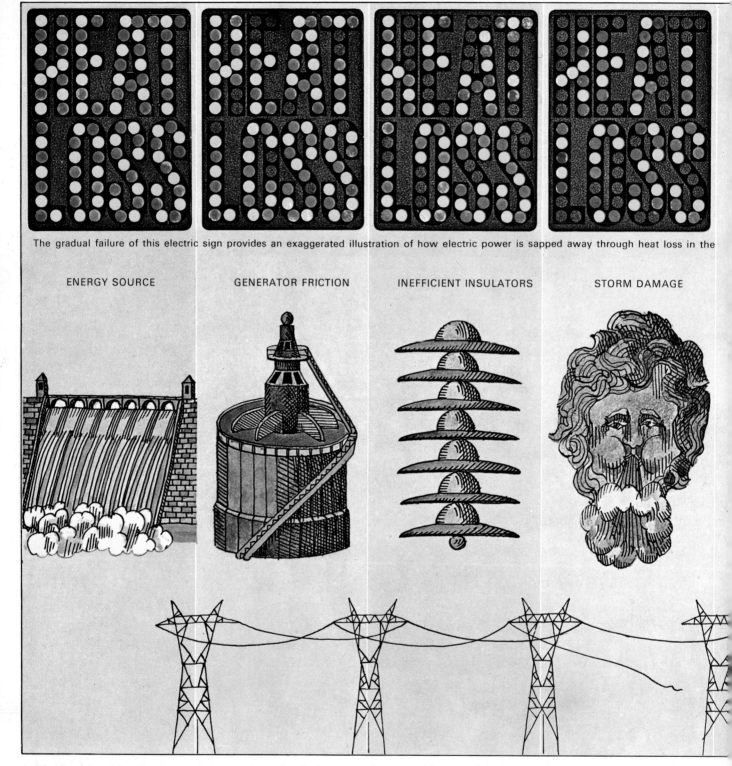

The gradual failure of this electric sign provides an exaggerated illustration of how electric power is sapped away through heat loss in the

ENERGY SOURCE

GENERATOR FRICTION

INEFFICIENT INSULATORS

STORM DAMAGE

Inevitable and accidental events conspire to rob an electrical network of power, with most of the losses seeping away to the atmosphere in the

The Incorrigible
Thief
of Power

The same perversity in nature that afflicts perpetual motion machines also robs man's electrical power lines of energy. No matter how perfect the conductor or how short the wire, there is always less power coming out of an electrical circuit than went in, because of some heat loss along the way (above).

As 19th Century experimenters coped

with inefficiency in their steam engines and other machines, they gradually came to the conclusion that heat was the culprit. They found heat to be nothing more than the external evidence of violent collisions of small particles within matter. The action of ordinary friction, for example, is similar to what would happen if oppositely moving streams of cars were

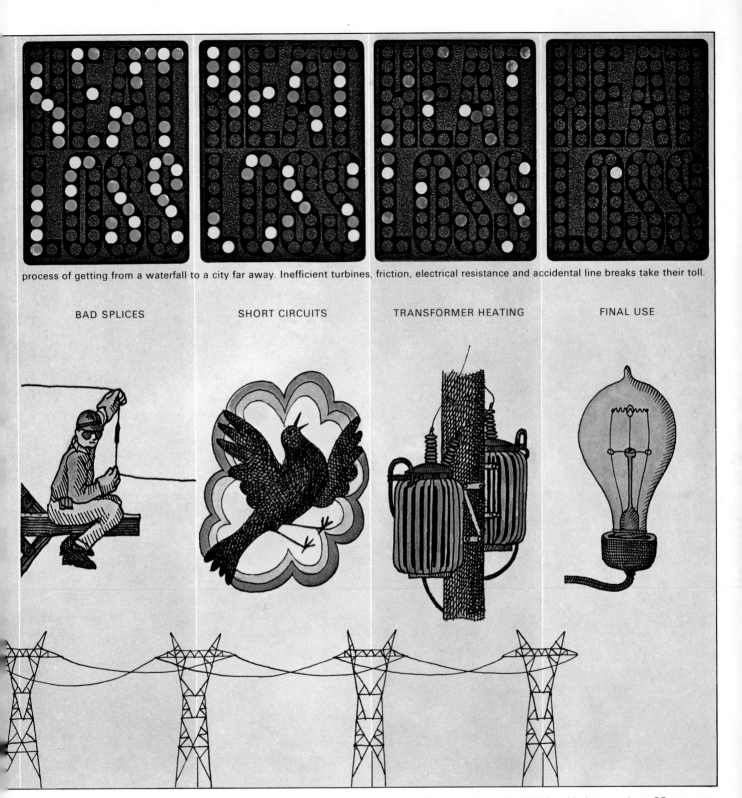

process of getting from a waterfall to a city far away. Inefficient turbines, friction, electrical resistance and accidental line breaks take their toll.

BAD SPLICES   SHORT CIRCUITS   TRANSFORMER HEATING   FINAL USE

form of heat. From the energy source in a waterfall to final use in a light bulb an efficient system will minimize this loss to about 25 per cent.

squeezed together. Their purposeful flow would be transformed into wild collisions and random swervings of automobiles that would communicate themselves through the swarm of cars.

The flow of electricity through a wire was found to be moving electrons—electrons that sometimes smash into other particles in the wire, setting them, too,

into the random motion characteristic of heat. The electrons themselves, of course, lose some of their energy in the process.

The longer the wire, the poorer the connections, and the less efficient the insulation between adjacent wires, the more rapid is this conversion of electricity to heat. As energy is thus sapped during electricity's journey, more power must be

"pumped" into the line, just as water is pumped into a leaky pipe. The energy loss in a power line can be so great that it is often cheaper to transport fuel to local electric generating sites than it is to send electricity out over long distances from the fuel sources. In current commercial practice, electric power is not generally transmitted for more than 600 miles.

Increasing entropy is represented here by a line of marching soldiers. Their perfectly ordered formation and single direction of march indicate

Entropy: Death Knell for the Universe

The squad of soldiers above represents the molecules of the universe as it heads toward ultimate death. For just as the soldiers break ranks and lie down, so will the molecules of the universe become disordered and "tired out."

When steam comes out of the spout of a teakettle, its molecules are predominantly headed one way, and they could easily be put to work pushing the piston of a toy steam engine. But within moments after it escapes into the air, the steam dissipates and its molecules go flying in every direction. As they spread, their heat goes to warm the cooler air, and they gradually lose their useful energy.

Nature's tendency to equalize temperatures as molecular disorder increases is a self-defeating process. If it were not for differences in temperature, none of our machines that convert heat to other forms of energy—steam engines, turbines or gasoline engines—could operate. In the same way that water can turn a wheel only if it runs downhill, so heat can do work only when it flows from a hot place to a cold one. This principle applies not only to machines but also to nature. The constantly

Stages in a possible entropy death of the universe are shown below as they might affect the earth. The sun grows to a "red giant" stage in

the state of least entropy, or greatest amount of usefulness. As the soldiers break ranks and gradually fall into disarray, entropy increases.

changing weather of our planet is dependent upon differences in heat levels around the globe. Wind, for instance, is largely caused by hot air rising and cold air rushing in to take its place.

The measure of just how evenly the heat of the universe is distributed is called entropy, a term invented by the German physicist Clausius in 1865. Increasing entropy—the continuous dilution of heat and order—has cosmic implications. For nearly a century, there has been widespread speculation that the whole universe might be running a self-destroying race toward maximum entropy. Ultimately, according to this traditional view, there must come a time when the whole cosmos will level out to absolutely uniform temperature. When this occurs, no more work will be done; all processes will stop; and so, some say, will time.

Recently, however, this doomful prospect has lost a little of the implacable certainty that once surrounded it. At least it is known that an entropy doomsday—if it happens—will not come for a long time. Physicists once said that the sun could last for no longer than 200,000 years before burning out. Now, with the realization that the sun's energy comes from nuclear fusion—the conversion of its matter to energy—they calculate it should keep burning for another 10 to 30 billion years. There has been an even more direct denial of the idea that our universe is a mortal one. Some astronomers have evolved the "steady state" theory—that new matter containing new usable energy is constantly being created in the voids of space between the stars and the galaxies. If this is true, the long-discussed running down of the universe may not happen after all.

the fourth frame, then shrinks to a "white dwarf" and finally winks out. Mountains decay and earth and space assume a common temperature.

4

The Search
for the Ends
of the Rainbow

IN 15 MINUTES the sun radiates as much energy on our globe as mankind consumes in every other form during an entire year. Although we now convert only the most minute fraction of this torrent of sunshine to use, an enormous wealth of radiant energy is available to us, and the time may come when we will be able to trap it and transform it at will.

Even now, specially designed houses use solar energy to cut fuel bills by two thirds. Inexpensive high-efficiency solar cooking devices are also being made in various countries. And while most of these are only big enough to barbecue a steak in the backyard, one mammoth solar furnace has been constructed on Mont Louis in the French Pyrenees. Under good weather conditions this device produces temperatures of over 5,400° F.—hot enough to burn a hole through a steel rail in 30 seconds.

Of all the new uses of solar energy, perhaps the most important today is in the field of space satellites. These complex payloads, both U.S. and Soviet, are studded with special solar cells which convert sunlight directly to electricity for powering instruments and radio transmitters. So reliable are these devices that one on board the grapefruit-sized Vanguard I operated without a minute's stoppage from the time it was launched in March of 1958 until May of 1964, when the natural radiation of outer space finally caused its cells to deteriorate.

Man has recognized that sunlight is a powerful source of energy since ancient times. For centuries it has been known that a simple magnifying glass will concentrate the light of the sun into a beam so hot that it will cause wood to catch fire; burning glasses not unlike modern children's toys have been found in the ruins of Nineveh dating from the 7th Century, B.C. In the Greek comedy *The Clouds* by Aristophanes, one of the characters speaks of focusing a burning glass on a wax tablet as a means to deface some written evidence. And there is a story, no doubt apocryphal, that Archimedes destroyed the Roman fleet attacking Syracuse by setting the sails afire with a battery of mirrors.

In the 17th and 18th Centuries, astronomers found evidence of the power of light in observing that tails of comets appeared to be blown by some mysterious wind, and they guessed that the effect was caused by a kind of light pressure. Trying to observe the pressure of light on earth, they suspended delicate pieces of paper in high-powered light beams. While the idea has since proved to be right, the existing light pressure was in a range too small to move the paper in the experiment. Not until the turn of this century were instruments developed which were sensitive enough to detect light pressure.

Soft as the touch of visible light usually is, it is one of the two forms of radiant energy that human senses can detect directly. So magnificent is the eye as an instrument, it can detect at a distance of one foot a

A COLD LIGHT FROM THE SEA
Deep-sea corals, opposite, subjected to ultraviolet rays, emit the ghostly glow of fluorescence. Most sources of light—such as an ordinary light bulb—produce infrared as well as visible radiation and therefore are quite hot. However, certain kinds of material, like these corals, when stimulated by ultraviolet rays, radiate visibly—fluoresce—but give off practically no heat. Thus fluorescence is often called "cold light."

light source one thousandth of the power of a single candle. The only other form of radiant energy that humans can sense is so-called infrared heat energy. For the skin of the human body is studded with nerve endings which detect heat and which, like the eye, are enormously efficient, responding to as little as 0.005°F. temperature change.

The fact that infrared energy is a form of invisible light was discovered at the turn of the 19th Century by Sir William Herschel, one of the greatest scientists of his age and a pioneer of stellar astronomy who became interested in sunspots and began examining light with a large variety of differently colored filters. In 1800 he discovered that though some produced the effect of heat, others did not, and he sought the cause of this difference. Using a prism he spread a beam of sunlight into the continuous band of color known as the spectrum, red at one end, shading through orange and yellow to green, blue and violet at the other end. He observed that yellow was the brightest light; that red in its turn gave off greater heat and, to his surprise, that the highest temperature of all occurred in invisible radiation just below the visible red light. This infrared—"beneath the red"—light is a prominent part of the radiation which we now recognize as being thrown off by any hot object.

Infrared as a private eye

In addition to its importance in household heat lamps and in other medical therapy where heat is helpful, invisible infrared has become, since the outbreak of World War II, increasingly important in photography. Newly devised films respond to infrared as does ordinary film to ordinary light, thus making it possible to take photographs in complete darkness. The image varies in its intensity on the film in accordance with the temperature of the various objects in the picture—the hotter the object the brighter it is in the finished photograph. In one test, for example, an infrared picture of an empty parking lot showed clearly where cars had been parked hours earlier, because the difference in the heat of the pavement—which had been shaded by the cars—showed clearly on the film.

For fairly obvious reasons the military is making widespread use of infrared photographs in night reconnaissance flights sent up to spot, from the heat they give off, installations so artfully concealed that they would be totally invisible by day. A further innovation of infrared, the so-called "sniperscope," permits a rifleman to see in the dark by means of a spotlight on his weapon which projects a beam of infrared that bounces back to a minute screen on the rifle, showing a TV-like picture of the landscape.

Just a year after Herschel discovered infrared, the German researcher Johann Wilhelm Ritter found that beyond the other end of the spectrum

A SUNLIT STILL

This solar furnace used for distillation was described by Athanasius Kircher, a 17th Century writer and illustrator. Reflected from a concave mirror, the sun's rays heat the liquid in the flask (center) so that some of it vaporizes and then condenses into the jar at right, leaving impurities in the first flask. The mirror pivots on its stand to keep sunlight on the flask, which also can be raised or lowered by the adjustable arm.

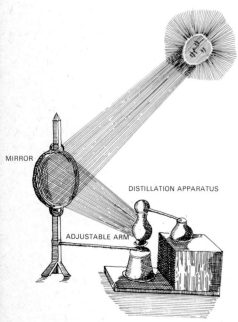

MIRROR

DISTILLATION APPARATUS

ADJUSTABLE ARM

there were other invisible rays which were especially effective in chemical reactions, and Ritter's discovery came to be called the "chemical spectrum." The fact that silver chloride, especially, was more affected by these rays than by ordinary visible light eventually brought about an explanation of the exact nature of this spectrum. However, this did not come about through scientific investigation but because of that highly commercial invention, photography. In 1839 the Frenchman Louis Daguerre popularized a process for taking pictures—the famous daguerreotypes of the Victorian era—on metal plates coated with silver salts. Science soon capitalized on Daguerre's process to make spectral photographs. Recorded on the silver plates beyond the violet band was a whole new sector of radiation invisible to the eye. Scientists named it ultraviolet, meaning "beyond the violet."

The human skin also reacts to ultraviolet radiation. Ultraviolet is the part of sunlight which causes suntans. Tanning is, however, purely a protective mechanism. Biologists have established that uncontrolled ultraviolet rays kill the cells of pure white skin: any fair-skinned person who overexposes himself to the first blaze of summer is likely to suffer third-degree burns. The white man's slowly acquired suntan and the permanent pigmentation of the dark-skinned races serve as effective ultraviolet filters which protect the body cells from damage by the rays which are present in sunlight.

Ultraviolet's effects are not all bad however. Among other virtues, it aids the body in synthesizing vitamin D, and in recent years it has been widely used as the so-called "black light" that causes special luminous signs to glow in the dark. Ultraviolet light can be generated artificially. The arc lights used to light movie and TV studios produce the radiation in large amounts. A simpler home "sunlamp" also has been devised which consists of a special quartz glass bulb containing a little mercury; when the electric current vaporizes the mercury, the resulting glow contains ultraviolet light. Quartz glass must be used because ordinary window glass is opaque to ultraviolet, as anyone knows who has tried to get a suntan through a closed window.

The forecast of waves to come

The fourth form of radiant energy is that of radio waves, first predicted by Clerk Maxwell in 1864. In his "Treatise on Electricity and Magnetism," one of the most important papers ever published in physics, Maxwell showed that a pulsating electric current would create a pulsating magnetic field in the space around it, and that this magnetic field would create another electric field and so on, ad infinitum. This chain of disturbances, he said, would flow across space until it contacted another piece of matter where it would generate an electric current sim-

**RADIANT HEAT TURNS
A MYSTERIOUS PADDLEWHEEL**

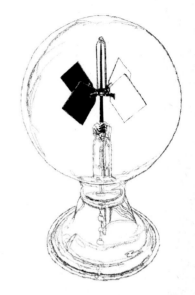

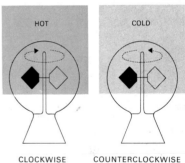

CLOCKWISE   COUNTERCLOCKWISE

THE REVERSIBLE RADIOMETER
Radiometers, found both in novelty shops and laboratories, are set twirling by radiant heat. Basically, they work because the black side of each vane absorbs radiant heat and gets warm; the light side, being shiny, reflects it and stays cool. Then, through "thermal transpiration," more gas molecules inside the bulb gather on the black sides, creating a pressure which pushes the vanes clockwise, much as heated molecules push a piston. When the bulb is cooled, the process is reversed and the vanes turn the other way until all the parts reach the same temperature.

ilar to the one that started the chain process. He then calculated that these undulations, having both an electrical and a magnetic component, traveled at the same velocity as light, and from this he concluded that light itself was a form of "electromagnetic" radiation.

Maxwell still had not discovered radio waves, nor had he invented radio. But Heinrich Hertz, a German physicist, was quick to apply Maxwell's theory and he found that it worked. When, in 1888, he made a spark jump between two terminals, he observed a smaller spark in a second circuit he had set up on the other side of the room. The waves traveling through the intervening space to cause the spark were, he recognized, electromagnetic waves of an entirely new sort. Still sometimes called Hertzian waves in his honor, they were today's radio waves. A 22-year-old Italian, Guglielmo Marconi, was the first to see commercial value in them. Reasoning that if current could be passed across a room it could be sent across miles of space, Marconi developed and patented the first radio transmitter and receiver in 1896.

The mystery ray called X

A year previously, Wilhelm Konrad Roentgen had discovered another form of radiant energy, identified as X-rays. A physics professor at the University of Wurzburg in Germany, he was working with a cathode tube in which a current of electricity was passed through a vacuum from one terminal inside the tube to the other. Because such a tube glows slightly when the current flows, Roentgen had darkened the room to see the glow better. Suddenly he noted that a piece of glass covered with a barium salt also glowed whenever the tube was operating—even though it was screened from the apparatus by black paper. He put a book in front of the tube and the screen still glowed. Then he substituted a piece of wood, and finally a piece of aluminum. The rays penetrated everything, including his hand. Furthermore, when he held his hand between the cathode tube and a photographic plate, the skeletal image was left on the plate. Roentgen's discovery created as much flurry in the press of his day as did the Russian satellite Sputnik in modern times. More than 1,000 scientific articles were published on the new X-ray in just the first year following its discovery.

The immediate scientific excitement over Roentgen's discovery had other effects as well. Among these was the impulse of the French scientist Henri Becquerel to reconsider the fact that certain uranium compounds fluoresce when they are exposed to light. Becquerel guessed that this glow, stimulated by sunlight, would produce a photographic impression as X-rays did. Wrapping such a plate in black paper, he topped his package with a sample of uranium ore and exposed it to sunlight. Then he found as he developed the plate that an image of the uranium showed

THE RANGE OF RADIATION
This scale plots the electromagnetic spectrum, from short gamma rays to long radio waves. All radiant energy is transmitted by electromagnetic waves at the speed of light. Though we feel some of them as heat and see others as light, the radiations basically differ only in wavelength. The electromagnetic theory of radiation, proposed by James Clerk Maxwell in Scotland in 1865, was proved by Heinrich Hertz in Germany 20 years later.

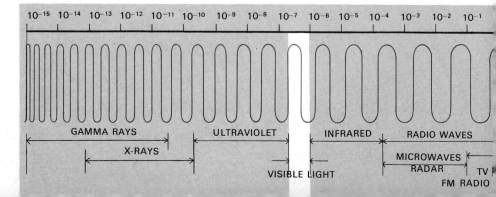

on the negative. He set out to repeat the test, but when the weather turned cloudy he put the package in a drawer with the ore still on top of it. Later developing one of these plates which had had no exposure to daylight, he found that the image of the ore was as clear as in his first experiment, and he thus established that uranium gives off radiation whether or not light strikes it.

An alphabet for radiation

Marie and Pierre Curie in 1897 were to find two elements, polonium and radium, which had precisely the same property. Analysis of the radiation later revealed three distinct types, which were called alpha, beta and gamma. Alpha and beta rays are electrically charged bits of atoms. On the other hand, gamma rays are similar to X-rays, though more energetic and of somewhat different origin. X-rays are produced by the electrons surrounding the nuclei of atoms whereas gamma rays are the result of changes within the atomic nuclei themselves. Gamma rays are produced both naturally—by decay of the earth's radioactive substances—and artificially—by the reactions that occur in atomic reactors.

While each of these forms of radiant energy—visible light, infrared, ultraviolet, radio, X-ray and gamma rays—was discovered separately and seemed to have different properties, the early work of Maxwell had made it clear that all were waves having both an electrical and magnetic nature which, when grouped together, could be called the electromagnetic spectrum.

Maxwell's convincing argument in favor of the wave theory of light seemed to end forever a centuries-old debate among scientists. The opposite view had conceived of light as beams made up of individual particles. Plato had asserted that the eye emitted particles which bounced back from objects encountered in normal vision. The first rejection of this Platonic view since ancient times came in 1666 when the Italian mathematician Francesco Grimaldi compared the reaction of light to the behavior of waves in a liquid. A dozen years later the eminent Dutch astronomer and physicist Christian Huygens published his "Traité de la Lumière," in which he also came out in favor of the wave theory.

Meanwhile, Sir Isaac Newton and Robert Hooke had taken up the debate, and after years of study Newton propounded the theory that all light phenomena could best be explained by considering light as consisting of particles. Although he pointed out further lines of inquiry, his followers for a century were adamant in holding to this corpuscular theory of light, until Thomas Young, making use of Huygens' postulate with extraordinary skill, announced unequivocally in 1801 that light is composed of waves. He had discovered that a beam of light, split in two, could be recombined to produce alternating bands of light and darkness,

A TRACER OF MISSING GASES
Within a span of five years, 1894 to 1898, Sir William Ramsay, professor of chemistry at University College, London, discovered five of the six inert gaseous elements—argon, helium, neon, krypton and xenon. He was awarded the Royal Society's Davy medal in 1894, was knighted in 1902 and received the Nobel Prize for chemistry in 1904. The caricature above, from *Vanity Fair* magazine, shows Ramsay in the classroom with some of his "family" on a chart of elements.

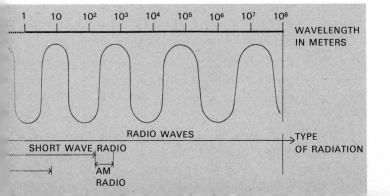

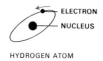

ELECTRON
NUCLEUS

HYDROGEN ATOM

HELIUM ATOM

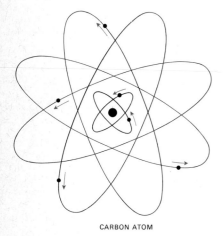

CARBON ATOM

THE TINIEST SOLAR SYSTEM
Niels Bohr, the great Danish physicist who died
in 1962, visualized the atom as a tiny solar
system with electrons traveling around a
nucleus in fixed circular orbits. German
physicist Arnold Sommerfeld suggested
elliptical orbits, as illustrated above in the
patterns of three common elements. Though
modern concepts of atomic structure are more
complex, the Bohr-Sommerfeld theory is
still considered a useful simplified visualization.

an effect known as the "interference phenomenon." This behavior could
not be explained by the particle theory.

Young, however, had antagonized the old guard of British science, and
the august *Edinburgh Review* thundered that Young's ideas were haz-
ardous to the progress of science and "destitute of every species of
merit." Confident of the accuracy of his observations, Young published
a rebuttal which sold one copy, but he was vindicated after a half century more of imaginative experimentation at last culminated in Maxwell's brilliant assertion that light is an electromagnetic wave.

Only 25 years after Maxwell had seemed to have settled the wave-
versus-particle controversy—in favor of the wave concept—a new piece
of evidence was discovered which reopened the argument all over again.
This was the discovery of the "photoelectric effect," a phenomenon used
today in the electric-eye devices that open and close doors in supermar-
kets and garages. Knowing that electricity is created when light knocks
electrons off the surface of metals, the German physicist Phillipp Lenard
found that increasing the intensity of an ultraviolet beam did not seem
to increase the speed with which the electrons left the metal. Furthermore, he observed no photoelectric effect at all in using a beam of pure
red or infrared light. It was almost as if a carpenter had found a nail that
could be driven only with a hammer blow of a certain strength—trying
to drive the nail with many smaller blows would not work. Lenard's
observations could not be explained by the wave theory and it was this
disquieting observation that caught the eye of Albert Einstein.

Energy in tiny packets

Einstein was aware of the recent discovery by the German physicist
Max Planck that heat radiation is absorbed or given off only in the form
of tiny packets of energy called quanta. In his revolutionary paper of
1905 Einstein said that light must behave the same way, and he asserted
that each color of light was made up of packets containing different
amounts of energy. These light quanta were later named photons.

Photons offered a partial explanation to Lenard's puzzling observations, for he said that a certain amount of energy was necessary to
knock an electron from the surface of the metal and additional energy
was necessary to send it flying into space. In Einstein's explanation, red
light did not consist of photons with enough energy to do the job, but
ultraviolet did; neither could two or more small photons gang up to do
the job. It was all or nothing for each photon.

Einstein's work was not intended to send physicists all the way back
to the particle theory; for wave and particle theories now coexist in almost perfect harmony. Waves seem more applicable as a term to describe
the radio sector of the electromagnetic spectrum, while the particle

description is more convenient for short compact waves like gamma and X-rays. Visible light—somewhere between in measurement—has a split personality, its behavior seeming sometimes like that of a wave, sometimes like that of a particle.

The discovery that light did consist of definite energy packets has been the key to answering the last remaining question about radiant energy: where does it come from? The first step toward the answer came about 50 years ago. In 1913, the young Danish physicist Niels Bohr, who was studying with Lord Ernest Rutherford at the Cavendish Laboratory, came up with a series of audacious assumptions about the nature of matter which placed him among the great physicists of our time.

An infinitesimal solar system

Starting with Rutherford's model of the atom and applying Planck's quantum theory, Bohr pictured the atom as a kind of solar system with a nucleus surrounded by orbiting electrons. But while planets are held in their paths around the sun by gravitation, Bohr knew that the gravitational effects between atom particles are too minute to keep electrons and nucleus together. The electrical attraction between particles positively and negatively charged served this purpose.

Bohr's contribution to the concept of the atom was to establish that the number and diameter of orbits permitted to electrons is fixed. For example, in hydrogen, an orbit is permitted which is approximately 1/250,000,000 of an inch in diameter, as well as orbits 4, 9, 16, and 25 times the diameter of this innermost orbit. In between these, all other orbits are forbidden. Ordinarily an electron remains in its permitted orbit without radiating or absorbing energy. However, electrons may leap from one permitted orbit to another.

When an electron does so, there is a change in its energy. If one jumps into an orbit farther from the nucleus, it has moved "uphill" electrically, which means that work has been done: it has had to absorb energy from some outside source. If it drops to an orbit closer to the nucleus, the leap "downhill" is accompanied by an instantaneous release of energy equal to the difference in energy level of the two orbits. These concentrations of energy are photons. And this is the general mechanism by which light is produced and absorbed.

The possible electron orbits surround the nucleus somewhat like concentric shells, one within the other. Electrons may jump not only to the next orbit, but to orbits quite a distance away. In hydrogen, transitions from the outer orbits to the innermost produce high-energy photons resulting in ultraviolet rays. Transitions from the outer orbits to the third orbit involve less energy and produce photons in the infrared.

When the atomic nucleus is more massive than the single proton, hy-

PRODIGAL ELECTRONS RETURN TO SHINE

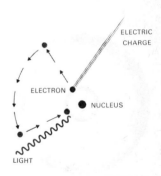

KEEPING BROADWAY BRIGHT
Main streets all across the country glitter at night because of the excited actions of tiny electrons in the neon gas of flashing signs. Struck by an electrical discharge *(above)*, an electron of a neon atom absorbs the energy and leaps from its normal orbit around the nucleus to a new but only temporary orbit. Upon returning, the electron gives off the absorbed energy as light. In other words, it glows.

ATOMIC HOPSCOTCH
The activated electron described in the margin above, right, may jump more than one orbit and then return in steps rather than in one leap *(right)*. On returning from an outer to an intermediate orbit, the electron, being farther from the attraction of the nucleus, emits less energy than on its next jump to an inner orbit. The wavelength of the light, which depends on the energy involved, is longer for the first step, shorter for the second.

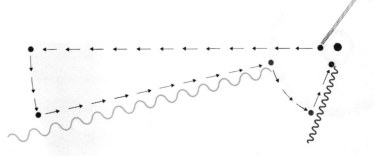

drogen, it is of course more highly charged. More energy is required to move an electron away from it, and therefore more energy is released in orbital transitions back to positions close to the densely packed nuclei of heavy metals. When electrons make transitions in this high-energy region, X-rays are produced, which is why the targets of all X-ray tubes are made of the heavier metals.

Orbits similar to those of hydrogen exist for all elements, their precise size depending on the volume and the strength of the electrically charged mass packed into the nucleus. The outermost orbit never contains more than eight electrons, and the innermost orbit never more than two, with some intervening orbits containing as many as 32. Sodium, for example, has 11 electrons: two in the innermost, eight in the second, and the remaining electron in the third ring. And because each element has a different orbital structure, the photons emitted are characteristic and account for the unique spectral colors of each element.

Though waves and photons sound completely contradictory, physicists have learned how to calculate radiation problems with astonishing accuracy. The modern theory of the electromagnetic spectrum, called quantum electrodynamics, is a striking example of the physicist's ability to predict accurately the results of experiments in spite of his inability to picture the basic concepts in nonmathematical terms, or even to defend, in a completely satisfactory way, the logical basis of the theory.

The Strange and Spectral World of Light

Because his world is largely defined by light, man has always been fascinated by its bewildering, dazzling antics. To the physicist, light is no more than a form of radiant energy, measured in matter-of-fact wavelengths. But to most people light means brightness and shade, a blending and a clash of colors as it plays upon the world *(opposite)*. Since ancient times, men have made lenses and other optical glassware to put light through its paces—and light rays have responded in a host of prankish ways, revealing curious worlds usually hidden from the eye: shapes that bend or break, enlarge or shrink, turn upside down or backward, grow distorted or disappear altogether; colors that turn into their opposites or appear where there was no color at all. In nature, this capriciousness results in such eerie phenomena as rainbows and mirages. In the camera it can be equally intriguing, as shown in the following portfolio by LIFE photographer Nina Leen.

SHEDDING LIGHT ON COLOR
In dim light, colors fade and appear to the eye as shades of gray and black. In the photograph opposite, in which only the apple is in a strong light, the right side shows how red roses would look to the eye in the low-intensity background light. Photographic film, however, is able to record color in conditions where the eye cannot, as illustrated by the left side of the picture.

Wavelengths
That Paint Man's
World

Color is present in all light. White light, which appears to have no color, is really the sum total of all color. In fact, although sunlight ordinarily seems white, in passing through the atmosphere it sometimes reveals its many colors spread out in a spectrum, or rainbow. By the same token, white light can be made by mixing colored lights together, as shown at the top of the eggshell at left.

Light consists of radiations, or electromagnetic waves, of various wavelengths. But the eye responds to these radiations by converting each wavelength into a specific color. In addition, the eye turns mixtures of radiations into new blends of color. In this way we perceive the egg at left to be decorated in more colors than the three actually shining on it.

Besides coloring our perceptions, the hues that we see everywhere around us can shape our moods and affect our tastes. A bizarre dinner party once proved this: when the guests were served under lights that made steak look gray, celery pink, peas black and coffee yellow, most could not eat and, though the food was superb, those who did try it became violently ill.

A SPECTRUM-SPECKLED EGG

On the shell of the egg at left, overhead beams of red, green and blue light overlap to produce the colors of the spectrum. The diagram above shows how the same pattern of colors looks when spread on a flat surface. At the top of the egg, where all three light beams are equally mixed, the "total color" of white is the result. Because red, green and blue light, besides adding up to white, can produce all other colors, physicists have named them the primary colors of light. There is another triad of colors —seen where the primary colors overlap above —which also can produce all other colors and which the artist has taken as his primary colors *(pages 82-83)*. But to the physicist, these are the complementary colors of light, for each can be formed by mixing two of light's three primaries. In the photograph at left, the colors of the three shadows cast by the egg are complementary to the pools of primary light around them.

Pigments:
Color
by Subtraction

The colors of almost everything we see are products of pigment, but pigments are not the source of colors. They are merely agents that screen out or "subtract" all but specific colors of light: green pigment, for instance, is green because in effect it absorbs all the colors of white light except green, reflecting the green wavelength that we see. The same is true of any other pigment. Thus black pigment looks black because it absorbs almost all light, while white pigment reflects light, absorbing very little color at all.

Most people may know from a high-school art class that the artist's names for the primary colors are red, blue and yellow. To the physicist, however, these are neither primaries nor properly named: the artist's primaries ought to be named magenta, cyan and yellow—for they are actually the complements of light's true primaries, as explained in the color wheel below. To add to the confusion, the photographer, in developing color pictures *(right and opposite)*, finds that the primary colors of pigment in his negative reproduce the primaries of light in a print.

COLORS TURNED INSIDE OUT

In the color negative opposite, light intensities are the reverse of those on the print above, as occurs in a black-and-white negative. This is due to a paradoxical property of photographic film: light becomes dark on the negative. Therefore another reversing step is required in order to produce a true image. In much the same way the colors on the negative shown opposite are reversed. For example, the colors of the clown's nose in the print and negative are complementary. The real nose is red with blue in it, so the negative nose is cyan minus that much blue.

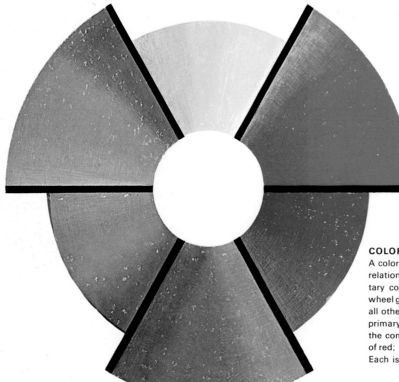

COLORS IN THE ROUND

A color wheel such as the one at left shows the relationships between primary and complementary colors. The three larger segments of the wheel give the primary colors of light, from which all other colors can be formed. Opposite each primary color is its complement. Thus yellow is the complement of blue; cyan the complement of red; and magenta the complement of green. Each is a mixture of the primaries next to it.

False Images in a Glass of Water

The amusing optical illusions pictured on these pages—the cat's face in a glass of water and the broken or disappearing spoons—are caused by the refraction, or bending, of light. A glass of water acts as a lens, and light is bent in passing through it as shown in the diagrams below. The spoons, seen through water, appear magnified and displaced. The cat's face is reversed so that the real whiskers, which can be seen outside and to the right of the glass, appear at the left inside the glass.

All lenses refract light. Their different effects depend on their curvature and refractive index—the power to bend light rays. In putting refraction to good use man has come up with all kinds of optical equipment—the eyeglasses, telescopes, microscopes, cameras and projectors by which he bends light to suit his needs.

A TURNED-AROUND CAT

Light from the figure of a cat *(below, top)* is bent passing through a glass of water as it would be bent by a lens *(blue area)*. Because of its curvature, the lens bends the light waves so that they converge on the other side— but in a reverse position. Thus, rays from the left side *(black)* focus at right, and rays from the right side *(red)* focus at left. Rays going through the center are unbent because they enter and leave the lens through virtually parallel surfaces. In the picture opposite, the glass is off-center, so the cat is distorted as well as reversed.

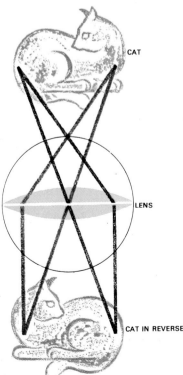

CAT

LENS

CAT IN REVERSE

WATER THAT BREAKS SPOONS

The apparent displacement of the spoons in the photograph above results from the bending of light, as shown in the diagram at right. The portion of a spoon above the glass is, of course, seen in its actual position. Light waves from the spoon in the water, however, are bent and sent astray by the lens formed by the water. (They are not focused as they are in the diagram at left because the spoon is much nearer the lens than the cat is.) The eye, when it sees the light waves, does not know they have been bent, but follows them straight back to where they appear to converge *(black lines)* and there sees an image of the spoon *(red circle)*. Note in the picture above that one spoon has been doubly displaced, and turns up in the wrong glass altogether.

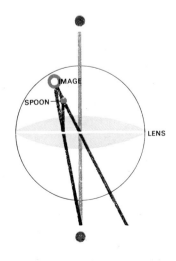

IMAGE

SPOON

LENS

White Light
Bent into
a Rainbow

When Isaac Newton in 1666 darkened his chamber and let a small slit of light pass through a triangular prism as pictured above, he observed "the most considerable detection which hath hitherto been made in the operations of nature." In the colorful spectrum produced from white light he beheld "the most surprising and wonderful Composition . . . of Whiteness."

Newton had not been the first to see white light so beautifully sundered, but he was the first to figure out that light is made up of separate colored rays which bend different amounts in passing through glass and so spread out to show their colors. He further proved that if the refracted rays were passed through a second prism, inverted to have the opposite effect of the first, the resulting beam would appear pure white again.

Physicists now know that such refraction takes place because each wavelength or color of light moves through glass at a different speed, as shown in the diagram at right. The same is true in other media: a rainbow, for example, is a spectrum formed as white sunlight is refracted by tiny droplets of water suspended in the air. Lens makers were long plagued by this feature of refraction, for lenses tend to produce a spectral color fringe, or "chromatic aberration," around an image. Today's refined lenses handle this by using one thickness of glass to correct the refraction of another—as Newton long ago restored the whiteness to refracted light.

SCHISM IN A PRISM

Light's passage through a prism is illustrated in the diagram at left. To simplify matters, only the wavelengths at each end of the spectrum are represented. At the far left, red and blue waves of light are shown moving in the same path toward the prism. The distance from crest to crest is greater for red than blue, because red light is of a longer wavelength than blue. What happens when light enters the prism is shown enlarged within the black circle. Light waves move more slowly in glass than in air and so are bent when they hit the prism. The blue wave is bent more than the red, making the two diverge. The waves are bent again on leaving the prism to produce the separation of colors in a spectrum.

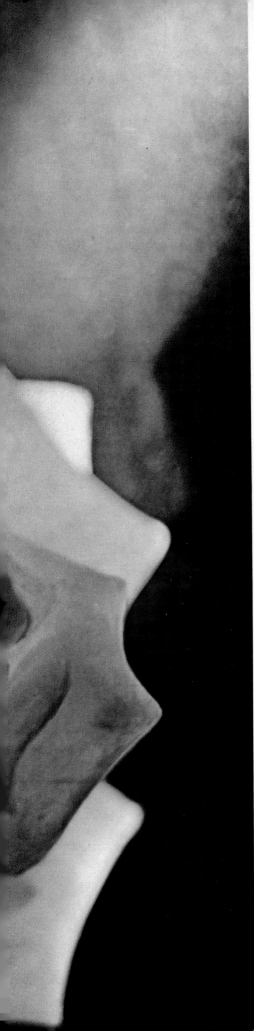

Making
Light Turn
a Corner

Like refraction, diffraction is a phenomenon based on the bending of light. The spectra hovering over the rose at left are products of diffraction. Because light travels in waves, it can bend around sharp edges or corners, as sea waves bend around a jetty. Light can be so bent with a diffraction grating—a plastic screen with thousands of opaque microscopic grooves separated by slits of clear plastic. Each wavelength of light bends at the grooves' edges to a different degree, thus splitting white light into colored spectra, as at left. The grating is so nearly transparent that it does not appear in the picture.

Similar diffraction spectra appear on an LP record held under a beam of light; the microgrooves of the disc diffract some of the light into small rainbows on its surface. The fact that a shadow is not as sharp as the object casting it, no matter how pinpointed the light, is also due to diffraction: since light waves bend around the edges of the object, the resulting shadow is blurred in outline.

The diffraction of light is proof that it moves in waves. But physicists have shown that in some instances light behaves as if made up not of waves but of particles. One of the hottest debates in the history of physics centered on this disagreement. It was settled in the 1920s by means of some illuminating mathematics that showed light to be both waves and particles. Now, in their lighter moments, physicists talk about "wavicles."

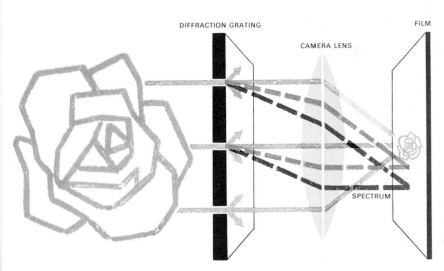

SPECTRUM FROM A ROSE

The spectra above the rose in the photograph at left are a striking demonstration that all colors are present in light. When, as shown in the simplified diagram above, a diffraction grating is placed between the rose and the camera lens *(shaded blue)*, some of the light *(solid gray lines)* passes straight through the slits and is focused on the film at far right to produce a reduced image of the rose. Other light bends at the slits: blue light, the shortest wavelength of visible light *(dark-blue dotted line)*, is only slightly bent and is focused by the lens just below the rose; the red, light's longest wavelength *(red dotted line)*, is bent more and is focused farther from the rose; the intermediate wavelengths not shown are bent within these extremes, to form the complete spectrum. The diagram shows only single rays of red and blue, but actually the light's countless rays spread in all directions to form many spectra, as in the picture at left.

Plastics That
Set Unruly Waves
in Order

Light, which can be reflected, refracted and diffracted, may be polarized as well. Ordinarily, as light waves move forward they also vibrate in all directions, radiating like wheel spokes around an axle. When polarized, however, their vibrations are restricted to a narrow plane, as shown in the diagram below. Polarization is produced by light's passage through molded plastic, crystals or even the upper atmosphere. The light reflected off mirrors is also polarized. Polaroid filters, used on cameras and as sunglasses, cut down glare because they too polarize light. Nevertheless, the naked eye cannot distinguish polarized from ordinary light.

When white light passes through molded plastics, in which it is both polarized and refracted, a polaroid filter will reveal its prismatic colors, as shown in the photograph opposite. Such colored patterns indicate internal stresses in the plastic. Thus plastic models of machine and missile parts are studied to pinpoint inner flaws, a technique employed in the design of nose cones and other space hardware.

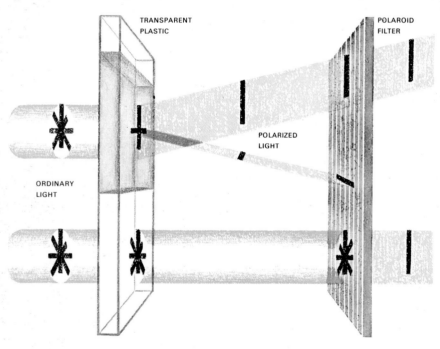

TRANSPARENT PLASTIC

POLAROID FILTER

POLARIZED LIGHT

ORDINARY LIGHT

SCREENING SCRAMBLED LIGHT
Light's vibrations, perpendicular to the wave's axis of forward motion, ordinarily occur in all directions, as depicted in black lines at the far left of the diagram above. In the lower portion of the diagram, an ordinary beam of white light *(shaded blue)* passes without being changed through clear plastic, and strikes a polaroid filter *(gray)* at the right. The filter permits only one plane of vibration to pass through it. Thus the light which does go through, vibrating only vertically, is polarized. In the upper part of the diagram, ordinary light is shown passing through plastic under stress, as in the photograph at right. In this medium the light is polarized in two planes at right angles to each other and the two polarized beams are refracted at different angles (a phenomenon known as "double refraction"). Only one polarized beam, the one in a vertical plane, can pass through the polaroid filter at the right; the other is screened out.

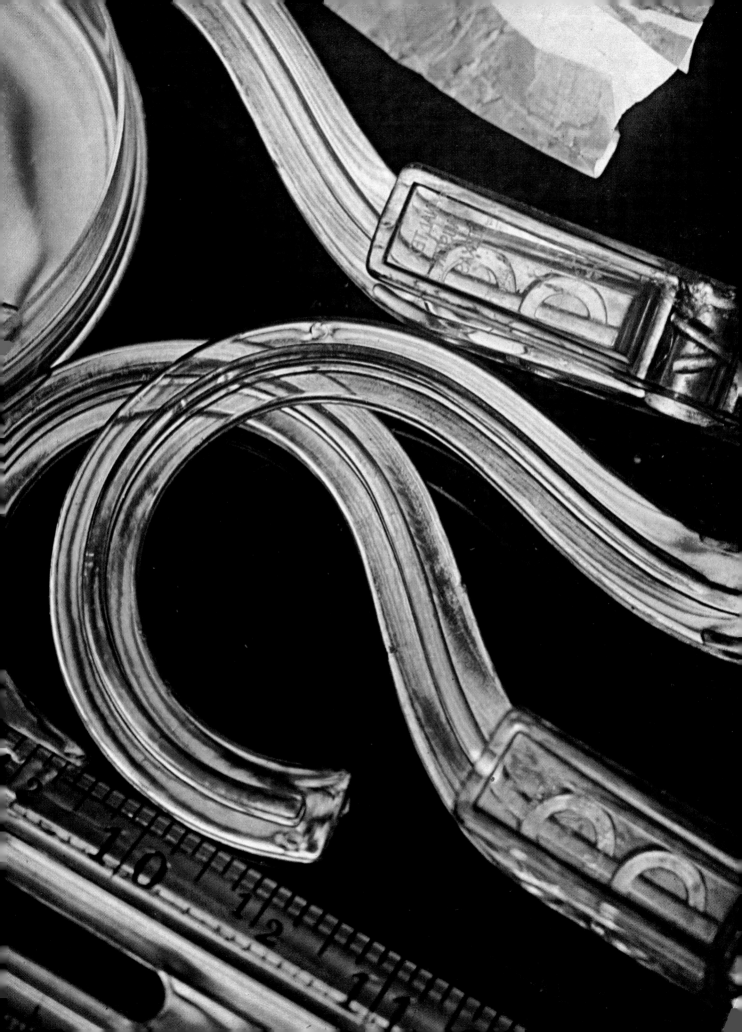

5

Rich Dividends
from
Chemical Bonds

FLY OVER AMERICA IN A PLANE and beneath you great highways thread the continent, beaded with moving cars. Powered by high-speed explosions of gasoline mixed with air, the engines of the cars pulse with chemical energy. Pistons, levers, gear and drive shafts smoothly convert the chemical energy of each explosion into the kinetic energy of the revolving wheels.

Along the highways sprawl farms, villages and cities. In winter a plume of smoke rises from the chimney of nearly every house below—a signal that burning coal, oil or gas is releasing its stored chemical energy in the form of heat to warm each dwelling.

Electric lights glow from the windows of houses and neon signs color each main street. But follow the web of electric wires over the landscape and more often than not they will end up at a giant generating plant where the chemical energy of coal, oil or gas is converted by burning into electrical energy.

Observe the tiny specks of life below: people, animals, plants. The energy that powers their motion, their growth, their reproduction, all comes from the chemical energy of food.

Of all forms of energy, none is so useful and vital to the life of man as chemical energy. Much of this utility stems from its tremendous versatility. Sometimes, as in ordinary fuels such as coal or wood, the chemical energy is so readily given up that a lighted match is all that is needed to release it. But there also is latent chemical energy in a diamond which does not burn until it is heated to 1,200°F. Chemical energy can be controlled so easily that a housewife can use it to toast meringue to just the proper shade of brown. Yet, it can be explosively uncontrollable, as it is when bound up in dynamite or TNT. The very page of this book is slowly releasing chemical energy as it combines with the oxygen of the air and becomes imperceptibly hotter than its surroundings. Should the book be kept for perhaps a hundred years, its pages will yellow as a result of this slow burning. In contrast, the fine strands of metal in a photographer's flash bulb burn instantaneously in a blinding flash of light.

Chemical energy is created when the complex bonds that cement matter together are altered. Atoms are tightly bonded together to produce molecules. And molecules are bound up into the larger pieces of matter that are big enough to see and touch. An atom of oxygen, for example, will join in a firm partnership with two hydrogen atoms to form a molecule of water. And many molecules of water will incorporate to form raindrops, snowflakes, oceans and icebergs. Every bonding between atom and atom, between molecule and molecule is a potential source of energy.

To understand why some substances have more chemical energy and give it up more readily, it is first necessary to recall some basic chemistry. As the last chapter explained, Niels Bohr had pictured the atom as a kind of miniature solar system. The sun is the nucleus and the planets are electrons. The nucleus has a positive charge and the electrons a negative charge. The positive and negative balance, and the atom is therefore electrically neutral.

As Bohr pointed out, electrons do not just whirl at random about the nucleus. They move in orbits only at certain distances away. If we could enlarge an atom about a hundred million times, we could say that some electrons orbit about an inch away from the nucleus; then another batch of electrons orbits four inches away, then more electrons orbit nine inches away, and so on. While electrons can go from the one-inch orbit to the two-inch orbit, they never circle permanently in the space between —say, a distance of an inch and a half. These orbits do not form two-dimensional planes like that of the earth around the sun; instead they form spherical shells like fuzzy ping-pong balls, one inside the other, surrounding the nucleus.

Building a shell collection

Not only is the size of the orbits limited, but so is the number of electrons each shell can hold. In any atom, the first shell, smallest and closest to the nucleus, is complete with only two electrons. The next shell holds eight. The third shell holds 18. The fourth contains 18 or 32. One of the most recently discovered of the man-made elements, Lawrencium, has atoms with 103 electrons in seven shells. But no matter how many electrons an atom has, the outermost ring never contains more than eight electrons.

These shells fill up with electrons the way cars fill the parking space around a supermarket. For the smallest atoms, at least, those closest to the nucleus will fill first, and only then are electrons found in the outer ones. Hydrogen, for instance, has one electron, circulating by itself in the first orbit which has room for two. Helium, a rare gas used in balloons and blimps, has two electrons, which completely fill the first orbit. Next in order is lithium, a light metal used in hydrogen bombs, which has three electrons, two in the first orbit and a single one in the second.

The way atoms behave chemically depends almost entirely on how many electrons are circling in their outer shell. This is an inordinate amount of influence for these few specks to wield and is only possible because of the intricacy of the forces that hold the atom together.

Overriding all other forces is the attraction of the positive nucleus for all of the negatively charged electrons around it. The nucleus constantly pulls electrons toward itself, and these electrons constantly whirl with just enough speed to keep from falling to the center, much the way an earth satellite must keep moving to prevent its falling back to earth. But in addition to this positive attraction, every electron in the atom

CHEMICAL COMBUSTIBLES

Burning or oxidation is an enormously useful form of chemical reaction. These drawings show three common substances which, when combined chemically with oxygen, emit heat energy which can be put to work. The amount of heat involved is given in kilocalories per pound (one kilocalorie, Kcal., equals 1,000 calories). Generally, these reactions need energy to get started—a match for a coal fire or a kerosene lamp, spark plugs for an automobile.

3.630 KCAL.　　　4.992 KCAL.　　　5.229 KCAL.

COAL　　　　KEROSENE　　　GASOLINE

repels every other electron. This is because they are all negatively charged, and negative charges repel each other. In a substance like helium, which has only two electrons, the two simply gyrate around in their own sphere, striving to keep poles apart from each other. But the situation is very complex in an atom like uranium, because there are 92 electrons, each being drawn as close to the positive nucleus as possible, yet each trying to maintain the greatest possible distance from each of the others. Such geometry would be difficult even if all 92 were not moving, but with all of them traveling at speeds averaging 1,500 miles per second, the balances become wildly complicated, changing from moment to moment.

The maximum numbers of electrons which can be found in each shell seem somehow to be determined by the over-all balance of the atom. From the point of view of the atom, it is the easiest, the most stable way of putting all these electrons together. The minute this pattern is disturbed with an unfilled ring, all of the difficulties of holding the atom together are tremendously increased. That does not mean that an atom cannot exist with unfilled outer rings—they simply make it harder.

In its precarious balance, an atom is something like a car parked on a steep hill. It is stable, but it could be a lot more so. One way an atom can "run downhill" is to join up with another atom. When two atoms join, the electrons in their outer rings are exchanged or shared. There are several ways this is accomplished, but the net result of it is that each atom has achieved *more* stability when its incomplete outer shell is filled. For example, sodium, with its one outer electron, mates readily with chlorine, which has seven. Seven and one make eight, the required number of electrons that make a complete outer ring.

In Chapter 1, the example of a car on an incline was used to demonstrate the phenomenon of potential energy. When the car rolled downhill, it released energy. And similarly, when an atom rolls downhill to combine with another in molecular bliss, energy is released. This is chemical energy, and the form in which it usually appears is heat.

Measurements in a bomb

There is no direct way to measure how much energy is locked up in the electrical bonds which hold a molecule together. But it is possible to determine how much heat is given off when a molecule forms or breaks up during a chemical reaction. Devices for making such measurements, called calorimeters, were invented in the 18th Century. One of the modern versions of this device is called the "bomb" calorimeter, and consists of little more than a well-insulated pot with a small container suspended inside. The pot is filled with water, and a chemical reaction between the substances being studied is started inside the container. The heat which

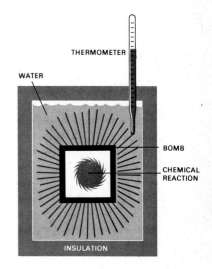

MEASURING HEAT WITH A "BOMB"
The schematic drawing above shows a bomb calorimeter, a simple apparatus that determines the amount of heat given off in a chemical reaction—such as the oxidation reactions described on the opposite page. Insulation prevents heat loss, and the thermometer measures the temperature rise of the water after the reaction has taken place. The inner box is called a "bomb" because the reactions in it are generally so rapid as to be almost explosive.

results as the substances react increases the temperature of the water, and the change is recorded on a thermometer. The calorie is the unit of measure, designating the amount of heat required to raise the temperature of one gram of water one degree centigrade. Indeed, the figures in all charts of the calorie content of food are made in this way—a sample of the food is burned and the number of degrees it raises the water temperature is measured. (The food Calorie, with a capital "C," is 1,000 times greater than the scientific calorie with a small "c.")

To describe chemical reactions in a quantitative way, not only must we calculate the amount of heat given off, but also each atom and molecule must be assigned a "weight." The measures commonly used are the gram-atomic weight and the gram-molecular weight. Every atom has a certain weight compared to every other atom, and the weight of a molecule is the sum of the weights of all the atoms that make it up. Common carbon has been taken as a weight standard and its weight has been arbitrarily set at 12. Compared to carbon, hydrogen, the lightest element, weighs 1.008, oxygen 15.999 and uranium 238.03. A molecule of carbon monoxide weighs 28, which is the sum of its components: one atom of carbon at 12, plus one of oxygen at 16. A gram-atomic or gram-molecular weight is simply the atomic and molecular weight expressed in grams. A gram-atomic weight of carbon is 12 grams; a gram-molecular weight of carbon monoxide is 28. The gram, although scientifically convenient, is an arbitrary choice of weights, for the unit of measurement could be an ounce-molecular weight or a ton-molecular weight. Indeed, American engineers still often use a pound-molecular weight.

The importance of a good draft

It is not easy to ascertain directly the heat given off in the oxidation of carbon to carbon monoxide, but for the sake of argument, let us assume that a gram-atomic weight of carbon is put into the calorimeter with *half* a gram-molecular weight of oxygen; when a spark is then passed through them, they combine violently to form carbon monoxide, the gas that is so dangerous in automobile exhausts. Could this union be isolated, we would find that 26,400 calories are given off. This is ordinary heat energy and could be put to work heating a house or running a locomotive. But carbon monoxide is capable of oxidizing further to carbon dioxide (the harmless gas that puts the bubbles in soda water), giving off 67,600 calories of heat. Thus in the oxidation of carbon to carbon dioxide, a total of 94,000 calories is produced. The same reaction—carbon combining with oxygen—goes on in any ordinary coal furnace, for coal is almost pure carbon. When there is a good draft of air supplying plenty of oxygen, the fire not only burns but it gives off

MOLECULAR TIES: BY GIVING . . .

With atoms represented as parents and an electron as a baby, the cartoons at right illustrate ionic bonding, one of two basic chemical bonds. The electron jumps from one atom to the other and forms two ions—atoms electrically charged by having gained or lost an electron—which are bonded together by electrostatic forces. An example is salt, in which one sodium electron joins a chlorine atom to make sodium chloride.

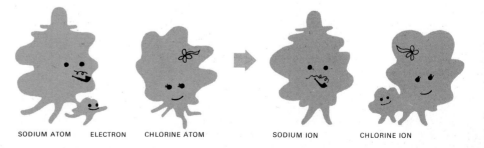

SODIUM ATOM   ELECTRON   CHLORINE ATOM   SODIUM ION   CHLORINE ION

more heat and is also less likely to produce deadly carbon monoxide.

Hydrogen also reacts with oxygen, and the result is hydrogen oxide—water. The reaction is explosive, emitting a loud bang when a spark is passed through the mixture of gases, and it results in minuscule water droplets—plus 68,400 calories of heat. Hydrogen might seem a less efficient heat producer than carbon because it gives off only 68,400 calories compared with carbon's 94,000, but, gram for gram, it is much more efficient. While it is too explosive a fuel for home use, rocketeers have an eye on it, and current plans for the American moon shot call for a hydrogen-oxygen-propelled engine in the rocket's second stage.

Though carbon and hydrogen are very simple molecular fuels, the same process of reaction occurs with more complicated molecules in the burning of petroleum, natural gas and a number of kinds of alcohol. Of all these, natural gas gives off the most heat on an ounce-for-ounce basis.

Each of the heat-producing reactions described above involves oxygen, yet this gas is not necessary for all chemical reactions. Hydrogen and chlorine react just as readily, giving off about 22,000 calories in the process, and in doing so produce a gas, hydrogen chloride, which in turn dissolves in water to form hydrochloric acid (the acid found in the human stomach). Sodium metal also reacts with chlorine to form common table salt and releases 98,000 calories. One of the most colossal heats of reaction results from the union of hydrogen and the horribly corrosive, pale-yellow gas fluorine—the most reactive of all the elements. Though fluorine compounds are so corrosive that they must be kept in specially coated bottles, small quantities of sodium fluoride are used in drinking water to prevent tooth decay. When hydrogen is combined with fluorine, the two give off more than 128,000 calories, and though this violent wedding is also attractive to rocket experts searching for new fuels, the problems of controlling fluorine thus far have made its use all but impossible.

Not all chemical reactions give off heat. In some reactions, heat from external sources must be added. Reactions are called exothermic when heat is emitted, and endothermic when heat is absorbed. Highly exothermic reactions produce very stable products.

While oxygen and hydrogen will react readily to form water, it takes the application of tremendous heat to break down water into hydrogen and oxygen again. When heated to 5,400°F.—twice the temperature needed to melt steel—only about one fourth of the molecules of water will split up. Just about the same is true for carbon dioxide, salt, or almost any other familiar compounds which are extremely stable because the molecules that make them up are more stable than free atoms.

Under any circumstances, all reactions follow the First Law of Thermo-

. . . AND BY SHARING

In covalent bonding *(right)* electrons are shared equally by the parent atoms. This generally occurs when each atom has several electrons in its outer orbit and needs one or more to become stable, as in the joining of carbon and oxygen to make carbon monoxide (CO) shown here. As in most relationships, the sharing results in a strong, stable bond. The covalent bond is generally stronger than the ionic *(opposite)*.

CARBON ATOM   OXYGEN ATOM

CARBON MONOXIDE MOLECULE

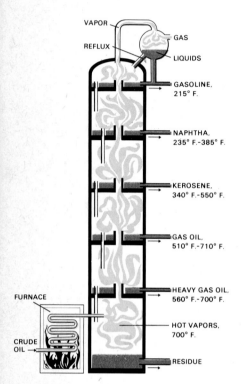

VAPOR

REFLUX

GAS

LIQUIDS

GASOLINE,
215° F.

NAPHTHA,
235° F.-385° F.

KEROSENE,
340° F.-550° F.

GAS OIL,
510° F.-710° F.

HEAVY GAS OIL,
560° F.-700° F.

FURNACE

HOT VAPORS,
700° F.

CRUDE
OIL

RESIDUE

A FRACTIONAL DIVISION

In refining crude oil, petroleum chemistry starts
with the fractional distillation shown here.
Heated to about 700° F., oil enters the
fractionating tower as hot vapors and liquids.
The vapors rise and condense on different
distillation trays, according to the temperatures
at which they change from vapor to liquid.
Lighter fractions, with lower boiling points, do
not condense until they get to the higher,
cooler trays; some gases are drawn off
and some condense to return as "reflux" (top);
heavier fractions condense on the lower
trays. Unvaporized residue goes to the bottom.

dynamics. Exactly as much heat is required to split a molecule as is given off when a molecule is put together. Since hydrogen reacting with oxygen produces water and 68,400 calories, it takes an equal number of calories to fragment water into hydrogen and oxygen. Chemical reactions also follow the Second Law of Thermodynamics, which implies that chemical energy in the universe tends to get less and less useful. As they occur in nature, these reactions move toward a point at which molecules contain the least amount of energy. In other words, chemical reactions really represent a quest for maximum molecular stability.

The American scientist Willard Gibbs, longtime professor at Yale University, worked out the formulation which finally put chemistry under the jurisdiction of the Second Law. His feat, announced in a pair of scientific papers in 1878 and 1879, is practically unknown to the public, but among scientists it is considered the greatest single achievement of American science. Gibbs's work founded a whole new branch of chemistry: physical chemistry, which deals largely with how energy behaves in chemical reactions. It is the development of physical chemistry which has made the whole of the modern chemical industry possible.

Fire without matches

At this point one might ask why a match is needed to start a fire if the union of carbon and oxygen is naturally supposed to result in a new and more stable molecular configuration. By the same token, why must a spark be passed through a mixture of hydrogen and oxygen in a calorimeter? The question is complicated, and the answer must begin with the statement that carbon will combine with oxygen without fire—and that hydrogen does the same with oxygen. But the rate of such combinations is extraordinarily slow, so slow as to be almost imperceptible. Old newspapers, for example, tend to get yellow and brittle. Because paper is a carbohydrate, the yellowing is the result of the oxidation or slow burning of carbon and hydrogen. If heat is not able to escape, its intensity will increase, which explains why the fire department constantly admonishes us not to leave oil rags accumulating around the house. For oil is another carbon compound that oxidizes in contact with air, and when enough heat accumulates (as it might if the rags were tossed in a wad in a closet) the heat may set the oil aflame—the process we know as spontaneous combustion.

The question might be phrased more concretely: Why does putting a flame to coal make it burn so much faster than not setting it aflame? A lump of coal is, in a manner of speaking, just one great big molecule of carbon atoms all arranged next to one another in a very orderly way and all held in position by the attractions of the carbon atoms for each other. Similarly, the oxygen of the air is made up of oxygen atoms held closely together. But chemical union operates strictly on an atomic scale. So before coal can combine with oxygen—or, as we say, burn—the coal molecule and the oxygen molecule must be broken down into atoms. This breakdown is what occurs when a flame is applied to the coal. The heat of the flame causes the carbon atoms on the surface of the coal to vibrate faster and faster at the same time that it causes the oxygen atoms around the coal to move faster too. Finally there comes a point when both are vibrating rapidly enough to separate from each other and recombine. As this process gets under way, the heat that is generated is enough to cause the other molecules to break up in chain reaction.

In addition to heat, light is an outside energy source that can start a chemical reaction going. The photographic process, for example, works on the principle that when certain unstable silver salts, such as silver bromide, are exposed to light, they begin to break down, freeing silver ions. On developed film the resulting specks of silver appear black. Hydrogen and chlorine, to cite another example, are so sensitive to light that they explode when placed together in a bright room. They will remain perfectly peaceful if kept in the dark.

It is also characteristic of chemical reactions that they are speeded up by substances called catalysts—including iron oxide (rust), platinum and copper—which may take part in certain reactions but always end up in an unchanged form. When a reaction has taken place in a chemical retort, the catalysts will remain—in exactly the same amount and completely unaltered, ready to be used in another reaction. A catalyzed reaction is as near as nature comes to a bargain, and, not surprisingly, catalysts are basic to most of the world's most important and most profitable industrial chemical processes.

Beating the Allied blockade

Before World War I, for instance, all nitrates for use in explosives and fertilizers were obtained from the few deposits of nitrate salts that exist naturally on earth, the best of them in the great niter beds of the Chilean deserts. When war came, one of the chief strategies of the Allies was to cut off German imports of this niter in order to stifle Germany's munitions-making and decrease its food production. But in 1913, just before the war, a German chemist, Fritz Haber, had developed a laboratory method of making ammonia, an important nitrogen compound, simply by passing hot air and hydrogen at 900°F. over finely ground iron. The nitrogen in the air combined with the hydrogen to form ammonia. This union is practically impossible without the catalyst. At temperatures necessary for uncatalyzed reactions, the ammonia comes apart almost as rapidly as it forms. The nitrate-starved Germans immediately seized upon Haber's laboratory apparatus and enlarged it to factory size,

OIL FROM A COAL MINE

Looking ahead to a day of dry wells, the oil industry is exploring this method of turning coal, a rich blend of hydrocarbons, into gasoline and other products. Pulverized coal, heated in a generator with steam and oxygen to 2,000° F. (below, left), produces a mixture of hydrogen and carbon monoxide called "synthesis gas." In a reactor, with a catalyst, this blend is converted into gaseous and liquid hydrocarbons—fuels and lubricants.

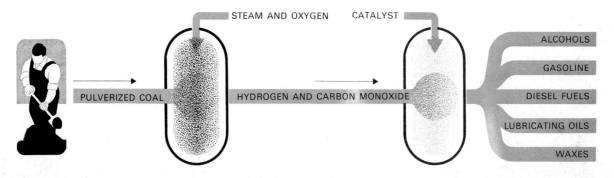

STEAM AND OXYGEN   CATALYST

PULVERIZED COAL   HYDROGEN AND CARBON MONOXIDE

ALCOHOLS
GASOLINE
DIESEL FUELS
LUBRICATING OILS
WAXES

eventually minimizing the effect of the Allied blockade. Indeed, the nitrate synthesis-process has since been developed so successfully that natural nitrates are of little importance today, and nearly all nitrogen compounds for explosives or for fertilizers are made from the air, with iron oxide still serving as the catalyst.

The catalyst works because it is able to act as a temporary middle-man in the reactions it expedites—much like the wholesale grocer who gets in a truckload of produce in the morning, neatly packages it for delivery to retail shops during the day, and then closes at night on an empty warehouse. The nitrogen and hydrogen of the Haber process exist as molecules which will not combine with one another if left to their own devices. Apparently the iron alters them in some way so that they are much more receptive to one another. Possibly both the hydrogen and nitrogen even combine for a moment with the iron and, finding themselves alongside one another, join up, leaving the iron free to combine with more molecules to continue the process.

While catalysts may seem to go against the grain of nature, they are careful to obey the Laws of Thermodynamics. When hydrogen combines with nitrogen in the presence of iron oxide, for example, the resulting ammonia is a more stable molecule. Without the application of external energy, no catalyst ever induces a reaction to go "uphill."

A synthesis from sunshine

Of all the compounds that exist in nature, by far the most important to mankind as sources of chemical energy are those containing carbon. All the important fuels—coal, oil, gas, wood, alcohol—contain carbon, as do all the principal foods—sugars, starches, proteins, fats. *All* chemical fuels and foods are the products of once-living things—the carcasses, the by-products, the decayed bodies of plants and animals. It is because all fuels and foods are the end products of plants, the primary storehouses of chemical energy which they have produced from the radiant energy of the sun. This transformation in plants takes place in the remarkable chemical process known as photosynthesis, which uses water and carbon dioxide as raw materials. The water is absorbed from the soil through the roots, the carbon dioxide from the air through the leaves. The plant then proceeds to split the water molecule and splices the hydrogen into the carbon dioxide to form a new molecule containing carbon, hydrogen and oxygen, a so-called carbohydrate. After a few finishing touches, this simple carbohydrate molecule is converted to one of the most common carbohydrates of all: sugar.

The remarkable thing about photosynthesis is that the plant achieves something a chemist finds hard to accomplish with 5,400 degrees of heat: it splits a water molecule. Behind this miracle is another kind of

DOUBLE-BARRELED FIREBOAT
"Greek fire," a highly combustible substance with pitch, naphtha or sulphur as a base, was used in naval and military warfare long before man even suspected that burning represented the release of chemical energy. Then someone thought of combining it with the battering ram, and the result was this bizarre vessel, probably of medieval origin. Blazing sulphur barrels flank the ram; the peaked roof protects oarsmen from fire fallout, arrows and spears.

catalyst—the green pigment, chlorophyll. In the process of breaking up the water, the plant expends a great deal of energy which it has previously absorbed from the sun. Excited when exposed to sunlight, the chlorophyll vibrates rapidly, acting as a sort of hammer to break the water molecule.

The inescapable First Law of Thermodynamics tells us that the energy required to break up a molecule is equal to the energy obtained when the molecule is put back together. When we eat carbohydrates and burn them in our bodies, we are putting the water molecule back together—and the energy we get from foods is the product of this reunion.

Plants and animals are able to build up their own tissues out of carbohydrates plus a handful of other substances. For example, many sugarlike molecules strung together form cellulose, the chief ingredient of wood. The formula for a simpler sugar is $C_6H_{12}O_6$ and for cellulose it might be $C_{6,000}H_{10,000}O_{5,000}$. No large animal has the necessary catalysts to break down wood to get at its energy. But certain microorganisms, not much bigger than bacteria, find wood very tasty and nourishing. These tiny creatures live in the intestines of termites, break down the wood the termite eats and share its chemical energy with their host. Similarly, cows eat grass, another high cellulose food, and microorganisms living in one of their four stomachs break the grass down so that the cow can digest it.

Fats can also be pieced together from carbohydrates. In processing sugar to make fats, the body manages to get rid of part of the oxygen in the sugar. If sugar has a formula of $C_6H_{12}O_6$, a typical fat is $C_{57}H_{104}O_6$. There are many fewer oxygen atoms per hydrogen atom in fat than in sugar. This means that when the body "burns" fat for energy, more energy is produced than when it burns sugar, since there are many more hydrogen atoms available to combine with oxygen. That is why fats are fattening and why they are such a good source of energy. A single gram of fat will contain more than twice as many calories as a gram of sugar.

The poverty of protein

Proteins are primarily used by animals to build up the flesh of their bodies and are not nearly as rich in usable energy as fats. In addition to carbon, hydrogen and oxygen, all proteins contain nitrogen. When the body breaks down proteins, it is faced with the problem of getting rid of the nitrogen. Since it cannot dispose of it as a gas, it ties it up in a compound called urea, which is excreted in the urine. Unfortunately the urea also contains a portion of the energy of the original protein molecule, which is wasted as far as the animal is concerned.

When a plant or animal dies, the precious chemical energy contained

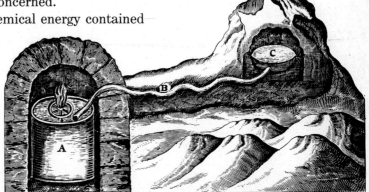

A LAMP FROM THE NILE
In his book *Notable Things Pertaining to the Egyptians*, medieval Arab writer Sciangia explained how to build an ever-burning lamp using a natural petroleum supply. From tub C, placed in a pool formed by oil seepage, a lead pipe, B, carries the fuel to tub A, enclosed and equipped with an asbestos wick. "It is obvious," wrote Athanasius Kircher, who reissued the instructions in 1665, "that such a lamp will never be extinguished."

within the cells of its body is suddenly available for re-use. Bacteria, molds and larger scavengers descend upon the corpse and devour it. But, sometimes, plant or animal remains are buried by a landslide or sink to the bottom of an ocean or swamp where the scavengers cannot get at them. Then they are preserved and their energy with them. Coal and oil are such fossilized remains. Coal generally is made up of the trunks, roots, twigs and leaves of gigantic trees that grew 250 million years ago in shallow swamps. As they died, they sank to the muddy bottom and were covered over. Time and the pressure of the accumulating earth over them gradually converted the tree forms into the homogenous black mass of a coal seam. Frequently, however, small portions of trees are still recognizable in chunks of coal. Oil is probably the remains of ancient aquatic animal life that sank to the bottom of some primeval ocean and was buried by sediment. Time and pressure turned these fishy remains into the viscous black liquid of petroleum.

The subterranean stores of coal and petroleum are really an energy inheritance from another age. As the earth's population has accelerated and as industrial needs for energy have climbed even faster, these irreplaceable stocks of fossil fuel have been ruthlessly exploited. Experts estimate there is insufficient coal and petroleum left in the earth to power man's machines for more than a few hundred years. To replace them, a new, more bountiful source of energy must eventually be harnessed.

The Vital, Versatile Bounty of Oil

Oil has been called "black gold," but no precious metal can match the infinitely varied uses of petroleum. Hidden in vast reservoirs in the earth—where it was formed millions of years ago from the remains of billions of microorganisms—oil was first found by man as it seeped to the surface in small quantities. From these natural pools it was eagerly scooped for use in medicine or fiery weapons, or for burning at temple shrines. Inevitably the demand for this marvelous substance grew, and in 1859 Edwin L. Drake sank the first commercial oil well to spark a boom that still goes on. In 1859 the per capita consumption of oil in the U.S. was one thimbleful. Today a 13-billion-dollar industry employing over one million people extracts almost four billion barrels of petroleum a year, sends its products through one million miles of pipelines and gas mains—enough for two round trips to the moon—and provides 75 per cent of all energy needs in the U.S.

SMOTHERED BY RICHES
When oil is found, nothing is spared. The uninhabited house fenced in by derricks opposite is a victim of the oilmen who swarmed over Signal Hill near Long Beach, California, in a 1921 oil rush. They changed the face of the land with this forest of thousands of rigs which stand over one of the country's most productive fields. It still puts out over five million barrels a year.

THE START OF IT ALL
Edwin L. Drake (in stovepipe hat) stands near the ramshackle wooden derrick and engine-house of his famous first well. Drake profited little from the giant industry he began. Despite a pension from the state of Pennsylvania, he spent his last years in ill health and near-poverty.

THE START OF IT ALL
Edwin L. Drake (in stovepipe hat) stands near the ramshackle wooden derrick and engine-house of his famous first well. Drake profited little from the giant industry he began. Despite a pension from the state of Pennsylvania, he spent his last years in ill health and near-poverty.

BURGEONING SHACKS AND SHAFTS
Drilling operations quickly spread from the first strike at Oil Creek in northwest Pennsylvania. This picture has its locale, the nearby Great Western Run area, scratched on it. Wells were often drilled in low areas on the theory that petroleum flowed from the coal seams higher up.

The First Lusty Stirrings of a Young Giant

Oil was not unknown in the U.S. before well drilling began. In areas such as Oil Creek, Pennsylvania, where it seeped naturally to the surface, it was scooped off with blankets and sold in small quantities for medicinal purposes. But interest in its enormous commercial potential began only with a scientific paper in 1855 which predicted that 90 per cent of crude oil could be distilled into salable products *(page 106)*. With this impetus, the Seneca Oil Company was founded by a group of New York investors determined to look for oil by drilling, which had never been tried. Edwin L. Drake, a retired railroad conductor, was put in charge of operations. With an assistant he erected an enginehouse and derrick on a farm near Titusville, Pennsylvania, and on August 27, 1859, at a depth of 69.5 feet, oil began coming to the surface. Drake's well produced an unexpected nine gallons a day which was hurriedly stored in tubs and whisky barrels. Within less than 24 hours the boom was on. Land around the site was at a premium. With a spirit reminiscent of the famous gold rush of 1849, boomtowns arose as scores of wells were drilled. Within a year, there were about 74 producing wells along Oil Creek, and in five years the daily yield reached 6,000 barrels. A new industry had been created.

PIPELAYERS' PORTRAIT
These rough-and-ready pipelayers were members of a "tong gang," so named for the tongs with which they plied their trade. The first successful pipeline was laid from the Oil Creek Railroad to a field about five miles distant. It undercut wagon haulage prices by two thirds.

LUBRICENE

CYLINDER OIL.

CHARDS CYLINDER OIL.

A Flood of Brand-new Wares

With crude oil gushing from the earth in apparently endless supply, businessmen began to look for bigger markets. The demand for motor fuel lay well in the future, but the pioneer producers, improving the techniques of refining *(above)*, could soon offer a large list of by-products and the buying public was wooed with tempting blandishments *(opposite)*. Many refineries distilled crude oil for kerosene for lamps, discarding what remained in the stills. But others reprocessed these "wastes" with profitable results: naphtha found use as a cleaning solvent and replaced turpentine in paints; petroleum jelly turned up on drugstore shelves in salves, lotions, unguents and pomades; while paraffin, besides providing cheap candles and better matches, was also used to seal jellies and coat pills—and by 1870 one New England concern was annually turning 70,000 pounds of paraffin into chewing gum.

ENGINE OIL

CHARD ENGINE OIL

BY-PRODUCTS BY THE BARREL

In the early refinery pictured above, heat is being applied to crude oil at left. The heaviest oil, a kind of asphalt, pours through the trough onto the table while the lighter oil vaporizes and rises through the pipe to the center vat. Further refining stages produce cylinder oil, for lubricating the moving parts of heavy machinery, while the process is repeated at the right to make a lighter lubricant known as engine oil.

LISTENING TO THE FAIRIES.

THE GLAMOR OF OIL

This coy ad failed to note that early engine oil, forerunner of motor oil, not only smelled bad but ignited at dangerously low temperatures.

A PITCH FOR PETROLEUM

The actress Lillian Russell endorses Carboline "for the hair." It promised a new growth on bald heads and a mustache within a few weeks.

CURE-ALL FROM CRUDE OIL

The first commercial petroleum product was marketed by Samuel Kier, a Pittsburgh refiner. His rock oil (a dollar a bottle and none genuine without his signature) was advertised as a cure for cholera, corns, toothache and neuralgia.

TEETH TO BITE OUT A WELL

This toothy drilling bit, its teeth emphasized by the camera's point of view, is called a rock drill. Revolved by the pipe to which it is attached, the bit bores down through hard rock layers. The interlocking wheels, turned by pressure against the bottom of the hole, crush the rock. The fragments are then flushed to the surface by a sludge of chemicals, clay and water called drilling mud, which can be seen dripping from the bit above. Drill bits range up to a foot in diameter, and some are coated with industrial diamonds for especially hard drilling.

The Tools and Techniques of a Costly Quest

The wicked-looking drilling bit shown opposite is the oilman's ultimate weapon in his assault on the earth's hidden store of oil. As shown in the diagram at right, the bit bores through the earth in a blind stab which is always chancy at best. Drilling for oil is no game for the fainthearted. The cost of drilling a well averages over $60,000 and requires such equipment as 25,000 feet of steel pipe, 4,800 sacks of cement and 3,000 barrels of diesel fuel. A wildcat well—one in territory where no oil has yet been found—faces eight-to-one odds of hitting pay dirt, and only three out of 100 wildcats are commercially successful. One well in Texas was drilled five miles deep at a cost of three million dollars. No oil was found.

Such are the hazards of an industry that spends close to two billion dollars a year just looking for oil. Some 14 per cent of U.S. land area is now available for that search, but only a small portion of it will prove economically significant. In the past decade the search has turned more and more to the sea and is luring oilmen farther and farther from shore. In some offshore operations, the rigs are sending bits down to 17,000 feet—some 70 miles out.

DRILLING IN THE DARK

The illustration at right shows a drilling rig and a cross section—not drawn to scale—of the earth it probes. Through the crown block atop the derrick runs a cable from the drum of the draw works back to the huge traveling block. This forms a great tackle to raise and lower the long "string" of drill pipes tipped with the bit. Hanging from the swivel and hook is the kelly, a square-shaped bar which, when threaded into the top of the drill pipe and locked into the spinning rotary table, turns the whole string. As the bit bores deeper, 30-foot lengths of drill pipe are added to the top, but when a bit wears out, the entire string must be hauled out of the hole. During drilling, a lubricating "mud" gets pumped down to the bit through the pipe and then returns inside the casing which lines the hole. The bit's unseen goal is a store of gas and oil, floating on water, which lies trapped in an underground pocket formed by layers of rock.

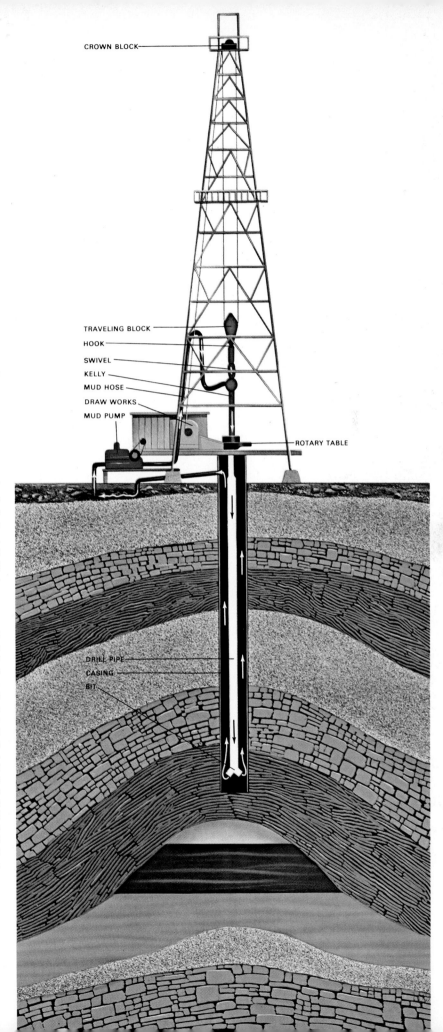

CROWN BLOCK

TRAVELING BLOCK
HOOK
SWIVEL
KELLY
MUD HOSE
DRAW WORKS
MUD PUMP

ROTARY TABLE

DRILL PIPE
CASING
BIT

Gushers:
Explosive Signs
of Success

No one is ever quite sure what is going to happen when the drilling bit finally crunches into an oil-bearing formation. The well pressure may be so low that the oil has to be pumped out. Even at high pressures, the upsurge can usually be checked. Yet sometimes the whole works are blown sky-high, as in the spewing gusher and flaming spout of gas shown here.

There are about 25 such catastrophes each year—a mere fraction of the world's 650,000 producing wells. Yet oilmen put the damage at about one billion dollars annually—and unchecked blowouts can reduce underground pressure so greatly that more billions of dollars in oil and gas are left stranded in the earth. Damage to equipment can be spectacular, too: a flash fire on a rig out in the Gulf of Mexico melted the 300-foot derrick in 40 minutes.

In the early oil fields, gushers were a common sight, and whole fields were often destroyed when they burst forth and caught fire. Nowadays, although special pressure valves, fittings and chokes are used to cap the well, a breached gas pocket can still erupt—and the smallest spark will then convert the jet into a geyser of flame, as happened in the Sahara blaze at right. When that one started, a frantic call was sent to Texan "Red" Adair who heads one of the most unusual businesses in the world. Using explosive charges, he and his men literally blew the fire out.

HERALD OF A BONANZA
The gusher at left, from a well "brought in" on January 10, 1901, in the Spindletop oil fields at Beaumont, opened up Texas as the greatest oil area in the nation. This well, spewing up some 100,000 barrels of oil a day for nine days, proved that petroleum could be secured in massive quantities. The derrick, unlike modern steel rigs, was made of wood and mounted on logs.

A FIRE SEEN FROM SPACE
At Gassi Touil in the Sahara *(right)*, "Red" Adair and associate in asbestos suits fight the biggest gas-well fire in history. It burned up more than $30 million worth of gas and if left unextinguished might have burned for centuries. Called "The Devil's Cigarette Lighter," the 450-foot tower of flame was visible for 90 miles and was seen by John Glenn from his space capsule.

Putting
Petroleum through
the Wringer

Before petroleum can be sent to market in its myriad useful guises, it must be subjected to an exhaustive going-over in a refinery. Here in giant stills, blenders and "cat crackers," heat and pressure are applied to the crude oil to pull it apart into its dozens of chemical components. These "fractions," ranging from cooking gas to asphalt, are then specially treated to tailor them for their various jobs. The brightly lit plant above, so fully automated that it takes only a few men to operate, is a gleaming example of the modern refinery. Its chief components are identified in the drawing at right; the refining process is illustrated on the following pages.

ROUND-THE-CLOCK REFINERY
Japan's Tokuyama refinery, the largest in the Far East, processes a whopping 140,000 barrels of crude oil every 24 hours. Some of its illuminated towers are numbered in the drawing at left: 1, gasoline-purifying unit; 2, crude oil-distillation towers; 3, vacuum-distillation asphalt unit; 4, crude oil boiler stack; 5, catalytic cracking unit; 6, gasoline-fractionating unit.

HOW A REFINERY SQUEEZES EVERY DROP OF USEFULNESS FROM OIL

CRUDE OIL

GAS

UNREFINED GASOLINE

NAPHTHA

CATALYTIC REFORMER rearranges the molecules of naphtha (also used as cleaning fluid) and unrefined gasoline, to produce high-octane, antiknock gasolines. Process takes name from catalyst, a substance which speeds chemical reactions.

GAS OIL

HEAVY GAS OIL

DISTILLATION PLANT separates complex crude oil into simpler "fractions." All crude goes through the still to be heated and vaporized. Once separated, the heaviest oils condense in lower, hotter part of tower, the lighter oils above.

POLYMERIZATION PLANT converts the lightest oils into giant-molecule compounds from which are derived gases, high-octane gasoline and petrochemical by-products such as detergents, plastics, synthetic fibers and synthetic rubber.

REFORMED GASOLINE

CATALYTIC GASOLINE

CATALYTIC CRACKER increases the gasoline yield of crude oil by a chemical process that breaks down the large oil molecules of heavier fractions to make lighter substances, which deliver energy more efficiently to automobile engines.

LUBRICATING OIL AND RESIDUAL PRODUCTS

BLENDED GASOLINE

GASOLINE BLENDING TANKS mix reformed, unrefined, cracked and polymerized gasolines into efficient motor fuel. Refining improvements have upped the gasoline yield of crude oil from 26.1 per cent in 1920 to 44.8 per cent in 1967.

END PRODUCTS WITH ENDLESS USES

COOKING GAS. Though most cooking fuel is unrefined natural gas, part of the growing demand is supplied by the refining process's lightest product.

GASOLINE. A useless by-product before automobiles, gasoline now is the oil industry's best seller. U.S. drivers use 76 billion gallons yearly.

JET FUEL. Kerosene, once the industry's chief product in its use as lighting oil, is fast gaining a new importance as the basis of today's jet fuels.

DIESEL FUEL. Having largely replaced locomotives, diesel engines pull 97 per cent of U.S. trains. Diesel oil also drives many ships and trucks.

FURNACE OILS. Consumption for domestic heating has increased over 400 per cent since 1940. The lighter furnace oils are similar to kerosene.

LUBRICANTS AND RESIDUALS. About 1 per cent of crude becomes heavy lubricating oil. Residuals range from heavy fuel oil to asphalt to wax.

6

Electricity:
Willing Genie
in a Wire

A MEDIEVAL SEAMAN'S CODE declares that any sailor caught tampering with the ship's lodestone ". . . shall, if his life be spared, be punished by having the hand which he most uses, fastened by a dagger or knife thrust through it, to the mast or principal timber of the ship. . . ." The punishment was designed to fit the crime—for the lodestone was a football-sized chunk of magnetic iron that served to magnetize the crude compass needles with which mariners navigated at the time. In the history of science, the stern code is vivid evidence of man's early dependence upon the phenomenon of magnetism, one of the most curious manifestations of what we now call electrical energy.

Thousands of years before its behavior would be accurately explained, magnetism was familiar to man. Indeed, the magnetic properties of lodestone—which is a variety of the iron ore called magnetite—were almost certainly known to the people of the Iron Age. No one can say where or when the word "magnetism" itself originated, but Pliny the Elder, the Roman naturalist, credits a shepherd named Magnes, who had expressed bewilderment at the attraction of lodestone to the iron nails of his shoes. On the other hand, the Roman poet Lucretius claimed that the magnet took its name from the ancient land of Magnesia, where lodestone was allegedly first discovered.

Considering its seemingly magic properties, it is not surprising that the magnet has inspired a wide range of farfetched explanations for its behavior. The Roman Claudian believed that a magnet drew iron to itself in order to gather "nourishment." Descartes, the 17th Century French philosopher, was no less fanciful when he suggested that magnetic substances were covered by minuscule screws whose constant rotations drew and locked themselves into innumerable threaded holes in the surface of iron.

The key to understanding magnetic power lies in an unfailing characteristic of a simple bar magnet. Mounted on an upright pivot or suspended from a cord on which it can swing freely, it will always line up in a north-south position. Because of this, the ends became known as north and south poles. Even in a magnet bent into the shape of a horseshoe, each end is similarly distinguished. Each end simply behaves differently from the other, and the difference is vividly demonstrated when *two* bar magnets are brought near each other. The north pole of one will attract the south pole of the other (and vice versa), the two ends being drawn together. On the other hand, when two north poles (or two south poles) are brought toward each other, they will exhibit a mutual repulsion that forces them apart.

The implications of all this become evident only when a bar magnet is cut in two. Each half becomes a new magnet, each with its own north and south poles. Had early scientists been able to conceive of slicing a

SPARKS ON A STRING
In 1752 Benjamin Franklin, as shown in the Currier & Ives print opposite, slipped a key over a kite string and risked electrocution to prove that lightning was electricity. His research into the nature of electricity helped pave the way for its practical use, resulted in the lightning rod and caused a French statesman to say: "He snatched the lightning from the skies."

magnet into smaller and smaller halves until each half consisted of only one atom, it would have been clear that magnetism is an atomic property of matter. Yet full understanding had to await the unfolding knowledge of electricity, of the electrical properties of atoms, and of the interrelationship of electricity and magnetism.

We now know that electricity is the cause of a wide variety of striking phenomena in nature, ranging all the way from the useful magnetism of lodestone to the destructive displays of summer lightning. But until the 19th Century, men surmised little connection between them.

One manifestation of what we call "static" electricity is recorded by the ancient Greeks, who observed that when a piece of amber is rubbed vigorously, it attracts small particles of dust and lint, and it is their word *elektron*, meaning "amber," from which we have derived our term for electricity. More than 1,500 years later, the same phenomenon attracted renewed attention, and the methodical study of electricity had begun.

Among the experimental pioneers was Otto von Guericke, a 17th Century German who is better remembered for his studies of atmospheric pressure and the effects of a vacuum. Seeking a way to observe static electricity, Von Guericke constructed a pumpkin-sized sulphur sphere, and mounted it in such a way that it could be rotated against the hand of the experimenter. Rubbed in this manner, the sphere would attract small pieces of paper, fabric and other substances. To his surprise, Von Guericke discovered that a linen thread attached to the sphere revealed the same power of attraction as the sulphur. He had succeeded in creating a modest but authentic generator of static electricity and the first fleeting electric current.

As experimentation progressed, it was discovered that objects rubbed against each other displayed properties not unlike those of magnets, except that their effect was much less powerful. When hard rubber was rubbed with fur, for example, the rubber would attract a piece of glass that had been rubbed with silk. On the other hand, *two* pieces of glass rubbed with silk would repel each other. As a result, the conclusion was reached that friction created a so-called "electrical charge" of two different kinds. The charge on the rubber was eventually called "negative," and the charge on the glass "positive," in much the same fashion as the terms for the north and south poles had been applied to a magnet.

In 1785 and 1786, a French physicist named Charles Coulomb described in precise mathematical terms how these positive and negative charges repel and attract each other. Coulomb's law, which closely resembles Newton's law of gravity, reveals that attraction and repulsion weaken very rapidly with distance—and increase just as rapidly as the charged particles get closer together.

Benjamin Franklin suggested the names of positive and negative for

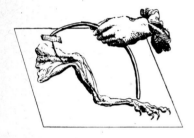

FROG'S LEGS BOLOGNESE
In 1786, Luigi Galvani, professor of anatomy at the University of Bologna, noticed that sparks from a nearby electric machine caused contractions in the leg of a frog he was dissecting. This chance discovery led him to numerous experiments. In the one illustrated here, he conducted electricity by touching the nerve of the frog's leg with a zinc rod and the muscle with a copper rod, then bringing the two metals into contact. Although Galvani wrongly credited the phenomenon to "animal electricity," his work led to the discovery of electric currents.

the two opposite charges. Franklin maintained that electricity consisted of a kind of fluid. When an object had more than its normal share of electricity, he reasoned, it had a plus, or positive, amount of fluid; when it had less than its normal share, it had a minus, or negative, quantity.

In his now legendary experiment, Franklin and his son set a kite aloft during a thunderstorm to prove that lightning is electrical in nature. The moment the kite disappeared into a menacing thunderhead, all fibers along the kite string stood erect, just as they did when a string was charged with ordinary static electricity in the laboratory. Suddenly a spark jumped to his finger from a metal key tied to the end of the string. Franklin had proved that the thunderhead, from which lightning strikes, is obviously electrically charged—though not without establishing a record for himself as one of the most foolhardy experimenters in the history of science.

Rearranging electrons

Modern atomic theory has superseded the fluid theory of electricity. Today, the generation of an electric charge by friction can be explained by the structure of atoms. As Chapter 5 revealed, atoms consist of a positively charged nucleus surrounded by a number of negatively charged electrons. Ordinarily, all the negative charges of an atom's electrons add up to a total charge equal to the positive charge of its nucleus. In this normal condition, the atom is electrically neutral. But some electrons —as in fur or glass—are loosely held and therefore can easily be detached when the object containing them is rubbed against another. As a result, these *free* electrons can transfer themselves to the atoms of other substances like rubber or silk. When this happens, the loss of an electron will leave one atom with an excess of positive charge, and the gain of an electron will give the other atom an excess of negative charge. In these changes, nothing but a *rearrangement* of electrons is taking place. Electric charges are moved from one substance to another, but none is destroyed—a principle that is known as the "conservation of charge."

The study of electrically charged bodies—today called "electrostatics" —is only a backdrop to the more complex study of electricity in *motion* —which is known as "electrodynamics." As a legacy of the 18th Century belief that electricity was a fluid, electricity in motion has come to be described as "current" electricity.

The origins of this study are credited to Luigi Galvani, an anatomy professor at the University of Bologna, who first encountered the effects of electric currents in 1780 as a result of a chance happening in his laboratory. Galvani was dissecting a frog with a steel scalpel when an assistant happened to produce a spark with a static-electricity machine located in the same room. As a spark sputtered in the machine the frog's

AN 18TH CENTURY RUBE GOLDBERG

To demonstrate static electricity, Dr. William Watson, an imaginative 18th Century English experimenter, devised this bizarre human chain. As the man cranked the wheel, it picked up a static electric charge from the woman's hand and transferred it to the feet of the boy suspended on silk ropes. The charge then went to the girl standing on an insulating tub of dried pitch. Her hand attracted chaff from the table.

legs suddenly twitched. Today we know that Galvani had witnessed a case of "electrostatic induction." It had occurred when negative electrons, leaping through the air to create the spark, caused a matching movement of other electrons in the scalpel, which was in contact with the frog's legs. The movement of electrons in the scalpel represented a momentary current whose electrical energy stimulated the frog's nerves and caused its leg muscles to contract.

Fascinated by the phenomenon, Galvani conceived other, similar experiments, including one in which he set out during a thunderstorm to see whether lightning would also cause a freshly killed frog's legs to twitch. He tied the legs to a brass hook and hung the hook over an iron fence in the front yard. Whenever the legs touched the iron fence, they twitched violently—even when there was no lightning. Misinterpreting what he had seen, Galvani concluded that the frog's legs contained what he called "animal electricity."

Galvani's work was followed almost immediately by that of Alessandro Volta, a professor of physics at the University of Pavia, who demonstrated in 1800 what had really happened in Galvani's experiment. He had discovered that the chemical action of moisture and two dissimilar metals—such as brass and iron—would generate a flow of electric currents. The frog's legs had simply been a source of moisture. Setting up a layer-cake arrangement of disks made of silver and zinc interlaced with paper or cloth, soaked in salt solution, Volta produced the world's first battery. In so doing, Volta also generated the first steady supply of current electricity made by the hand of man.

Invisible, superior power

In time, man would come to regard the invisible currents of electricity as a new source of power, serving him even better than the majestic currents of rivers and brooks he had long harnessed to turn the water wheels of the world. Today, indeed, we realize that currents of electricity behave in many ways just like currents of water. Both, for example, flow in a single direction. Just as water runs downhill if left to its own devices, electricity seeks its own kind of "downhill" path.

Movement occurs only from a place with greater amounts of electrons to a place with fewer electrons. What we call electric current is, therefore, nothing more than a movement of electrons trying to even out an electron inequality. The measurement of this inequality—the difference between two concentrations of electrons—is called "voltage." In terms of water running down a hill, "volts" are a measurement of the height of the hill. A volt and a half—the strength of an ordinary flashlight battery —corresponds to water flowing down a very small incline. In this situation, the amount of electrons at one battery terminal is not far

BREAKTHROUGH IN A CLASSROOM
Depicted on the medal above is the only known occasion when a major scientific discovery was made during a classroom experiment. While lecturing in 1820 the Danish scientist Hans Christian Oersted chanced to place an electrified wire parallel to a magnetized needle. The needle responded by swinging so that it was perpendicular to the wire, revealing that electricity had created a magnetic field around the wire. The Oersted Medal is now given to superior teachers by the American Association of Physics Teachers.

different from the amount at the other. On the other hand, 220 volts—the amount required to operate an ordinary electric stove—may be likened to water racing down a steep hillside.

In this analogy between electric current and running water, one important qualification must be made. Although the very word "current" suggests that electricity runs uninterruptedly, like water in a hose, physicists now know that the movement is more comparable to the way in which water is passed along by a fireman's bucket brigade. The electrons which comprise the current are passed along, one electron after another, from atom to atom. In the flow along a piece of wire, for example, electrons move relatively slowly, sometimes not more than an inch a second. On the other hand, in a bolt of lightning electrons may travel at a speed of 61,000 miles a second.

Just as voltage measures the *pressure* which causes the current to flow, so "amperage" measures the *amount* of flow. Thus, every time 6,242,000,000,000,000,000 electrons move past a given point of wire in one second, one ampere of current has passed. The two measurements, voltage and amperage, offer widely different clues to the behavior of currents. It is easily possible, for example, for a great number of electrons to flow through a wire at a very low pressure, much as the Mississippi River flows past New Orleans as a voluminous but sluggish body of water. Such a current is said to be high in amperage but driven by low voltage. On the other hand, a current may be just the opposite—driven by high voltage but low in amperage, behaving much like a mountain rivulet that plunges at top speed down a precipice. A welding machine may use a low voltage and high amperage electric current, as low as 15 volts and as high as 1,200 "amps" (short for "amperes"). A static-electricity machine generates sparks with discharges of high voltage but low amperage. To leap a single inch of air, for example, a spark requires 15,000 volts regardless of amperage. Combining the most fearful aspects of both voltage and amperage, a single stroke of lightning may be rated at 100 million volts and 160,000 amps.

Still another factor affects the flow of electric current: the nature of the substance through which it passes. In certain substances, like copper and silver, electrons are more loosely bound than in others, such as porcelain and glass, and they more readily permit the flow of electricity. Copper and silver are thus said to be good "conductors." Porcelain and glass, which are poor conductors, are called "insulators." In determining flow, the size of a substance—as well as its nature—is of importance. For just as larger pipes permit water to flow more freely than smaller pipes, the bigger the diameter of a wire conductor, the more readily electrons can flow along its length.

Everything which tends to impede the flow of electrons contributes

LIGHTING THE WAY TO THE FUTURE

THE MASTER INVENTOR

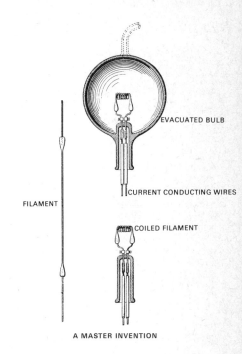

FILAMENT

EVACUATED BULB

CURRENT CONDUCTING WIRES

COILED FILAMENT

A MASTER INVENTION

GLASSING IN A GLOW

Thomas Alva Edison, shown in his laboratory in Menlo Park, New Jersey, held patents on thousands of inventions, ranging from the mimeograph to the phonograph to the incandescent light bulb *(above)*. In his first successful bulb, Edison used a charred, coiled cotton thread to make a filament. When enclosed in an evacuated glass bulb and connected to an electric current, it glowed brightly for 40 hours before burning out.

to "resistance." Its nature was first studied in detail by Georg Simon Ohm, a German schoolteacher of mathematics and physics. After extensive experiments in which he compared conductors of various substances, shapes and lengths, Ohm arrived at an understanding of electrical resistance that would one day bring him fame.

But trouble dogged Ohm's early work. When he published his findings in 1828, the article was largely ignored, and in the following year when he published in Berlin a book containing his theoretical derivation of the law, his ideas were misjudged by those who had passed up the article which described his laboratory work. The result was a widespread impression that there was no experimental basis at all for his book, and it was dismissed as ". . . an incurable delusion whose sole effort is to detract from the dignity of nature. . . ." But over the years, his electrical researches won recognition. By the time of his death in 1854, he was famous throughout Europe, and today the law of electrical resistance he first formulated bears his name.

A historic milestone

Ohm's law stands as a historic milestone in man's application of electricity to the needs of civilization, for it is resistance which transforms electricity into heat. The transformation occurs, for example, in an electric toaster whose nickel-chromium alloy wires convert current electricity into heat. A whole range of household appliances, from heaters to stoves, utilizes the principle of Ohm's law—that the amount of heat developed by a conductor varies directly with its resistance. Ohm's law accounts, too, for one of the great discoveries of man: artificial electric light. For it was the phenomenon of resistance heating which enabled Thomas Edison to raise a charred piece of thread to white-hot incandescence in his invention of the light bulb.

In their effect upon civilization the reciprocal transformations of electricity and heat are overshadowed by the transformations of electricity and mechanical energy. To achieve these, man first had to discover the relationship between two seemingly independent phenomena: electricity and magnetism.

In 1807, trying to relate the two, a Dane named Hans Christian Oersted began a long series of experiments. He reasoned that if electric current was allowed to flow through a wire, it should turn the wire into a kind of magnet with the properties of north and south poles. Such magnetism, like that of a conventional bar magnet, should be detected with a regular compass. Placing a wire in a position across the length of a compass needle, he formed a simple cross with the two objects. He expected that, if the wire became magnetized, the compass needle would have to swing around a quarter turn to line up with the wire—as it

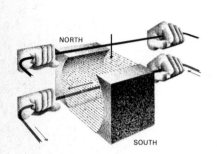

CURRENT ATTRACTIONS

Passing a wire through a magnetic field created between the opposite poles of two bar magnets demonstrates the phenomenon of electromagnetic induction. As the wire moves down, electric current flows along it to the left (arrows); when it moves up, the current reverses. The speed of the moving wire and the strength of the magnetic field determine the strength of the current. When the movement stops, the current also stops, even if the wire is still within the magnetic field.

would with an ordinary bar magnet. But when he turned on the current, nothing happened. Years later, while he was lecturing at the University of Copenhagen, Oersted accidentally placed the wire *parallel with*—instead of *across*—the needle, and turned on the current. As if by magic, the needle moved, swinging around a quarter turn so that it lay precisely at right angles to the wire. Electric current did, indeed, create a magnetic field around wire, and Oersted years earlier had only misjudged the direction in which it would appear. At last the connection between electricity and magnetism had been discovered.

One year after Oersted's remarkable discovery, André Marie Ampère—the French physicist for whom the ampere was eventually named—discovered that one electrical wire produced a magnetic effect upon another electrical wire next to it. Parallel wires with currents flowing in the same direction attracted each other, while those with currents flowing in opposite directions repelled each other. Ampère's results reinforced the proof yielded by Oersted's experiment that an electric current could create a magnetic field around itself. But the opposite and more promising question remained to be answered: could a magnetic field create an electric current?

In 1830, about a decade after Oersted's experiment, Joseph Henry in America and, a year later, Michael Faraday in London discovered that a magnetic field could indeed induce a current—if only a transient one—provided the magnetic field was kept in motion. The proposition can be demonstrated when a magnet is moved in the vicinity of a coil of wire, thereby inducing a brief electric current to flow around the coil. When the motion of the magnet is stopped, a current no longer is evident in the coil.

The discovery of "electromagnetic induction"—the creation of a current by a constantly changing magnetic field—was destined to be one of the most fruitful observations in the entire study of electricity. Once the principle was fully understood, it became clear that the battery was not the only source or even the most convenient source of electricity. Instead, the generator would become one of man's greatest machines for generating power.

Power from spinning coils

In an electric generator, mechanical energy—from water power or the heat of a steam engine—is used to spin a coil of wire within a magnetic field. As the coil revolves, pulses of electric current are generated in exactly the same manner as in the primitive experiments of Henry and Faraday. An electric motor, on the other hand, is just a generator in reverse. Current from the generator creates a magnetic field in a coil of wire known as the armature. The armature spins as it is alternately

TO LIGHT A LAMP

One of the major applications of electromagnetic induction *(opposite page)* is in generators, which convert mechanical energy into electrical energy. By means of a turbine and shaft, the kinetic energy of the waterfall below turns a wire loop in a magnetic field. This creates a constant flow of current in the loop that is conducted to a light bulb. Commercial generators use a huge coil instead of a single wire, and several electromagnets.

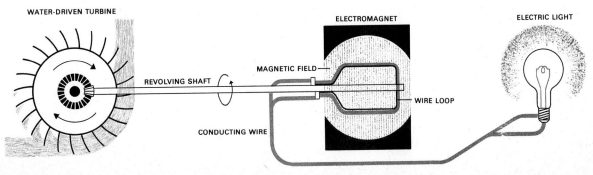

WATER-DRIVEN TURBINE   REVOLVING SHAFT   MAGNETIC FIELD   ELECTROMAGNET   WIRE LOOP   ELECTRIC LIGHT   CONDUCTING WIRE

attracted and repelled by other magnets surrounding it. Connected to the end of the armature is a shaft which delivers mechanical energy which the motor has converted from electricity.

The electrical motor is one of the most efficient of all energy converters, transforming into work over 90 per cent of the energy that reaches it. By contrast the steam engine is only about 30 per cent efficient and the gasoline engine 50 per cent.

No survey of electricity, however brief, can fail to pay credit to James Clerk Maxwell, the great English physicist of the mid-19th Century already mentioned in earlier chapters for his work in thermodynamics and his pioneer studies of the nature of light. But Maxwell is perhaps best known for his contributions to electricity. Building on Faraday's discovery that electric current and magnetism are related, he went on to unify all of the electrical phenomena known in his day into four brief equations. The work of Coulomb, Ampère, Oersted, Ohm, Henry and Faraday, among others, was neatly drawn together by his mathematics.

Maxwell's equations were one of the brilliant achievements of the science of the Victorian era. The physicists who followed Maxwell understandably held his word to be law. Yet he could be wrong. As the next chapter will show, many of the greatest scientific advances of our own age came about because, ironically, in one fundamental hypothesis, Maxwell was indeed wrong.

The Miracle of Tamed Lightning

"We call that fire of the black thundercloud electricity," said Thomas Carlyle in 1841. "But what is it? What made it? Whence comes it?" The questions have never been completely answered: the real nature of electricity is not yet understood. But we are fairly certain that electrical phenomena lie at the very core of life—that the atom itself is an electric entity. In any event, electricity has surged into the daily affairs of men within the last century, sparking changes as far-reaching as those wrought by the steam engine. For in his insatiable quest for energy, man has found electricity to be unbeatable. It is clean, convenient, convertible; its generators, motors and solid state devices make feasible a great many of civilization's casually accepted accouterments—from television to skyscrapers. Benjamin Franklin said it in a prophetic understatement nearly two centuries ago: "Electrical fluid . . . may . . . be of use to mankind."

ELECTRICITY'S SIGNATURE
The crackling veil of electricity opposite is formed by high-tension arcs leaping from one insulator to another. Each 600,000-volt discharge leaves a glowing trail and heats the air to create convection currents which waft the trails out from the insulators. Each electric trail glows for a mere fraction of a second, yet this is long enough to make a dazzling tracery of man-made lightning.

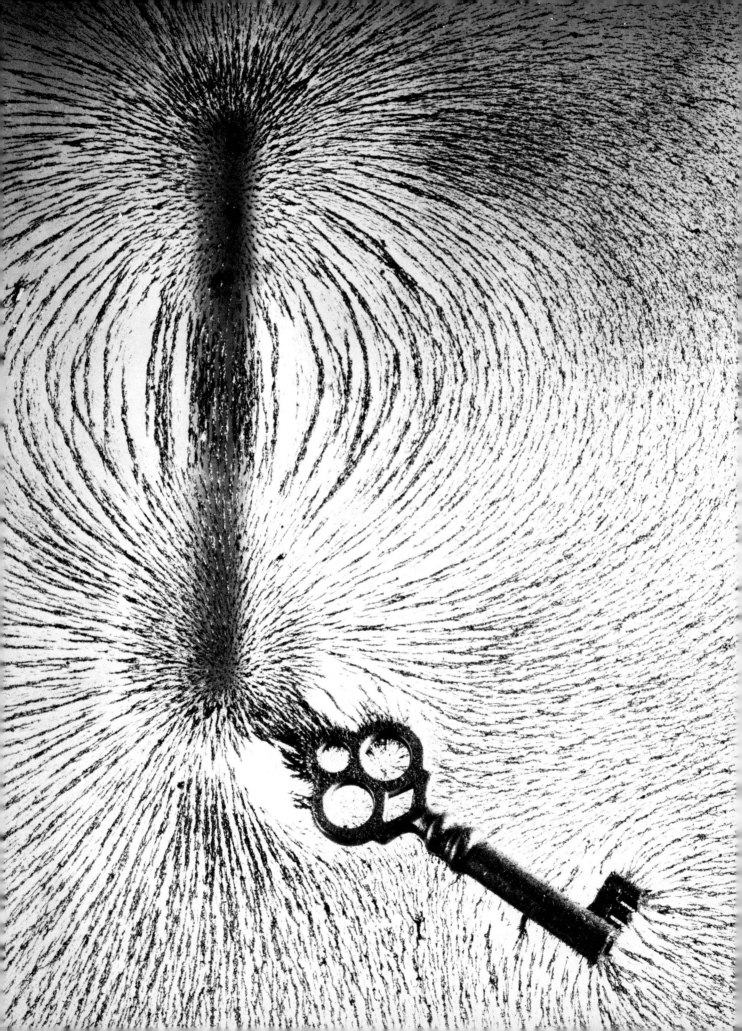

The Age-old Mysteries of Magnetism

The mysterious power of a cold lump of metal to reach across empty space and attract or repel other lumps of metal has intrigued the scientist and schoolchild alike for centuries. Magnets were known to the ancient Greeks in the form of an iron ore called lodestone, and later they were used by the Chinese to make the first navigational compasses. The earth itself, in behaving like a huge magnet, makes these compasses possible.

Scientists know that a magnetized substance has many atoms, each like a magnet, aligned so that they exert their force together. All magnets, including the earth, have two opposite poles which are called north and south. The strange lines of force that curve from pole to pole (*opposite and below*) are inseparably intertwined with electrical forces. The most powerful magnets, in fact, are not the so-called "permanent" magnets shown here, but are "electromagnets" operating on electricity. Nonetheless, with all the knowledge that has been accumulated, the occurrence of natural magnets remains a mystery.

A GLOWING ARC OF FORCE
A special tube built to produce electrons demonstrates to a student the symmetrical force lines curving between the poles of a permanent horseshoe magnet. Streams of electrons, pulled from the perforated, electrically heated core of the tube, stream along these lines and create a crescent of bluish light when they collide with floating molecules of gas sealed in the tube.

MAGNETISM'S SIGNATURE
Sprinkled on paper, a powder composed of iron filings aligns itself in swirling patterns to reveal the magnetic "lines of force" that arc from one end of a bar magnet to the other. Similar lines also emanate from an iron key magnetized by its proximity to the bar. The varying densities of the pattern show the relative strength of the magnetic field at different points.

Static Electricity: A Pesky, Ghostly Shocker

In the past, frightened mariners voyaging at night sometimes saw ghostly phantoms of bluish light dancing on the masts of their ships. They called the effect St. Elmo's fire, after the patron saint of sailors, but it has now become the unwanted companion of aviators as well *(top)*. Not really fire at all, it is merely one of the guises taken by that form of electricity known as *static* electricity because it remains stationary on the surface of an object, as opposed to the familiar *current* electricity that flows in a wire. At the heart of both is the negatively charged electron. The shocks one gets after shuffling across a wool rug on cool, dry days come from a static electricity charge—a charge composed of electrons rubbed from the rug onto the shoe soles. The rug's atoms, with their electron deficiency, become positively charged, while those in the shoe—and hence one's body—are negatively charged. A spark made up of these excess electrons will jump from the fingers to a grounded object such as a radiator or a less-charged human being. Furthermore, any object charged this way tends to attract another object with an opposite charge and to repel one with a similar charge *(opposite)*.

Besides administering shocks, plaguing mariners and pilots, static electricity can also cause more serious troubles; gasoline trucks usually have a dangling wire or chain to drain off any charge that might ignite their cargo. In 1937, static electricity may have sparked the explosion of the hydrogen-filled dirigible *Hindenburg* as it was docking at Lakehurst, New Jersey.

GETTING AN ELECTRIFIED LIFT
The lightweight ping-pong balls suspended from thread at left are poised around the charged metal globe of a toy electrostatic generator. Having been first attracted in to touch the globe, they acquired the same charge as the globe and were then repelled away from it. At the same time, they also repel one another and so remain balanced in their gravity-defying formation.

STREAKS OF FEATHERY FIRE
The model airplane above has been charged with static electricity so that researchers may study the effects of the St. Elmo's fire that streams from sharp corners such as wing and tail tips. Frequently seen by pilots flying in dry, falling snow or ice crystals or in the vicinity of thunderstorms, the fire can cause noisy static on radios or induce lightning to strike the plane.

A HAIR-RAISING SENSATION
Suitably insulated from the ground by standing on a stool, the girl at right is touching the globe of a powerful static electricity generator. She is being charged with as much as a million volts—and all she gets is a tingle and a new and fuzzy hairdo. Since the hairs all have the same powerful electrical charge, they repel one another to produce this hair-raising effect.

Motors Bigger than a Room and Smaller than a Grain of Sand

In simplest terms, an electric motor is a machine for converting electrical energy into mechanical energy by exploiting the intimate relationship between electricity and magnetism. If a wire is coiled around an iron bar and a current sent through the wire, the bar will be converted to a magnet. Such an electromagnet, when made to rotate on an axle, is called a rotor, the heart of any electric motor. It can weigh over 300,000 pounds (right), or it can be a part of the smallest motor in the world (below). The rotor turns out mechanical energy by being made to rotate constantly between two stationary "field magnets."

Like poles repel, and if the rotor's south pole is face to face with the field magnet's south pole, it is pushed around through the 180 degrees toward the stationary north pole. Just as the rotor's south pole gets there, however, the direction of the current in its coil is reversed by a device called a "commutator." This reverses the rotor's poles so that the stationary north pole gives the rotor another 180-degree kick to complete its turn. This continuous switching of current makes the rotor spin on and on—like a frustrated rat on a treadmill—and its rotation can operate in any number of ways to perform useful work.

A ROTOR TOO SMALL TO SEE
The world's smallest motor—weighing one half-millionth of a pound—is shown with the head of a pin. It was built by William McLellan of Pasadena, California, who used a toothpick, a microscope and a watchmaker's lathe. It is 1/64 of an inch on all sides, has 13 parts and generates one millionth of a horsepower. Its operation can be seen only through a microscope.

A ROTOR TOO HEAVY TO CARRY
A 169-ton rotor (right) is gently lowered, with bare clearance, into one of the world's largest motors at Grand Coulee Dam on the Columbia River. Capable of generating 65,000 horsepower, this gigantic magnet had to be built at the dam itself because no train or truck could have carried its huge weight. Its power pumps water for the irrigation of arid areas of Washington.

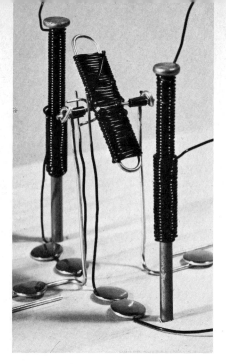

The finished motor.

A Do-It-Yourself Recipe for a Simple Homemade Motor

Although the giant motor shown on the preceding page is obviously a costly and complex machine, a primitive motor can be easily constructed with nothing more than the commonplace tools and materials shown in the photograph below. The basic ingredients are eight thumb tacks, three two-inch paper clips, two three-and-a-half-inch nails, needle-nosed pliers, electrical tape, two one-and-a-half volt dry cell batteries, a wooden board five inches wide by six inches long, a small spool of #20 insulated copper wire and a knife to scrape it with. Most of this equipment can be found at home. But even if it all has to be bought, the total cost should not exceed four dollars. These and the following pages outline in 15 illustrated steps the procedure for putting together the simple motor shown assembled above.

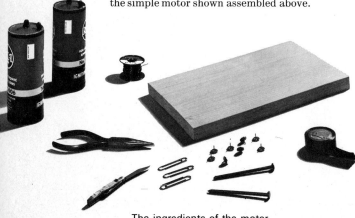

The ingredients of the motor.

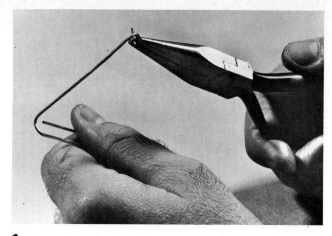

1 The first step in making a motor is taking one of the paper clips and straightening its smaller loop, and then twisting it so that it stands upright at right angles to the larger loop. Then use the pliers to bend a tiny loop in the upright end.

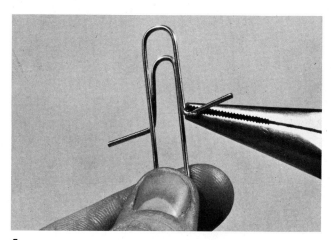

4 Next make the rotor. With pliers, bend the ends of the third paper clip so that they are perpendicular to the clip's loops, as shown in the photograph above. The ends, which will serve as the rotor's axle, should each be a half inch long.

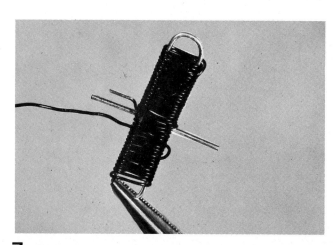

7 When the copper wire has been wound around the second half of the rotor clip as shown above, it is brought back to the center of the clip as in step 6. The ends of the wire will serve as the rotor's commutator, which reverses its current.

2 Next, attach the paper clip to the board with two thumb tacks as shown above. The clip should be positioned near the center of the board and parallel to its longer side. Then prepare another clip in the same way described in step 1.

3 Take the second clip and attach it about one inch from the first clip. It is important to leave the tacks loose enough so that the clips can be moved freely back and forth. These clips are the two supports for the axle of the motor's rotor.

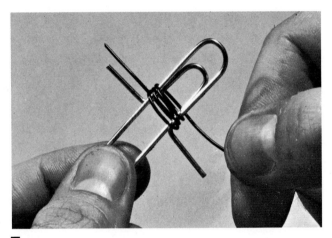

5 Leaving one inch free, wrap the copper wire tightly around the rotor clip, working out from the middle. Wind the turns of wire closely together, but it is important not to wrap them so tightly that the clip is bent out of shape.

6 Wrap about 20 coils out toward the end of the rotor clip. Then take the wire back to the center and wrap—*in the same direction*—an equal number of turns around the other half. These coils will make the clip an electromagnet.

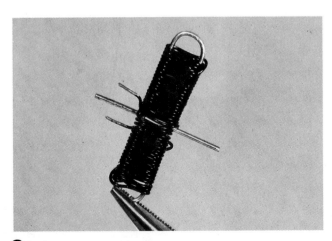

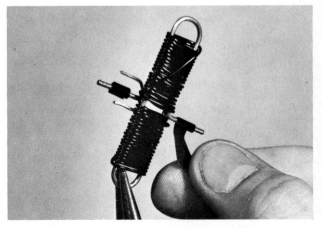

8 The next step is to cut the ends of the wire so that they are slightly shorter than the projecting ends of the clip. Then scrape the coating off the wires' ends to expose the bare copper. These two ends should bend off in the same direction.

9 Take two strips of electrical or adhesive tape—each about a quarter of an inch wide and two inches long—and wrap one around each end of the axle—or projecting ends—of the rotor clip. This tape keeps the axle in the paper clip supports.

133

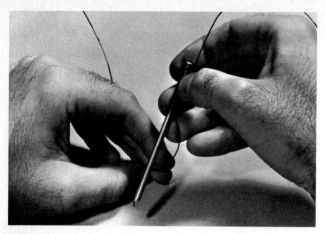

10 To make the two stationary magnets, wrap each nail with wire, leaving about nine inches of wire free close to the head. Wind the wire evenly for about two and a half inches down from the top, then back up again for about half that.

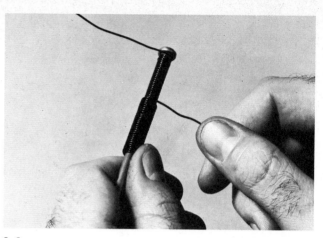

11 Leave about six inches of wire sticking out from the middle of each nail and cut it. Each nail should now have a nine-inch tail and a six-inch tail. Hammer the nails into the board approximately two and a half inches apart as shown in step 12.

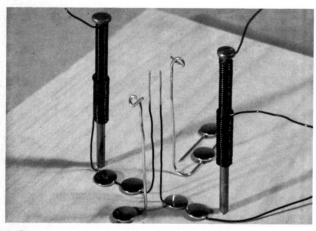

12 Tack the six-inch tail from one nail to the board. Lead it to within one quarter inch of either support and bend it up so its tip is slightly higher than the support. Do the same with an unattached, 12-inch length of wire. These form the brushes.

13 After scraping three quarters of an inch of insulation from the two upstanding wires (the brushes), fit the axle of the rotor into the loops of each support so that the rotor's commutators, when twirling, will make contact with the brushes.

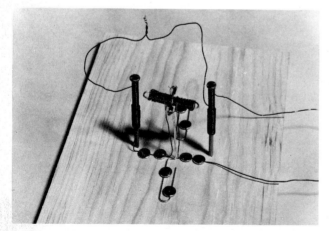

14 Twist the end of the six-inch tail from the second nail around the nine-inch wire from the first nail. (Scrape the ends to achieve solid metal-to-metal contact.) The nine-inch wire from the second nail will connect with one of the batteries.

15 Fasten the wire from the second nail to the center terminal of one battery. Link the free end of the 12-inch wire to the side terminal of the other battery. A short wire connecting the two remaining terminals completes the circuit.

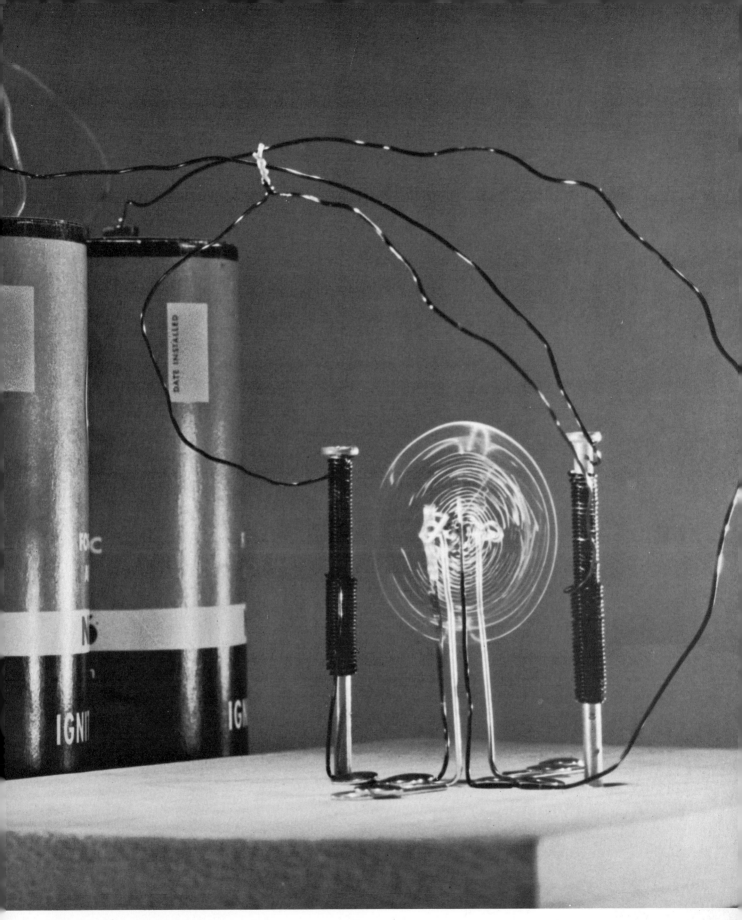

THE FINISHED MOTOR. It may be necessary to give the rotor a gentle nudge. As the rotor spins, both commutators should touch the brushes simultaneously, so the supporting clips must be bent back and forth to put the rotor in position.

7

The Fantastic
World of
Dr. Einstein

"THE MOST INCOMPREHENSIBLE THING ABOUT THE WORLD," Einstein once said, "is that it is comprehensible." Yet no man in history has made it more difficult for the ordinary man to understand his world. Time expands, lengths contract, the substance of the world explodes and vanishes. Experience and common sense no longer count. The real world tends to become the world of the mathematician. This is the course of science and of man's understanding of energy—from 1905, the date of Einstein's first important scientific publication, until the present day.

This venture into a new and abstruse world begins with the demolition of one popular 19th Century concept promulgated by Clerk Maxwell in his electromagnetic wave theory of radiant energy. "We have therefore some reason to believe, from the phenomena of light and heat," he wrote in 1865, "that there is an aethereal medium filling space and permeating bodies, capable of being set in motion and of transmitting that motion from one part to another, and of communicating that motion to gross matter so as to heat it and affect it in various ways."

That archaic word, "aether," had a precise meaning for Maxwell. In explaining his electromagnetic theory, he had postulated its existence to help visualize how light is transmitted through space. In his definition, ether was the medium through which radiant energy was transmitted and through which electromagnetic waves vibrated—much as the air is a medium for sound. Some of his 19th Century colleagues actually used the term "aether wind," as if they were speaking of a breeze blowing through a grove. And because this medium was thought to permeate all space in the universe, the earth itself was supposedly speeding through "aether" while spinning on its own axis and orbiting around the sun.

By the time of Maxwell's death in 1879, the need to confirm the ether's existence had become a nagging concern of many physicists. Whatever it was, it was a very versatile substance. On one hand, a medium so universal and so invisible had to be tenuous enough to allow celestial bodies to circulate freely through it; on the other hand, it must have elasticity greater than that of steel in order to sustain the vibrations of light and radio waves.

Maxwell had suggested that the presence of ether would be proved if it could be shown to slow the speed of light. But this is an extremely difficult measurement to make, because light travels so fast that an airplane at the same speed could circle the earth at the equator roughly seven and a half times in one second. The time elapsed in the passage of light from one wall of a laboratory to another is so infinitesimal as to be practically unmeasurable. Yet, the quantity to be evaluated in Maxwell's problem was even smaller: he had proposed to establish the *difference* between the time spent by light to pass from one point to another and the time it would spend on the return journey. It was clear that the ex-

THE FAITH OF A PHYSICIST

In 1905 Albert Einstein *(opposite)* recast the classical concept of the universe in two brief papers. From then on it was his lifelong desire to fit all the forces of nature into a unified set of equations. He never completed this work, but held firm in his faith that order, not chaos, ruled the cosmos—for, he said, "God doesn't play dice with the universe."

periment could not be carried out utilizing conventional timing devices.

If, however, some means could be found to show that there is actually a difference in elapsed time, regardless of its exact amount, this would be sufficient proof of the ether's existence. This aspect of the problem was tackled in 1887 by two American physicists, Albert A. Michelson and Edward W. Morley, who used an ingenious piece of apparatus (illustrated in the margin) called an interferometer.

Ripples, waves and undulations

The effect caused by dropping stones in water is something like the phenomenon of interference which is observed in light. Each stone sets off a pattern of ripples in ever-widening circles. Eventually the ripples emanating from different stones must come in contact. When crest meets crest, the undulation of the water is deepened; but when a crest meets a trough, the ripple flattens out. Similarly, if two identical light waves travel simultaneously at the same speed over equal distances, they are in step, or in phase, when they reach a common destination. Crest meets crest and the two waves combine their strengths. If these waves travel at different speeds or over different distances, however, it is most likely that they will be out of phase at their destination and thus will tend to cancel each other out. The result is generally an alternating pattern of brightness and darkness called "interference fringes."

Michelson and Morley suggested that if space were filled with ether, then a light beam projected in the direction of the earth's motion must be retarded just as a boat is slowed down when it sails against a current. To test their idea, they conceived what is regarded as one of the most elegant experiments in the history of physics. Their apparatus had at its center a mirror which could split a beam of light and send each half of the beam in a different direction. Two other mirrors, placed at a very carefully measured distance from the first, flashed the split beams back to an eye piece where they recombined into one. The apparatus was adjustable so that one half of the beam could be sent in the direction of the earth's motion and one half in another direction.

The reasoning behind the experiment was this: If the light that was beamed in the direction of the earth's motion was slowed by passage through the ether, it should be out of phase with the other half of the beam when the two recombined. This would be detectable by studying the interference fringes of the recombined beam. When the experiment was made, there was no evidence that the beams were out of phase. Such experiments were repeated year after year in different places by different scientists, but the results were always negative. If ether existed, it had no effect on the velocity of light.

The Michelson-Morley experiment was a body blow to the ether the-

THE ETHER WIND: A MYSTERIOUS PHANTOM

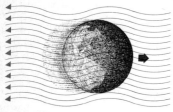

EARTH MOVING THROUGH ETHER

BOAT MOVING AGAINST CURRENT

THE INVISIBLE MEDIUM
Scientists of the 19th Century thought light waves were carried by an invisible medium, "ether," and that the movement of the earth through it created an "ether wind" *(top)*. Light, they supposed, was affected by this wind as a boat is by water current—it moves faster with the wind than against it. In 1887, to try to prove ether's existence, Americans Albert Michelson and Edward Morley conducted the test described opposite.

ory. But a way to save the theory was suggested in 1893 by G. F. Fitz-gerald of Trinity College in Dublin, and an almost identical solution was offered independently by H. A. Lorentz of Leyden University. An object moving through the ether, Fitzgerald and Lorentz postulated, would shrink in the direction of its motion by an amount that depended on how closely its speed approached that of light. The "Lorentz-Fitzgerald contraction"—as it came to be known—was given a simple mathematical expression. In these equations the speed of the earth around the sun allowed for a contraction of the Michelson-Morley apparatus of one part in two hundred millionths. However minute, this change was sufficient to explain the apparent failure of the experiment. The contraction of the apparatus, its actual physical shrinkage, would have concealed any decrease in the speed of the beam that had been slowed down by pas-sage through the ether.

Neither Lorentz nor Fitzgerald made any successful attempt to inter-pret this contraction. Theirs were merely mathematical hypotheses which—for the moment—seemed to offer right answers. But the idea that solid matter could contract because of movement attracted popular at-tention, and a limerick of the day satirized the theory:

> There was a young fellow named Fisk
> Whose fencing was exceedingly brisk;
> So fast was his action,
> The Fitzgerald contraction
> Reduced his rapier to a disk.

While Lorentz and Fitzgerald had seemingly saved the ether theory, it was at a cost of introducing a worse puzzle than the one it solved: How could motion cause an object to shrink? The answer was to come from Albert Einstein, who once explained his attraction to natural sci-ence in these words:

"Out yonder," he wrote, "there was this huge world, which exists in-dependently of us human beings and which stands before us like a great eternal riddle. . . . The contemplation of this world beckoned like a liberation. . . ."

Mystery in a pocket compass

The call of scientific inquiry had moved Einstein to question the mys-teries of a pocket compass even before he began his schooling in Munich, and soon he was deep in his new-found world. At 16, when he applied for admission to the Swiss Federal Polytechnic Institute in Zurich, he was turned down because of his inadequate training in modern lan-guages, zoology and botany. A year later, however, having studied on his own, he was finally admitted.

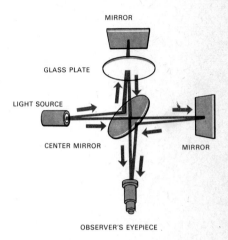

SHUTTING OUT THE ETHER WIND
To prove the existence of ether (opposite page), Michelson and Morley devised an interferometer, which split a beam of light and sent it two ways at one time. Part passed through the thinly silvered center mirror and part was reflected through a clear glass plate, which compensated for the mirror's retarding effect on the other beam. Bouncing off the outer mirrors, the beams reunited at the center. Had the ether wind affected the speed of light, the beams would have been out of phase as they returned. But they were not— and the ether theory was on its way out.

At the Institute, where he began the schooling that was to help shape his thinking, Einstein met the great mathematician Hermann Minkowski (who was later to say on his deathbed, "What a pity to die on the eve of Relativity"). As a theoretician Minkowski conceived an important contribution to the Special Theory of Relativity, but he had few talents as a teacher. Still, as Einstein's biographer says, ". . . it was Minkowski, whose mathematical lectures Einstein found so uninteresting, who put forth ideas for a mathematical formulation of Einstein's theories that provided the germ for all future developments in the field."

Prodigy in a patent office

After his graduation from the Institute, Einstein found work as a clerk in the Swiss patent office at Berne. Here, called upon to grasp quickly the basic concepts of inventions submitted for patents, he developed his unusual faculty for grasping the chief theoretical consequence of scientific experiments. In addition, his patent office duties fostered his bent for the construction of scientific apparatus, a reminder of which still exists at Berne in a device he developed for measuring small electric charges. "Such work," wrote one biographer, "was for him a kind of recreation from his abstract theoretical investigation in much the same way as chess and detective stories serve to relax other scientists." His enthusiasm for inventions was such that, after he left the patent office, he augmented his income as a consultant to a number of industries in Europe, charged with the investigation of new devices.

Out of this brief period in Switzerland came a number of epochal papers, written on a variety of scientific subjects, each of which would create its own revolution in physics. One of his papers, "On the Electrodynamics of Bodies in Movement," published in 1905 when he was only 26 years old, contained the essential ideas of Einstein's Special Theory of Relativity. Its conclusions went straight to the heart of classical mechanics and electromagnetics. First, Einstein dismissed the ether theory. Second, he said that there is no such thing as a fixed space, i.e., one in which a distinction can be made between relative and absolute motion. In other words, there is nothing in the universe that we can be sure is stationary. Anyone who has been sitting on a stopped train while another train passes by the window has noticed this. Suddenly it is impossible to tell which train is moving and which is standing still. Last, and perhaps most important, was his conclusion that light always has the same velocity, no matter how it is measured. Einstein considered the speed of light a universal constant.

Reasoning from these postulates, Einstein stated that every observer must perform his own measurements in his own frame of reference—his house, his planet or his galaxy. For all practical purposes, all things are

LIGHT'S SURPRISING CONSTANCY
If bullets are fired simultaneously from two rockets, each equidistant from an observer and traveling at the same speed *(right),* the bullet from the approaching rocket will strike first. Its velocity is increased by the speed of the rocket while the second bullet is slowed down by the same amount. On the other hand, if lights were flashed simultaneously from the rockets *(opposite),* both beams would arrive at the same time—an example of Einstein's postulate that, regardless of the motion of its source, light always moves through empty space with constant speed.

BULLETS' DIFFERENT SPEEDS

adrift in space at various speeds. There is no ether or other fixed sign-post anywhere in the universe by which one can locate himself or measure his movement. The only common ground is that *everyone everywhere, regardless of his state of motion, will obtain the same answer if he attempts to measure the speed of light.*

Einstein's idea has interesting consequences. Suppose a space platform has been put into orbit over the earth and a scientist is aboard to check the speed of light with a ruler and a clock. Surprisingly enough, these two instruments are, in principle, all he needs in the way of equipment because speed is simply a measurement of how far something will go in a given length of time. The scientist carefully performs his measurements and finds light is moving at 186,272 miles a second just as it does when the speed is measured on earth.

A second expedition is sent up from earth to make exactly the same measurement. But the second scientist does not enjoy the comforts of a relatively slow-moving space station. He is instructed to make his measurements from a rapidly moving rocket ship using a ruler and a clock which, when compared on earth, were absolutely identical to the ones aboard the space station. Just as the rocket ship flashes by the space station, the scientist makes his measurements while, across the way, the scientist on the space station watches through the telescope.

He notices that the rocket ship, his colleague, and the ruler he uses have all diminished in size in the direction in which they are moving. But more disconcerting, he overhears the report from the rocket ship on the speed of light. According to his colleague, light is traveling at exactly 186,272 miles a second. How can this be? Using the short ruler for the measurement should have produced some different answer. The inescapable conclusion is that the other variable in computing speed has also changed: that time has "slowed down."

A journey in slow time

This slowing of the clock in the rocket ship is an example of what physicists call time dilation. It is predicted by Einstein's equations and is a natural result of light having a constant speed. At first glance this might seem no more than a clever exercise of the mind, some sort of useless mathematical idea without any application to the real world. Yet Einstein always felt that it was more than mental gymnastics. He believed that time dilation was an authentic property of the real world. Einstein insisted that a man speeding away from the earth in a rocket ship would actually experience the slowing of his clock.

Moreover, the man on such a journey might come back to earth to find that everything he valued—his family, his country, his civilization—had completely disappeared. A trip to a neighboring star at nearly the speed

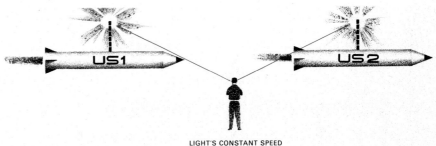

LIGHT'S CONSTANT SPEED

of light might seem to him to take only a few years, and indeed he would be just a few years older in biological age. Yet when he returned to earth, he might find that centuries of earthly time had elapsed, changing everything that he had known before he left.

Like Lorentz and Fitzgerald's contraction theory, Einstein's assault on common sense attracted the satirical pen of a limerick writer who carried time dilation to the ultimate in this poem:

> There once was a lady called Bright,
> Who could travel faster than light;
> She went out one day,
> In a relative way,
> And came back the previous night.

Time dilation remained an unproved theory for 31 years after it was first proposed by Einstein. Then, however, actual physical examples of this retardation began to be observed by physicists at a subatomic level. It occurs, for instance, in the decay of certain small subatomic particles called mesons, which have a mass intermediate between an electron and a proton. Under ordinary circumstances these mesons are extremely short-lived and transform themselves spontaneously into two other particles, an electron and a neutrino. But at extremely high speeds approaching the speed of light physicists have discerned a noticeable delay before this spontaneous decay occurs.

At odds again with the status quo

In addition to the peculiar behavior of time and length predicted by his equations, Einstein's theory also suggested a most unexpected new possibility for the transformation of energy. By his time, scientists had accepted not only the principle of the conservation of energy, but another principle called the conservation of mass. This stated simply that matter could neither be created nor destroyed. Any change in a particular sample of mass could come only from some mechanical or chemical diminution or augmentation. In other words, a quantity of mass either had more mass glued, nailed or fused to it in order to enlarge it or it was vaporized, dissolved or chipped away to make its quantity smaller. However, the sum total of matter in the universe was considered forever constant. Until Einstein, physicists also would have said that movement of matter could not alter its basic nature. But this idea turned out to be completely at odds with Einstein's findings.

Scientists do not always assess matter by weighing it on a scale. More often they will define it according to the rate at which it picks up speed when it is pushed or pulled by some known force. The result of such a measurement is not called weight, but mass. Given the same push, a

THE LONG AND SHORT OF IT
Although it is not apparent to the driver, the car shown below is shorter when speeding than when stationary, according to Einstein's relativity theory. This effect is exaggerated here—the amount of contraction in the fastest-moving car would actually be imperceptible to the observer. Even at 18,000 miles an hour, a rocket ship in space would shrink by only .0000000003 per cent. If an astronaut should ever attain 90 per cent of the speed of light, however, both he and his craft would contract by a little less than half their length.

STATIONARY CAR

MOVING CAR

142

large mass will pick up speed much more slowly than a smaller mass. Scientists had no reason to doubt that, given a big enough push, a piece of matter could be accelerated to a point at which it was traveling faster than the speed of light.

This is where Einstein said no. Nothing, he asserted, could go faster than the speed of light. Not only were length and time affected by speed, but so was mass. As a body approached the speed of light, its mass would increase. It would be harder and harder to push. At the speed of light, its mass would become infinite and no amount of energy could make it go faster—a fact now supported by actual observations.

At conventional velocities the increase in mass predicted by relativity is imperceptible. Even a jet plane traveling at the speed of sound would experience an increase in mass of only one ten-billionth of one per cent. However, mass increases rapidly as the speed of light is approached. At 90 per cent of the speed of light its mass increases more than two times. The effect is very important in designing some of the larger atom smashers. Atomic particles in these machines are spun around and around in a circle, picking up a little speed with each revolution and also a little mass. The timing of the electrical forces, which are pushing the particles, therefore, has to be adjusted with each cycle to keep the slightly heavier particles moving properly.

Up to this point, Einstein had only stated that the mass and the movement of matter (kinetic energy) are related. After equating them in this restricted sense, he then took the bold leap forward that would eventually lead to the atomic age. Mass, he asserted, is the equivalent of energy in all its manifestations. Thus energy and matter are not the two faces of the universe, but simply two sides of the same face. Increases and decreases in energy, according to this theory, are always associated with a change in mass. Even heating an object—filling it with heat energy—increases its mass by an imperceptible amount.

Riches out of reach

These alterations of mass that accompany ordinary changes in energy —heating on a stove, speeding on the highway—are so minute that normal weighing could not hope to disclose the change. But this connection between mass and energy suggested to Einstein that a direct conversion of mass into some useful form of energy might be possible. The means for making this transformation were totally unknown, however, when he first published his theory.

According to Einstein's equation, the now famous $E = mc^2$, the total amount of energy (E) locked into a mass (m) is equal to m multiplied by the square of the velocity of light (c). As in all equations relating physical quantities, care must be taken to express all numbers in the proper units. In the above equation, E is the number of ergs if m is expressed in grams and c in centimeters per second. For example, one gram of any substance, if totally converted into energy (taking the speed of light at its rounded value of 30 billion centimeters per second), would yield:

$$E = 1 \times 30,000,000,000 \times 30,000,000,000 \text{ ergs}$$

or 900 billion billion ergs, equivalent to 25 million kilowatt-hours. In more striking terms, one might say that the mass of a railroad ticket contains enough energy to run a large train around the world several times. A similar calculation reveals that a pound of matter entirely converted into energy would be the equivalent of ten million tons of TNT.

In the years that followed the publication of Einstein's theory, his statement of the equivalence of mass and energy was the subject of much debate and wishful speculation. For if Einstein was right, untold riches lay trapped in familiar substances that surround us—a new El Dorado, more fabulous than all the gold fields of the world, if only man could one day learn to release this energy and use it for his service.

The idea appeared absolutely fantastic to Einstein's friends in Berne, who hotly refused to accept his theory. A typical exchange was described in the recent biography by Peter Michelmore:

"You're saying there's more horsepower in a lump of coal than in the whole Prussian cavalry," they complained. "If this were true, why hasn't it been noticed before?"

"If a man who is fabulously rich never spent or gave away a cent," Einstein replied, "then no one could tell how rich he was or even whether he had any money at all. It is the same with matter. So long as none of the energy is given off externally, it cannot be observed."

"And how do you propose to release all this hidden energy?"

"There is not the slightest indication that the energy will ever be obtainable," said Einstein. "It would mean that the atom would have to be shattered at will. . . . We see atom disintegration only where nature herself presents it. . . ."

In the same conversation, according to Michelmore, Einstein was asked if he had worked out his energy equation from his experiments, and his friends were horror-struck when he told them he hadn't been inside a laboratory for years. Laboratory work was not necessary, Einstein said:

"Physics is a logical system of thought in a state of evolution. Its basis cannot be obtained merely by experiment and experience. Its progress depends on free invention. . . . I haven't the faintest doubt that I am right."

Despite its critics, the theory slowly gained acceptance as experimental evidence in its favor began to accumulate. The most dramatic confirmation of the equivalence of mass and energy occurred in 1932

KEEPING THE BALL ROLLING

The little man in the comic strip below is attempting to fight Einstein's Special Theory of Relativity. As he pushes the load faster, it gets heavier because, according to the theory, mass increases with speed. Thus, more effort is needed to keep the ball rolling. Also, as it moves faster, the ball contracts in the direction of its motion. These effects, exaggerated here, become noticeable only near the speed of light.

with the discovery of a new fundamental particle called the positron. It was to turn up in investigations of high energy photons, which had been studied in two forms—as gamma rays emanating from radioactive substances here on earth, and as cosmic rays bombarding the earth from outer space. Cosmic ray photons, which revealed energies far greater than those of gamma ray sources, had first been studied only three years before by the British physicist C.T.R. Wilson, in an instrument called a "cloud chamber." In this device, the passage of a charged particle through a mist of water vapor leaves a track of tiny water droplets which can be photographed. When the cloud chamber is placed between the poles of an electromagnet, the magnetic field makes the charged particles move in a curved path through the mist, and the direction of this curve is used to evaluate the electric charge of the particles.

In 1932 C. D. Anderson, a physicist at the University of California, observed a track curved in a direction opposite to that taken by ordinary negatively charged electrons. The density of the track showed that the mass of this apparently misbehaving particle was that of an electron, but the track's opposite curvature indicated that the particle was positively charged. Anderson named this new particle the "positron."

What happened was this: cosmic ray photons were transforming themselves from packets of electromagnetic energy *without mass* into electron and positron pairs *with mass*. This energy-to-mass conversion was absolutely in accord with Einstein's equation.

Further study of cosmic ray phenomena revealed that the reverse of photon annihilation also takes place: mass too can become energy. Experiments showed that free positrons and electrons can use and annihilate each other, their mass transforming into the energy of photons. Here was further evidence that Einstein's equation holds true whichever way the transformation goes.

A clue in the stars

As yet, scientists had little inkling of the means by which the conversion of mass into energy could be effected for practical purposes. On the other hand, it was becoming progressively evident that the vast output of energy by the stars, including our own sun, must originate in some kind of nuclear transformations akin to those observed in cloud chambers.

In 1938 Hans Bethe, professor of physics at Cornell University, developed a theory explaining what these nuclear transformations might be. According to Bethe, the extremely high temperatures found in the sun and the enormous pressure exerted by its great bulk cause protons to join together in the process called fusion. In the fusion reaction, four protons are combined to form the nucleus of a helium atom. The mass of this nucleus is very slightly less than that of the four pro-

$E = mc^2$

The theoretical conversion of mass into energy on the basis of Einstein's famous equation, $E = mc^2$ (energy equals mass times the square of the speed of light), results in astonishing figures. Each of the illustrations listed below represents the equivalent of just one pound of any substance completely converted into energy:

- **11 billion kilowatt hours**
- **15 billion horsepower hours**
- **40 million million BTUs**
- **An electric iron running for one million years**
- **A room air conditioner running for 500,000 years**
- **A home furnace operating continuously for 25,000 to 50,000 years**
- **A car driven 180,000 times around the earth**
- **The largest oil tanker propelled 300 times around the world**
- **The electric power needs of the United States for five days**

tons. The missing mass has been converted into the energy of the sun.

The next year two German chemists, Otto Hahn and Fritz Strassmann, made an accidental discovery that at long last was to give man the means to unlock the energy of the atom. While bombarding a sample of uranium with neutrons in the hope of creating heavier elements—a favorite pastime of atomic research in that epoch—they found to their surprise that the resulting mixture actually contained barium, a substance much lighter.

The mystery was unraveled by Lise Meitner and Otto Frisch, then refugees from Nazism working in Sweden. They showed that the uranium nucleus had split into lighter elements whose combined weight was less than that of the uranium. The missing uranium mass had been converted into energy!

Although scientists were quick to grasp the significance of this discovery, they still were not yet ready to apply it to practical purposes. So far, the only means by which they could reproduce it in their laboratories was by applying more energy than was released in the reaction itself. A method had yet to be found whereby the reaction could be made self-sustaining. But the die had been cast. By 1945, only six years later, the greatest concentration of scientific minds ever applied to a single task, brought together by the war effort of the U.S. Government, had solved the riddle. Man had unleashed the explosive energy of the nucleus.

From a Mite of Matter, a Mighty Force

When Dr. Enrico Fermi set off the first nuclear chain reaction in 1942, a colleague capsuled the meaning in the nine words of a symbolically coded phone call: "The Italian navigator has landed in the new world." The new world, of course, was the atomic age. In 1905, Albert Einstein had theorized that a tiny amount of matter could yield an enormous amount of energy. When the team of scientists led by Fermi found a practical way to pry open the heart of matter, the nucleus, they turned Einstein's theory into reality. Twelve years later a single H-bomb exploded at Bikini had five times the destructiveness of all the conventional bombs dropped in World War II. Today nuclear power is serving man. Reactors like the one opposite produce useful forms of elements called radioisotopes; they are also generating electricity. And the new power may soon create harbors and canals as well as propel space vehicles far beyond the moon.

FEEDING AN ATOMIC FURNACE
More than 1,200 fuel openings dot the face of the world's oldest reactor *(opposite)* at Oak Ridge, Tennessee. With a long rod a technician is poking a slug of uranium fuel through a channel into the core of the reactor, while at left a health physicist measures radioactivity with a Geiger counter. For 15 years the Oak Ridge reactor was the nation's primary source of useful radioisotopes.

A SALUTE IN BRONZE FOR FERMI

The bronze plaque at left, at Chicago's Stagg Field, commemorates Dr. Enrico Fermi's historic fission chain reaction. Fermi, criticized in Italy for not giving the Fascist salute when presented with the 1938 Nobel Prize, never returned to Italy, and became an American citizen in 1945.

CRADLE OF AN AGE

The picture at right shows the now-demolished stands of the University of Chicago's Stagg Field as they looked in 1942 when, in the squash court beneath them, a small group of scientists inaugurated the atomic age. They toasted in solemn silence by sipping wine from paper cups.

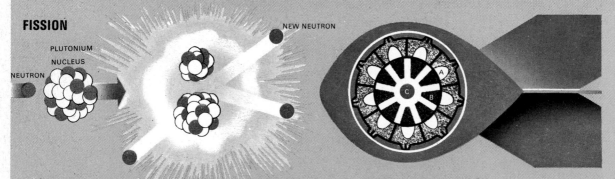

FISSION

PLUTONIUM NUCLEUS

NEUTRON

NEW NEUTRON

THE EXPLOSION OF AN ATOMIC BOMB is the result of fission *(above, left)*. In an A-bomb the nucleus of a fissionable element such as plutonium is hit by a neutron and it splits into two smaller nuclei, releasing energy plus two or three other neutrons. If there is enough plutonium present to make what physicists call a "critical mass," these new neutrons will bombard enough other plutonium nuclei to set off a spontaneous chain reaction—a fission explosion. In the bomb itself, shown above in a schematic drawing, TNT charges, A, explode simultaneously, pushing separated wedges of plutonium, B, together into a critical mass. Blown into the neutron source, C, it explodes immediately.

FUSION

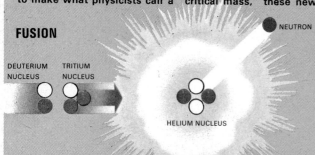

DEUTERIUM NUCLEUS

TRITIUM NUCLEUS

NEUTRON

HELIUM NUCLEUS

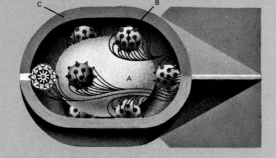

IN AN H-BOMB, two nuclei fuse, just the opposite of fission. Deuterium and tritium are two different kinds of hydrogen. If their nuclei can be made to unite, the marriage produces a helium nucleus, a neutron and more energy per pound of reacting material than any other reaction in the universe. Fusion, however, takes place only at temperatures of at least 180,000,000° F.—unheard of until man had built an atomic bomb. The H-bomb is composed of a core, A, of lithium hydride—a source of deuterium and tritium—and is triggered by several small atomic explosive devices, B. The outer casing, C, is uranium 238, whose fission, produced by the blast, adds to the bomb's explosive power.

The A-Bomb's Awful Extravagance

If an atom were the size of a room, its nucleus would be no larger than a grain of sand. Yet this tiny speck of matter is held together by forces so powerful that when an unstable nucleus like that of uranium 235 is split—as in the fission reaction opposite—the energy unleashed from a few pounds of that metal is equivalent to the explosion of thousands of tons of TNT. And the incredibly high temperatures released in such atomic explosions made possible the even more fearsome fusion reaction (*opposite*) of the hydrogen bomb.

When European physicists in 1939 first discovered that uranium emitted neutrons as its nucleus split, they wondered if these could be made to split other nuclei to start a chain reaction. This was finally done under controlled conditions in Chicago in 1942. But could an uncontrolled chain reaction be used to make a bomb? To answer that question, the U.S. launched a massive scientific and industrial effort. The result was a devastating blast over the desert of New Mexico in 1945: the first atomic explosion in history.

A LADY WITH A FIERY TIARA

The mushroom cloud from a nuclear explosion erupts 43,000 feet into the air over the Nevada desert in a 1957 military test called "Priscilla." The brilliant streak in the upper cloud is the edge of the luminous fireball, showing through the cloud. Part of a series of 24 tests, this 37-kiloton blast was exploded from a balloon 700 feet high. (One kiloton equals 1,000 tons of TNT.)

An Atomic Gnome to Carve a Cave

"Atoms for Peace" is a popular layman's slogan in the postwar world, and the U.S. Government's "Plowshare Program" is aimed at making it a reality. In December 1961, Plowshare's "Project Gnome" sank an elevator shaft 1,200 feet into the New Mexico desert, dug a horizontal tunnel 1,116 feet long and planted a small (3.1 kiloton) atomic bomb. Closing a blast door at the elevator end, the Gnome scientists detonated the bomb. The result was the first man-made atomic cave (left).

Five months later, scientists crawled into the cave through a tiny hole and found a scene of eerie beauty (left). The cavity was 170 feet wide and 80 feet high.

The temperature was still a torrid 140° F., but practically all the radioactivity had either already disappeared or been trapped beneath the rubble.

Gnome provided hopeful guides to the feasibility of using such blasts for mining ore, extracting oil and providing water reservoirs. It also proved there was one scheme which would *not* work. Water was poured into the cavity soon after the explosion in the hope that high-pressure steam would jet to the surface, where it could be used to generate electricity. But much steam escaped through cracks and vents, and what did come up was too full of corrosive minerals to be used.

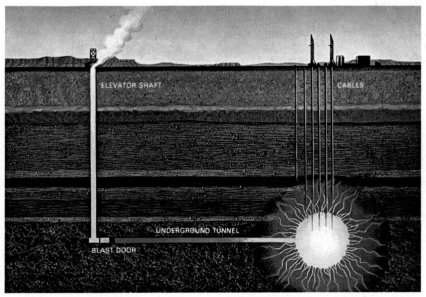

A NUCLEAR SALT BUBBLE
As deep in the earth as the Empire State Building is high, the scientist at left stares in awe at Gnome's handiwork. Exploded in a bed of rock salt, the bomb blew a huge bubble that fused the salt, forming an almost perfectly spherical cavity. The bottom half is filled with rubble; the domed roof, with its slender stalactites, was tinged with green and violet by intense heat.

A CAVE DIGGER'S BLUEPRINT
This cutaway diagram of the first underground atomic explosion shows the elevator shaft, the underground tunnel to the blast site, the fiery explosion and the cables which relayed information about the blast. Dozens of instruments were buried in the ground at various levels. Seismic stations around the world recorded the tremor, which was equal to a minor earthquake.

These four movie frames show the desert floor erupting to a height of 290 feet after the "Project Sedan" explosion. The first frame was taken

A Quarter-Mile
Crater Dug by
a Nuclear Shovel

The exploding dome of sand above is the blast of a hydrogen bomb that was buried 635 feet underground. The desert boiled, seething with radioactivity. When the dust settled, the huge hole at right, a quarter mile across, bore testimony to the power of thermonuclear bombs.

Another of the Plowshare Program's tests, this one was called "Project Sedan." It differed from the Gnome explosion described on pages 150 and 151 in that its purpose was to construct a gigantic open crater rather than an underground cave. It was a "clean" explosion because at least 70 per cent of its energy came from fusion rather than "dirtier" fission; and the rubble that fell back into the crater made a

blanket that buried radioactive debris hundreds of feet below.

Like all of Plowshare's programs, this was nonmilitary. By 1980, cratering explosions like these will probably be safe enough to take on mammoth excavation projects such as the construction of a new shipping canal through the Isthmus of Panama. That job would be done with 651 H-bombs having a total power of 42 megatons. (One megaton is equal to one million tons of TNT.) To build it with conventional explosives would cost nearly six billion dollars—using nuclear blasts just a little over two billion. Excavating, which took almost 20 years for the old Canal, might take only five for the new one.

THE WORK OF A BURIED H-BOMB
This crater in the Nevada desert *(right)*—320 feet deep and 1,280 feet wide—was created by the underground explosion of a 100-kiloton hydrogen bomb. The blast displaced about 12 million tons of earth, but was so clean that scientists were able to visit the lip of the crater five days later. At bottom left is the work-site of a research team checking for radiation.

one quarter second after the detonation; the last, two and three quarter seconds later. The small black box in the first frame is the detonator.

From the Control of Fission, a Global Bounty

Not all nuclear chain reactions result in devastating explosions like those pictured on the preceding pages. In fact, the peaceful harnessing of atomic energy is based on the fact that a fission chain reaction *can* be easily controlled—by slow fission in nuclear reactors.

Unstable uranium in a reactor's core begins disintegrating when hit by neutrons—generating new neutrons as well as heat. These neutrons bombard and split other uranium atoms in a chain reaction which can be controlled by rods that move in and out of the reactor's core. The rods are made of substances which absorb neutrons, such as boron, cadmium and hafnium. This control, releasing the atomic energy slowly over a long period of time, is what makes the nuclear fission in a reactor different from the uncontrolled instantaneous explosion of an atomic bomb.

Two decades after the first chain reaction in 1942, there were almost 400 nuclear reactors in the world: 285 in the United States, 39 in Great Britain, 39 in the Soviet Union, 18 in West Germany, 14 in Italy, 11 in Japan and 10 in Canada. Most of these are low-power reactors built for research, such as the three in Scotland, India and Portugal shown on these pages. Many, however, are high-power reactors for the generation of electricity, such as the New England Yankee at top. The operation of such a nuclear generating plant is described on the next pages.

THE U.S.: A HARD-WORKING YANKEE
A white dome in the icy New England winter, the Yankee Atomic Electric Power Plant at Rowe, Massachusetts *(above)*, is New England's first nuclear power station. Yankee went to work in 1961 and churned out enough power with its first load of 23 tons of uranium to supply all the homes of Boston for two years. Yankee is a joint project of 10 power companies.

PORTUGAL: A SIGN OF FISSION
The workman at right holds a sign which reads "Portuguese Reactor for Research" and refers to Portugal's nuclear research center in Sacavem. The Sacavem reactor is available to students at the Universities of Lisbon and Coimbra. Completed in 1961, it was the 15th nuclear reactor built in foreign countries under the U.S. Government's "Atoms for Peace" program.

INDIA: A COMMONWEALTH GIFT

The laborers in the photograph at right are leveling ground for the building of the "Canada-India Reactor" near Bombay. The equipment and employee-training for this international project was supplied by Canada, the labor and building by India. Completed in 1960, it was described by Prime Minister Nehru as "a symbol of the manner in which the world has shrunk."

SCOTLAND: A WELCOME SURPLUS

On the site of an old air base in northern Scotland, the Dounreay experimental reactor overlooks the North Atlantic. Dounreay, which started operating in 1959, was built for research; any electricity it can spare, however, is fed to the power lines of Scotland. Faced with a diminishing fuel supply, the United Kingdom has more nuclear power plants than any other country.

Building an Atom-fired Steam Boiler

The pictures on these pages are of the great nuclear reactor in Shippingport, near Pittsburgh, Pennsylvania. This was the first large-scale atomic power plant in the U. S. devoted exclusively to generating electricity. It was built in 1957 as an experiment to probe the problems and costs of converting the heat of atomic fission chain reactions into electric power.

The reactor began its work with 165 pounds of enriched uranium surrounded by a 14-ton blanket of uranium dioxide. At first, half of the reactor's power comes from the enriched uranium. But the fission reaction slowly converts the uranium dioxide into the highly radioactive plutonium, which produces an increasing share of the power. The first load of U-235 kept the reactor going for two years and a day.

The reactor is being stepped up from an output of 60,000 kilowatts—enough power for 225,000 people—to 100,000 kilowatts. The plant has an operating force of 240 people, many of whom are involved in reactor research.

Guiding spirit of the project was Admiral Hyman Rickover, father of the U.S. Navy's nuclear fleet. The reactor, sponsored by the Government, was produced by Westinghouse and the Duquesne Light Company at a cost of $110 million. Its success in providing both knowledge and electricity has proved that nuclear power plants, while still costly, are here to stay.

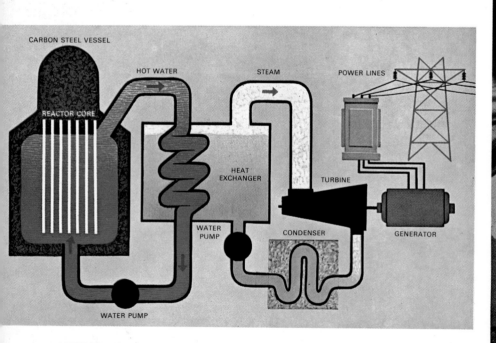

ATOM TO WATER TO WIRE

The radioactive core of the nuclear reactor *(above)* heats water—under pressure, to keep it from becoming steam—to a temperature of 550° F. In a heat exchanger this water transfers its heat to a second water system, where steam forms to operate a turbine. This drives the generator, which sends electricity into the power lines. Meanwhile, the steam is reconverted into water by a condenser and pumped back to the heat exchanger for another round. The water from the reactor, cooled by the exchanger, returns to the reactor for reheating.

COOLER FOR A HOT HEART

The shell shown above contains the heart of the Shippingport reactor: the radioactive core. Some 26 million pounds of water circulates through the shell every hour, carrying the extreme heat of the reactor to the heat exchanger *(diagram opposite)*. Made of carbon steel —carefully X-rayed to detect flaws—the shell alone weighs 235 tons and is 32.5 feet high.

AT THE CORE OF THE MATTER

Shown under construction at left is the Shippingport reactor's core. Engineers in white coats —to protect the machine from dirt—adjust the long cylindrical rods containing hafnium, an element which slows down uranium's chain reaction. The core is now shielded by layers of stainless steel, water and concrete, and the whole is encased in the shell pictured above.

Bridling the Atom
for Travel
in Air and Space

The most powerful rockets in the world today will someday seem like toys compared to those powered by engines such as the one called "Kiwi," shown being tested at right. The secret of this revolution in rocketry is nuclear reactors small and light enough to be boosted into space. Reactors for transportation were first put in ships and submarines, and small reactors have even been suggested for aircraft engines *(opposite)*.

But so far the most dramatic progress in light, miniature reactors is being made in "Project Rover," whose purpose is to test the mettle of nuclear reactors for use in rocket engines. Knowledge gained from these tests will be used to construct a nuclear rocket that may propel a vehicle through space sometime in the 1970s.

A rocket reactor must have qualifications not required of ordinary reactors. Though light in weight, it must be high in power. Out in space, a nuclear rocket delivers up to twice the thrust per pound of propellant as a chemical rocket. Like many non-nuclear rocket engines, Kiwi uses hydrogen. But in conventional engines, the hydrogen is burned and the expanding combustion products provide the thrust. In a nuclear engine nothing burns; the enormous heat of the reactor is all that is needed to blast the hydrogen out of the nozzle. And in a few years it will be the concentrated power of such rockets that will enable man to boost himself past the moon to the depths of the solar system.

A HIGH-STRUNG REACTOR
In a test to study how the crew of a nuclear-powered aircraft might be shielded from the deadly rays of its own engine, this atomic reactor *(opposite)* hangs between two 324-foot towers in Oak Ridge, Tennessee. Scientists underground watched through television cameras and measured its radiation with instruments in the barrel-shaped detector suspended nearby.

AN UPSIDE-DOWN REACTOR
The "Kiwi A" *(above)*, first in a series of nuclear rocket engines used for test purposes, is fired off at its Nevada testing grounds. Kiwi's heart is a nuclear reactor whose job is to heat hydrogen to a high temperature so rapidly that its expansion thrusts it violently out of the nozzle. To keep it from leaving the ground, the Kiwi is tested upside down. Although smoke is normally not produced by the reactor's operation, it is injected into the engine to track the otherwise invisible radioactive exhaust cloud. Kiwi is named for a New Zealand bird that does not fly.

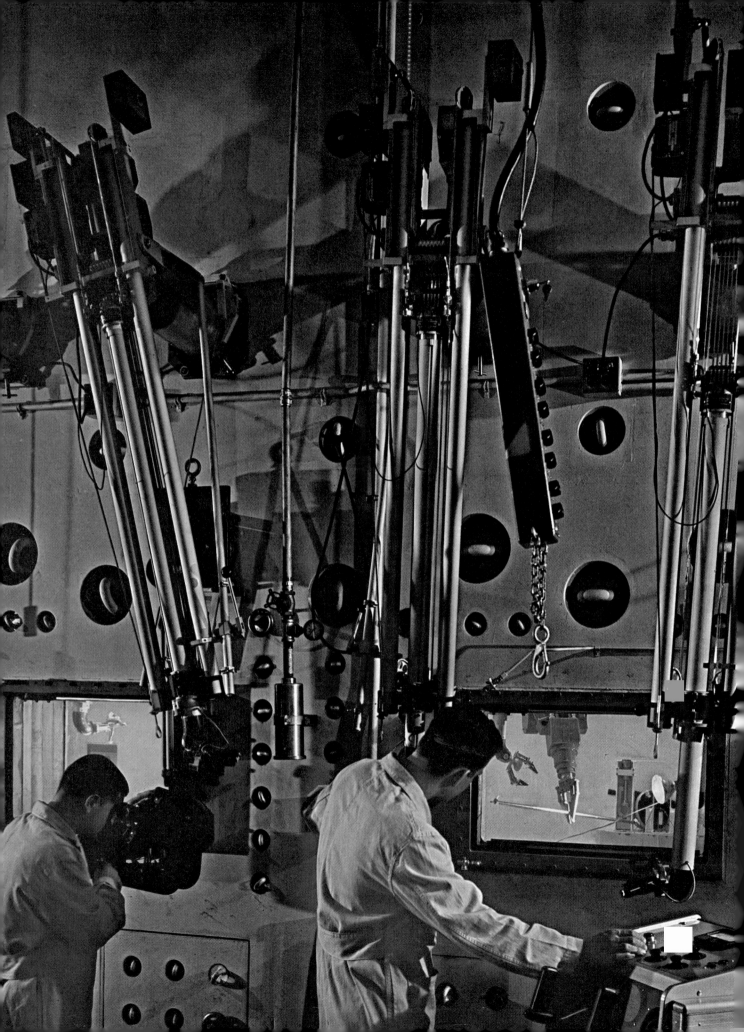

Keeping Invisible Death at Bay

When radioactivity was first discovered in 1895, scientists were generally unaware of the dangers of this new form of invisible radiation. They soon learned. Experimenters and technicians working with radium received bad burns from overexposure, and radium's discoverer, Mme. Curie, eventually died from the effects of her work. Radiation can cause cancer and destroy bones and vital organs. It can also insidiously damage the genes, the structures in the body controlling heredity, and children born to parents exposed to radiation may be harmed.

The coming of nuclear bombs and the useful harnessing of atomic energy made the radiation problem so acute that Congress in 1959 set up the Federal Radiation Council to protect workers in the new industry. Long before this date, however, there had been safety devices such as the portable Geiger counter for measuring the intensity of radiation. Then came a host of industrial safeguards like the protective plastic suit at right, bells that ring when the radiation in a room gets to the danger point and robot "masterslaves" to handle dangerous objects (opposite). The size of the job of making nuclear energy safe is indicated by the fact that an atomic energy plant estimated to cost 12 million dollars could be built, without its elaborate safeguards, for one million. Yet the cost is worth while. Since the U.S. atomic program began, only four workers have died of radiation exposure.

HOMER'S HIDEOUS HALLUCINATION
The technicians at right are protected from the deadly plutonium dust of a "hot room" by an ingenious polyethylene suit that makes them look like visitors from a far planet. Nicknamed Homer's Hideous Hallucination for its inventor, Homer Moulthrop, the suit has a long hollow tail stretching to an adjoining safe room. The worker crawls through the tail to get to his suit.

A ROBOT TO BEAT RADIATION
Behind a radiation-proof window a yard thick (opposite), the pincer hand of a robot device called "master-slave" manipulates a radioactive rod. The robot, in a laboratory in Pleasanton, California, is guided by the technician at right, while a metallurgist observes through a magnifying periscope. Robot hands are delicate enough to pick up an egg without cracking it.

FISSION'S GRAVEYARD

A 6,000-cubic-foot "coffin" *(above)* containing 15 tons of obsolete plutonium reactor machinery is interred by bulldozers while a radiation-shielded workman checks for radioactivity. The 20-acre cemetery is a final resting place for "hot" wastes from the Hanford Atomic Plant in Washington. For each radioactive burial, details are noted and a concrete marker is set up.

A PRISON OF CLAY

The four clay balls held casually in the technician's hand at right have been impregnated with dangerous radioactive liquid. But heating the clay to 2,372° F. effectively locked the radioactivity inside the balls to make them safe. Called "sponge fixation," this promising new method for solidifying and disposing of "hot" liquid wastes is still in the experimental stage.

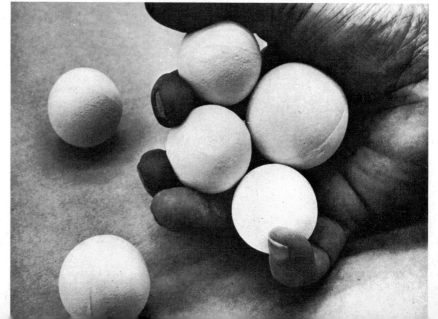

A Hot Garbage Disposal Problem

Getting rid of the inevitable fission by-products that are too "hot" to handle is one of the nuclear engineer's thorniest problems. A varied list of contaminated items comes out the back door of a nuclear worksite: laundry water from workers' uniforms, towels, broken glass—and such major refuse as radioactive chemicals, machinery and reactor cores. Since only time—about 100 years—can neutralize most of these wastes, they must be carefully bundled up and put where they can cause no harm. So far the only practicable answer is an old one: bury them.

Just about all of fission's leftovers are being interred either in the earth or at sea (*left and below*). The latter is an obvious dumping ground, but the dangers of leakage and contamination of large areas of the ocean make it such a tricky business that only low-level radioactive waste gets this treatment. Most really "hot" stuff is stored underground in special steel and concrete tanks or vaults which must be continually checked for leakage.

Progress is being made in finding new storage methods (*below, opposite*), and there is a chance that underground salt mines could be effective traps. But the problem remains pressing: by the year 2000, nuclear plants will be yielding 50 million gallons of "dirty" garbage a year.

A BRINY BURIAL
The concrete burial vault about to be dumped overboard from the U.S. Coast Guard cutter *Cherokee* at right contains a dangerous load of radioactive debris. It is part of a 25-ton cargo of radioactive waste from atomic research projects in the District of Columbia. The vaults, dropped into the sea 120 miles east of Norfolk, Virginia, are designed to last at least 100 years.

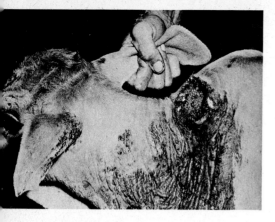

A calf's wound *(above)* festers with larvae.

Screwworm flies are a half inch in length.

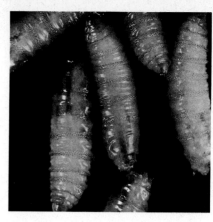

Larvae *(above)* hatch in the cattle's flesh.

A Radioactive Prescription to Keep Cattle Fit

The screwworm fly has been a scourge of Southern cattle. Hatched from eggs laid in scratches and cuts *(above)*, the maggots can kill a steer in 10 days. Yet in the last few years, planes have dumped over eight billion *live* screwworms over the South.

The reason? The eight billion had all been sterilized. And if a female screwworm unites with a sterile male, she lays sterile eggs. Southern cattlemen believe the screwworms will be eliminated. On the island of Curaçao, a project like this exterminated them in a year.

The secret of this pest control is radioactive isotopes. Offbeat unstable cousins of ordinary chemical elements, radioisotopes are constantly disintegrating and emitting rays. Like all radioactivity, these rays are dangerous; but they can be put to good use, as in the laboratory sterilization of the screwworm *(below)*. Radioisotopes can also kill cancer cells; and since their radioactivity can be detected, they are used as tracers to report on the flow of digestive juices or of oil in pipelines. They even power unattended weather stations in the Arctic. In fact, the enormous versatility of the radioisotopes has given man optimistic notice that the specter of radioactivity also has its benign features.

ATOMS VERSUS THE SCREWWORM
When screwworm eggs evolve into pupae, they are packed into a can like the one at the left in the photograph above and are sterilized by the gamma rays of the radioisotope cobalt 60. The sterile males compete successfully with virile males in mating with the female screwworms.

NO ESCAPE FROM STERILIZATION
In the largest screwworm "factory" in Texas, Dr. W. L. Tarver *(opposite)* releases 4,500 sterile screwworm flies in the middle of his plant. Purpose: so that they might mate with and thus sterilize any flies that have escaped from their cages and are wandering around near the plant.

8

$E = mc^2$:
Substance Put
to Work

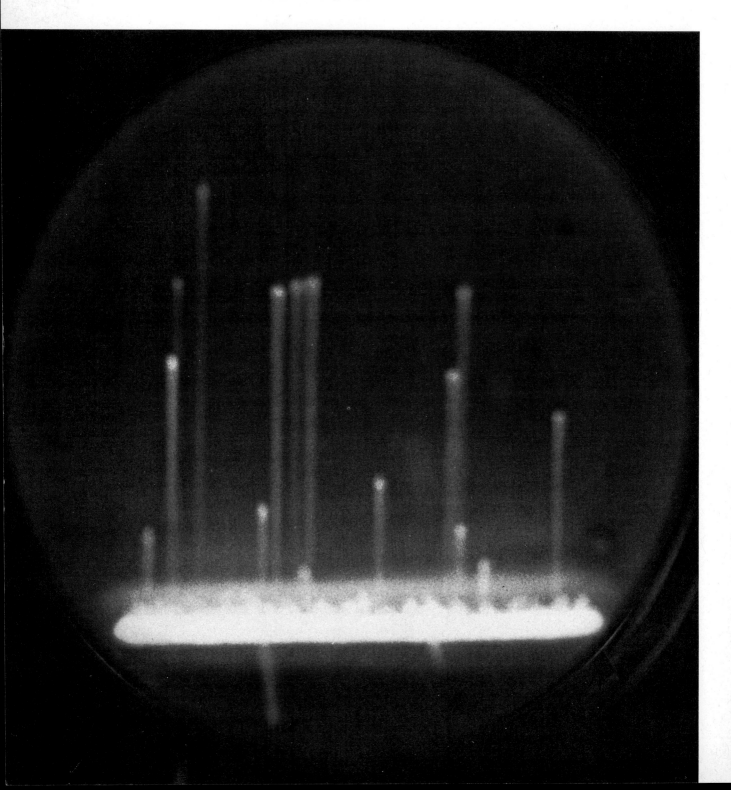

ON DECEMBER 2, 1942, a group of 39 scientists, including one woman, surrounded the great Italian-born physicist, Enrico Fermi, in a squash court of Stagg Field at the University of Chicago. They stood tensely as a huge pile of uranium and graphite was slowly subjected to a crucial test. At 3:25 p.m., as the group grew silent and neutron counters ticked away, Fermi began to relax. "The chain reaction," he said, looking around at his fellows, "is self-sustaining."

This was the climax of three years of effort to twist the arm of nature. The experiments in 1939 of Otto Hahn and Fritz Strassmann had established that when uranium is bombarded with neutrons some of its atoms split into lighter fragments. Some mass disappears in the breakup, as part of the uranium atom is converted into energy. One neutron is enough to split an atom, and even that neutron is simply invested, not lost; among the debris are, on the average, between two and three additional neutrons. These new neutrons can in turn split two or three other atoms, releasing more energy and from four to nine more neutrons. If each of these succeeds in splitting just one atom, the next step in the reaction will produce between eight and 27 neutrons, and so on. Thus the whole "chain reaction," as it came to be known, would proceed at an ever accelerating rate.

But what happens in theory and what actually happens are two different things. Many of the neutrons will simply fail to split another atom, and each time they miss their target the chain reaction is weakened. The atomic scientists very soon realized that if energy was to be released from uranium on a large scale, some means had to be found to make the chain reaction self-sustaining. Some method had to be devised to make sure enough neutrons got to enough nuclei and split them.

In 1942 Fermi's uranium-graphite pile managed to do just that. Fermi had found from experiment that slower moving neutrons were more effective at causing fission than those traveling at higher speed. But most neutrons released by the breakup of a nucleus are fast ones. If the chain reaction was to be a reality, a way had to be found to slow these neutrons down to speeds where they were effective.

Fermi knew that the nuclei of certain materials such as graphite, a pure form of carbon, show almost no inclination at all to absorb neutrons—which simply bounce off these nuclei like a rubber ball off a concrete wall. On the other hand, there are substances with spongelike nuclei that will absorb any passing neutron without any apparent ill effects from their aggressiveness. A combination of the impervious and the absorbent nuclei gave Fermi the tool he needed to control nuclear breakup with a delicate touch.

Fermi embedded the uranium fuel for the reaction in a huge mass of graphite, his reasoning being that fast neutrons created by nuclear splitting would, in ricocheting off the graphite, be slowed into more efficient projectiles for hitting the tiny uranium nuclei and breaking them in two. But if the experiment were successful, the possibility of a runaway nuclear reaction arose. In order to control the progress of the reaction, Fermi decided to insert some rods of a neutron-absorbing substance into the pile. In this case, the material chosen was cadmium, a rather rare metal related to ordinary zinc. The rods were arranged so that they could be pushed into and pulled out of the pile, depending on whether the reaction needed to be slowed or speeded.

The situation in delicate balance

When Fermi announced to his colleagues that the chain reaction was self-sustaining, it meant that just enough neutrons were being slowed by the graphite to keep the reaction going. And enough were being taken in by the cadmium to keep the situation from getting out of hand.

The success attained at the Stagg Field court proved that both the atom bomb and the peaceful harnessing of the atom were feasible. If a pile were built without the cadmium rods, the chain reaction could proceed unbridled. On the other hand, controlling the reaction by the use of cadmium, or any other absorber, offered the key to an orderly generation of atomic power. This would become the major principle of the atomic reactors that now are producing electric power for an increasing number of cities around the world.

But from 1942, when the first chain reaction was achieved, it would take more than two and a half years until the first atomic bomb was detonated in 1945. In between, the labor of 500,000 men and women and two billion dollars were poured into the vast Manhattan Project—the greatest industrial effort ever undertaken by man—which was charged with converting the Stagg Field experiment into the reality of an atomic bomb. Not the least of the problems that faced the Project was to get the materials they needed in their experiments. Graphite, for example, is a quite common substance, widely used in pencils and lubricants, but in the early 1940s it was practically unavailable in the purity needed for an atomic pile. As a result, in the very depths of wartime shortages, the graphite industry had to revamp its production techniques.

Uranium metal was another critical material. Before World War II, uranium was little more than a laboratory curiosity. In the whole world there was not a single pound of pure uranium. In the United States none was mined and only a little was available as the unwanted by-product of big vanadium metal refineries in the Rockies. In 1942 about 500 tons of these uranium wastes were on hand. In the Canadian Arctic there were a few uranium-radium mines, including the famous Eldorado mine on Great Bear Lake, which was capable of producing about 300 tons of ore a year.

But by the greatest stroke of good fortune the United States found itself in custody of 1,200 tons of uranium oxide which had been stored on Staten Island by mining interests in the Belgian Congo. Before the war the Congo was the prime producer of radium and uranium; when the Germans took over Belgium, the mines were shut down and allowed to fill with water to keep them out of the hands of the Germans should they move into the Congo. Thus, as the atomic program got under way in 1942, the United States was holding some 2,000 tons of uranium ores—luckily quite enough for the entire atomic bomb project.

But a supply of uranium was not itself the answer. Even when 100 per cent pure, ordinary uranium was too bulky and too stable to be used in making a bomb. In Fermi's Chicago pile, for example, seven tons were required to achieve a relatively slow chain reaction. For a weapon which had to be carried in an airplane, something lighter and more potent was needed. Fortunately such a highly reactive form of uranium exists. But before the physicists could make use of this elixir, they had to develop a large-scale industrial process to separate it from the more stable uranium, with which it is always intimately mixed.

The story of this accomplishment has its roots as far back as the turn of the century. Following the discovery of radioactivity by Henri Becquerel in 1896, physicists had defined as one of their major goals an understanding of how an atom is put together. In the first decade of the 20th Century, it was generally accepted that an atom was a positively charged, submicroscopic spherical mass in which negatively charged electrons floated rather like raisins in a pudding. The sum of the negative charges of the electrons equaled in magnitude the positive charge of the atom; viewed from outside, the atom as a whole was electrically neutral.

Farewell to the raisin pudding

In 1911, this view was abruptly shattered when Lord Rutherford published a discussion of experiments performed by him and his associates at the famous Cavendish Laboratory at Cambridge, England. At Cavendish the scientists had set up an apparatus in which a piece of gold or platinum foil was sprayed with a stream of alpha particles (large, relatively slow-moving products of radioactive decay which carry a positive electrical charge). Most of the particles went right on through the foil, but to everyone's puzzlement more than had been expected bounced back toward the source. As Rutherford observed later, it was as incredible as a 15-inch artillery shell bouncing off a piece of tissue paper.

From the results of the experiment, Rutherford deduced that the atom must be a very open structure since so many of the alpha particles had gotten through. But he also realized that it must have a massive nucleus at its center with a positive charge, because only a positively charged body could have repelled positively charged alpha particles so effectively. If the nucleus were positive, Rutherford concluded, the electrons could not be embedded in it; they must be far enough away so that their negative charge did not cancel out the positive charge of the nucleus. It was apparent that the raisins-in-the-pudding view had to be abandoned.

Today, thanks to the work of Rutherford and his successors, we know that, even though the preponderance of mass is concentrated in the nucleus of an atom, the volume of the nucleus is minute in comparison to the total volume of the atom which encompasses the electrons. The radius of an atom is now considered to be about one two-hundred-and-fifty-millionth of an inch. Buried deep within is the atomic nucleus with a radius so small that its measurement ranges from one ten-thousandth to one one-hundred-thousandth of the radius of the atom. If a ball of uranium just an inch in diameter were blown up to the size of the earth, a single uranium atom would be only an inch across. And the nucleus of the atom would be only one ten-thousandth of an inch in diameter.

The nature of the nucleus itself has been revealed only after a series of highly imaginative hypotheses. The first postulated the existence of a particle inside the nucleus called the "proton." We now know that it has a mass about 2,000 times that of the electron. The proton also has an electric charge equal to that of the electron, but its charge is positive while that of the electron is negative. For instance, hydrogen, which is the simplest atom, has one electron revolving about one proton and, because the electric charges are equal and opposite, they neutralize each other for any outside observer. The mass of the hydrogen atom is practically the same as the mass of the proton.

The number of protons in the nucleus of an atom varies from substance to substance. Helium nuclei, for example, contain two protons; carbon nuclei, six; uranium nuclei, 92—each nucleus being surrounded by as many electrons as it has protons. Except for ordinary hydrogen, however, the weight of each nucleus is always considerably higher than the combined weight of its protons. The nuclei contain something else besides protons, something which has no electric charge, for, if it did, the atom would no longer be neutral.

A prediction and confirmation

As early as 1920, the existence of such a chargeless component of nuclei had been predicted by Rutherford. But for another decade, physicists were unsuccessful in their attempts to find this particle, which was given the name neutron. Then puzzling results cropped up in a number of experiments performed on the substance beryllium during the years 1930 to 1932 by Walter Bothe and Hans Becker in Germany, and by Irène and Frédéric Joliot-Curie in France. When beryllium had been bombarded

DEADLY SPHERES OF INFLUENCE

In an air explosion over Manhattan, the destructive power of a fusion bomb equivalent to 10 million tons of TNT would probably kill every unprotected human within a circle four miles in diameter. The primary death-dealing effects are neutron particles, gamma rays, a flash of heat and light, and a blast wave of high-pressure air. Secondary effects are fire storms—the result of many separate fires joining to make one huge blaze.

A 10-MEGATON BLAST

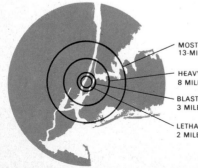

MOST FRAME HOUSES DAMAGED—
13-MILE RADIUS

HEAVY DAMAGE TO BRICK BUILDINGS—
8 MILES

BLAST DAMAGE TO LUNGS—
3 MILES

LETHAL DOSE OF RADIATION TO MAN IN THE OPEN—
2 MILES

with alpha particles, it emitted a mysterious radiation, at first interpreted as a type of gamma ray. Finally James Chadwick in England demonstrated that the radiation consisted of particles having a mass roughly equal to that of the proton but without any electric charge. Without a doubt, these were the neutrons that Rutherford had predicted.

Since then, experiments have revealed that nuclei of a given substance always have the same number of protons but may have different numbers of neutrons. For example, the nucleus of the element carbon, which has six protons, sometimes has six neutrons and sometimes seven. Such forms, which differ only in the number of neutrons, are called "isotopes." Their chemical symbols are written with the combined number of protons and neutrons (roughly their atomic weight) following the symbol for the element. In the case of the carbon just described the two forms can be written as C-12 and C-13. C-12 is the more common form; C-13 appears only once in every hundred carbon atoms.

Uranium, like carbon, exists in various isotopes, and it was this characteristic that the U.S. atomic project put to good use. The most common uranium isotopes are U-238 and U-235. The latter is the fissionable isotope, but the former is by far the more abundant—accounting for about 99.3 per cent of the uranium mixture in which both exist. Since both isotopes have identical chemical properties—as do all isotopes of the same substance—there is no simple chemical method by which one may be separated from the other. The Manhattan Project was in large part a mammoth scheme for sifting them apart. This was based on atomic weight—on the fact that U-238 is slightly heavier than U-235 because—as the numbers 238 and 235 indicate—its nuclei contain three more neutrons than the other's.

Atoms are, of course, too small to be sifted individually. But when uranium combines with the gas fluorine it forms a gaseous compound whose molecules can be separated. Knowing that lighter molecules travel slightly faster than heavier ones, scientists devised a "gaseous diffusion" process in which uranium hexafluoride is pumped against an extremely fine screen. The lighter and faster molecules pass through the screen a bit more quickly than the heavier and slower ones. As a result, the gas that collects on the other side of the screen has a greater concentration of U-235 than the gas that remains behind. By repeating this operation several thousand times, using on each occasion the refined gas obtained from the previous operation, it is possible—theoretically, at least—to increase the concentration of U-235 from 0.7 per cent of the mixture to an astonishing 95 per cent. With this process, the U.S. had now found a way to create a concentrate of uranium that could be used in a bomb—or so it seemed at the time.

One of the major accomplishments of the U.S. wartime atomic pro-

THE BIG BOMB'S DANGER RANGE

Unleashed over Manhattan, an H-bomb with 10 times the megatonnage of the 10-million-ton bomb on the opposite page would actually cause less than 10 times the damage *(below)*. A 100-megaton bomb has never been exploded, but the U.S.S.R. has tested a 60-megaton device and it is believed that a similar bomb could be souped up to deliver 100 megatons of energy.

A 100-MEGATON BLAST

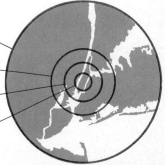

MOST FRAME HOUSES DAMAGED—
28-MILE RADIUS

HEAVY DAMAGE TO BRICK BUILDINGS—
11 MILES

BLAST DAMAGE TO LUNGS—
6.5 MILES

LETHAL DOSE OF RADIATION TO MAN IN THE OPEN—
3 MILES

gram was the construction of a gigantic gaseous-diffusion plant at Oak Ridge, Tennessee, to undertake the concentration of U-235 on a vast scale. The plant was almost half a mile long and ended up costing more than $500 million.

In an attempt to develop additional methods of refining U-235 so that it could be used in an airborne bomb, the government constructed another series of plants alongside the Oak Ridge gaseous-diffusion plant. Built at a cost of more than $300 million, these plants were designed to concentrate U-235 by passing uranium tetrachloride gas in an electrically charged state through a strong magnetic field. In the process, the paths of the slightly heavier U-238 particles would be less bent by the field than those of the lighter U-235. The two uranium isotopes would thereby be separated.

In the end, it was the magnetic process that first succeeded in creating a concentrate of U-235 that was 85 per cent pure—more than adequate for use in a bomb.

But long before the Oak Ridge plants were completed, the government decided to launch a wholly different project as a backup measure in case the others did not succeed. And so, at an isolated spot on the Columbia River near the hamlet of Hanford, Washington, a new plant was constructed to produce a substance called plutonium. The heart of the Hanford installation was several gigantic atomic piles evolved from the Fermi prototype at Stagg Field. Unlike an airborne bomb, the piles could be built with ordinary uranium. When completed, a pile was allowed to simmer slowly in a controlled chain reaction, which was cooled by water from the Columbia River. Inside the pile, a strange transformation took place. Bombarded with neutrons, part of the uranium—the U-238—was converted into plutonium, a man-made element even more fissionable than U-235. And all that remained was to separate it from the uranium, a step readily accomplished by conventional chemical processes since the plutonium and uranium were two different chemical elements—unlike the chemically similar isotopes U-235 and U-238.

Instant success for the new element

As things worked out, plutonium was used in the first bomb, exploded at Alamogordo, and for the Nagasaki bomb. The Hiroshima bomb used U-235. It was a success story of a high order for plutonium, an element that had been discovered only five years earlier. The credit goes to a University of California team of scientists led by Dr. Glenn T. Seaborg, now Chairman of the U.S. Atomic Energy Commission. They had begun their work with another man-made element, neptunium, which had been discovered in 1940 by Edwin M. McMillan and Philip H. Abelson, who were also on the California faculty. Taking up where McMillan left off

SIFTING MOLECULES

In the gas diffusion process for separating the rare and valuable isotope uranium 235 from less usable uranium 238, the two are first combined with fluorine to form the gas uranium hexafluoride. When the mixture is pumped through a fine porous screen, the slightly lighter and faster-moving molecules with U-235 penetrate more readily. Many repetitions of the process result in a sufficient concentration of the U-235.

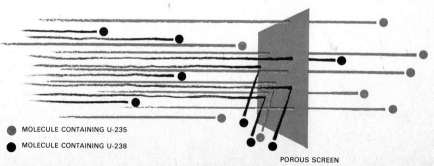

MOLECULE CONTAINING U-235

MOLECULE CONTAINING U-238

POROUS SCREEN

when he was called away to work on the development of radar, Seaborg and his associates found that neptunium decayed radioactively into the element they named plutonium. Among other things, they established that one isotope of the new element would fission under neutron bombardment, just as U-235 did. It was the beginning of a remarkably fruitful period, during which Seaborg was to become the codiscoverer of nine other transuranium elements and the winner—along with his friend McMillan—of the 1951 Nobel Prize in chemistry.

But before plutonium could be exploded over Japan, scientists still faced serious problems in the design of the bomb itself. Some plan had to be worked out to keep stray neutrons from automatically triggering off a chain reaction in the bomb while it was in storage or aboard an airplane. Yet the same design had to be flexible enough to permit a rapid chain reaction to start once the bomb was dropped. The solution was found in dividing the fissionable material into two or more parts, each of which by itself was too small to undergo a chain reaction. To create the explosion, the parts would be brought together by the detonation of small TNT charges.

By summer of 1945, all of the industrial and design problems connected with the atomic bomb had been solved. Then on July 16, 1945, just over 31 months after the first chain reaction in the squash court of Stagg Field, man's first nuclear weapon was exploded in a test on the desert wastes of Alamogordo, New Mexico. Three weeks later, on August 6, 1945, another version of the bomb was dropped on Hiroshima and the nuclear age had begun.

Not long after the atomic bomb had ended World War II, an even more powerful nuclear weapon was proposed by scientists. This was the hydrogen bomb. Seven more years of intensive work would go into making it a reality, climaxed by its first successful explosion at Eniwetok Atoll in November 1952.

The hydrogen bomb is not just the atomic bomb's big brother. It involves a nuclear transformation that seems to be the antithesis of the other. Whereas the atomic bomb depends on the phenomenon of "fission," which *divides* nuclei, the hydrogen bomb depends on "fusion," which *joins* them—and does so with an even more powerful release of energy.

At first glance, one might consider this a contradiction in nature. How is it possible that fission—the breakup of a nucleus into smaller fragments—and fusion—the build-up of a nucleus from smaller fragments —are *both* accompanied by the release of energy?

The answer to this puzzle lies in the extraordinarily complex forces that hold the nucleus together. The first of these is gravitational force— although the masses of protons and neutrons are so minute that the gravitational effects are almost zero. Then there is the electrostatic force

—i.e., the electrical effect of one particle on another. But since all the electrically charged particles are protons with positive charges which repel each other, the electrostatic force would seem to be an agent for breaking up the nucleus rather than for holding it together. The fact is that there has to be yet another force responsible for the nuclear cohesion. Hypothesizing its existence, physicists call it the "nuclear force."

This nuclear force behaves in such a complicated way that scientists have not yet fully understood it. Whatever it is, it has a most peculiar nature: (1) it treats protons and neutrons alike; (2) it acts over an extremely short range, becoming negligible at distances in excess of about four times the radius of a proton; (3) it is normally a force of attraction, which can be 35 times more powerful than the electrostatic force between two protons; and (4) it turns into a force of repulsion at distances shorter than about two thirds of a proton's radius.

Scientists believe the nuclear force and the disruptive electrostatic force play against each other, depending on the number and arrangement of protons and neutrons in the nucleus. In some elements, the forces of attraction far outweigh the forces of repulsion, and the nucleus remains stable and tightly bound. In other elements, the forces of repulsion almost counterbalance the forces of attraction, and the nucleus thus becomes a loosely bound assemblage, ready to fly apart at the slightest derangement of its components—as with the intrusion of a neutron in the phenomenon of nuclear fission. In both U-235 and plutonium, the nuclei are of the unstable variety.

The energy linked with the combination of electrostatic and nuclear forces that hold the nucleus together has been given the name of "binding energy." In a sense, a nucleus held together by strong binding energy is like a screen door with a heavy spring on it. It takes a lot of energy to open it, but it gives a tremendous slam when it closes. By the same token, it takes a lot of energy to pry apart a nucleus with strong binding energy, but a tremendous amount of energy is given off when such a nucleus is put back together again.

Atomic triggers and fusion heat

In this concept of binding energy, scientists have found an explanation of why fusion and fission both release energy even though they seem to be exact opposites of each other in principle. The crucial fact is that if the atoms of all 104 elements are laid out in a row according to weight, from lightest to heaviest, the binding energies per proton and neutron are found to increase gradually from the lightest element, hydrogen, up to the middleweight element, iron. *Then they gradually decrease again toward the heavier elements.*

When two hydrogen nuclei join up in the process of fusion to produce

CURING A LEAK WITH IODINE

Radioactive isotopes like uranium 235 and strontium 90 are best known for their role in atomic bombs and their presence in atomic fallout. But other isotopes have come to serve man in a wide variety of domestic ways, ranging from treatment of cancer to tracking down pipe leaks *(right)*. Having added radioactive iodine to the water, engineers can follow its flow by "watching" the radioactivity through the walls of a building or under a sidewalk with a Geiger counter *(gray arrows)*. When the radioactivity stops, the leak has been pinpointed.

RADIOISOTOPE   RADIOACTIVITY   NO RADIOACTIVITY

CONCRETE

a single nucleus of the slightly heavier helium—which is what happens in a hydrogen bomb—the screen door is slamming. A new nucleus with high-energy bonds is being formed and energy is given off.

On the other hand, when a nucleus of U-235 splits up in the process of fission, it forms smaller nuclei which also have higher energy bondings than those of the original nucleus. Once again the screen door is slamming, and energy is being produced.

Getting hydrogen nuclei to the point where they will fuse requires fantastically high temperatures in the range of millions of degrees. Normally, such temperatures occur only in the interiors of stars such as our sun—which, incidentally, is cool as stars go and has a rate of fusion sufficiently low so that it does not explode like a colossal hydrogen bomb. No ordinary device produced by the hand of man could possibly generate temperatures hot enough to produce a fusion reaction on earth. But such temperatures are momentarily produced by the explosion of an atomic bomb. And so, with a kind of awesome simplicity, a hydrogen bomb is triggered by one or more atomic bombs built into its mechanism. The combination, because of its dependence on heat, is known as a "thermonuclear" device.

Like so many inventions born of war, man-made nuclear reaction has proven itself readily adaptable to peacetime use. Ironically, its chief benefit has come from the heat which was considered only an incidental byproduct of nuclear fission until it was turned to advantage to achieve the thermonuclear fusion of the hydrogen bomb. Heat does, of course, add to the destructive effects of an atomic explosion, but the explosive blast and the ensuing fallout of radioactive debris are principally responsible for the damage. On the other hand, this very generation of heat is the sole purpose for which peacetime nuclear reactors are built, because it can be used to turn water into steam which then powers the turbines that generate electricity or provide propulsion.

Mobile steam plants operated by scaled-down nuclear reactors can be employed to run machinery otherwise powered by conventional steam engines. The cars of the future, for example, might well be nuclear-powered Stanley Steamers. At present, however, the most dramatic use of such nuclear reactors is certainly to power submarines—a possibility suggested as early as March 1939 by Enrico Fermi. His idea—almost forgotten during the war years—was stubbornly championed by Admiral Hyman Rickover, and eventually the U.S. Navy was convinced of its extraordinary advantages. The first U.S. atomic submarine, the *Nautilus*, was launched on January 21, 1954, at Groton, Connecticut, and on its maiden voyage it far outdid its Jules Verne namesake when it traveled 62,500 miles without refueling. Under conventional power, such a voyage would have consumed upward of two million gallons of diesel oil.

What nuclear power has given the submarine, it can give to society as a whole: a new and vastly more efficient source of energy than ever before harnessed by man. For many reasons it is the most promising source of power for the future. Nuclear reactors, employing fission reactions, have been erected in many scattered parts of the world. In an attempt to stretch the global reserves of uranium to the extreme limit of their usefulness, some have been designed as "breeder reactors" to produce plutonium from U-238.

Still untapped for peacetime purposes is the heat of the hydrogen-fusion reaction, which will find its limitless raw material—hydrogen, the most abundant of all elements—in the oceans of the earth. But before this power is harnessed, scientists first need to find a container in which such a reaction can safely take place, even though every known solid substance on earth evaporates at temperatures only a minute fraction of those involved in the fusion process. Thus far, the most ambitious attempt at solution has been the design of so-called "magnetic bottles" —devices employing powerful magnetic fields that continually deflect electrically charged hydrogen particles into a prescribed enclosure. In these experiments, scientists have so far met with only limited success. Nevertheless, if there is any lesson to learn from the history of science, it is that the problem will be solved in less time than is estimated conservatively and by means which will seem astonishingly unconventional.

For the Future: Potent New Sources of Power

With the world's consumption of fuel energy increasing at an astronomical rate, man is overtaxing the organic fuel sources he depends upon so heavily now—coal, petroleum, wood, agricultural wastes. The use of these fuels in the last century alone amounted to almost half the total used in all the preceding 19 centuries; consumption is now expected to double and then double again before the year 2000. A worldwide hunt goes on for new fuel reserves, and scientists are looking for new ways to get more use from the fuels we have. An even greater challenge is the search for entirely different sources of energy which will be needed to sustain the expanding populations and complex technology of tomorrow. Among the exciting developments outlined on the following pages are efforts to harness the untiring push of the tides, extend the use of sunlight and earth heat, and control the elusive but dramatic energy of lasers and nuclear fusion.

FUELING A FIRE AT 76° BELOW
A scientist watches closely behind glass as experimental rocket fuel gets a crucial ignition test under simulated flight conditions. The chamber is cooled to 76° F. below zero, the temperature at altitudes of 50,000 feet and above. In a rocket engine, the fuel must ignite instantly, since otherwise the volatile unfired fuel particles could accumulate, then explode to demolish the engine.

Two Projects to Harness the Surge of the Tides

Back in the 1920s, while watching the formidable rush of the tides in Passamaquoddy Bay between Maine and Canada, Franklin Roosevelt became intrigued with the possibilities of harnessing tidal energy to make electric power. The tide wells in from the sea and ebbs away again in a 12-hour cycle, moving two billion tons of water as it rises and falls an average of 18 feet. Roosevelt's scheme to put this force to work got a false start in the 1930s, but has been recently revived as the Passamaquoddy Tidal Power Project (opposite).

The cost of construction is estimated at about $600 million, and if the project is finally completed as planned, it will attain a peak daily output of 500,000 kilowatts. This power will be delivered to users as far away as Boston, Massachusetts, and will easily take care of an expected 40-million-kilowatt increase in New England's annual electric power consumption.

But long before Passamaquoddy's pride and joy is built, the French will have become old hands at using the tides. The dam (below), spanning the tidal Rance River on the Brittany coast, began producing electrical power in 1966. While less ambitious than Passamaquoddy—its peak daily output is 240,000 kilowatts—it bears the distinction of being the world's first successful tidal-powered electric plant.

CHANNELING THE CHANNEL
The concrete caissons of the world's first tidal-power dam arc across the Rance River in northern France. Completed in 1966, the plant's 24 specially designed turbine generators effectively harness the tides in the English Channel, which rise and fall as much as 44 feet. A lock (far right) provides the river's shipping traffic with access to the busy nearby port of St.-Malo.

A TORRENT OF POWER FOR FRANCE
An ebbing torrent returns to the Channel through one of the Rance dam spillways, emptying a nine-square-mile pool behind the dam (above). Electricity can be produced both by the falling and rising of the tides. The spillway gates serve to concentrate the power of the sea, holding back its ebb and flow until the water levels on either side of the dam differ by at least 30 feet.

PASSAMAQUODDY: A COMPLEX PLOT TO TRAP THE SEA

THE TIDE COMES IN. The Passamaquoddy Tidal Power Project will create power in a two-step process linked to the rise and fall of the tides in the Bay of Fundy between Nova Scotia and the Canadian mainland, as illustrated in the map diagrams above and below. The first step *(above)* will consist of trapping water in Passamaquoddy Bay, the "High Pool," by opening the gates at (1) and (2) to let the rising tide flow in, and then closing the gates just before the outgoing tide begins. Differences in water level between high and low tides along the Bay of Fundy are the greatest in the world, ranging from Passamaquoddy's 18 feet to as much as 50 feet at the head of the bay. Wharves are built high and harbors are dredged deep to accommodate the tides, but boats are often left stranded at dockside when the tide goes out *(pictures above and below).*

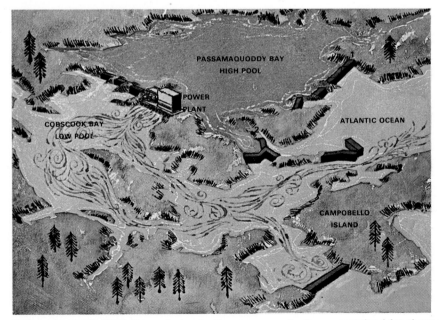

THE TIDE GOES OUT. Second step in the power-production process comes during low tide when water in Cobscook Bay, the "Low Pool," empties through the gate at (3), creating a maximum water-level difference between the High and Low Pools. Now water from the High Pool can flow downward into the Low Pool through a bank of 50 turbine generators in the power plant. The tremendous surge of power produced can be sustained for about one hour. By closing the gates at (1), (2) and (3), thus cutting off both pools from the sea, engineers will hold this power surge in reserve to coincide with known daily periods of peak consumption. To supplement Passamaquoddy's delivery of big, brief loads, power for periods of low consumption during the rest of the day will be supplied by a hydroelectric station to be built 175 miles away on the St. John River.

From Deep in the Earth's Crust, a Plume of Energy

As long ago as 1904, Italian engineers near Lardarello in Tuscany happened on a means of manufacturing cheap electric power which remains a promising reserve of energy for the future. The source of this energy is steam—created deep underground by earth heat—which gushes from specially drilled wells and is diverted to drive turbine generators. Today Lardarello's steam plants produce two billion kilowatt hours of power a year, enough to operate most of Italy's railway system.

Earth steam is put to other uses in other areas, too. In Iceland 45,000 people use

it to heat their homes. In Kenya it hatches chickens. In New Zealand and the state of California it is a source of electric power. Installation costs for a steam plant are high, but savings in fuel make such power substantially cheaper to produce than electricity from conventional plants.

A SCALDING RUSH OF POWER

A roaring jet of steam at 350° F. hides the sun as a workman wearing protective mufflers on his ears releases pressure from a steam well near Lardarello, Italy. The product of surface water seeping into volcanic fissures, the steam is routed via pipelines to turbine generators and thence to condensing towers *(background)* for recovery of commercially valuable chemicals.

Sunlight:
A Vast but Fickle
Power Source

As fossil-fuel supplies go on dwindling, scientists show increasing interest in one of the most readily available fuel sources of all: sunlight. Delivered in payloads of fantastic magnitude, sunlight provides the U.S. every two days with energy equal to all our remaining fossil-fuel reserves. But how to use this energy is something else again. Since it comes to us in such diffuse form, about the only direct use of it that can be made is for evaporation (above). To turn it into an effective power source it must be gathered and concentrated, as in the solar furnace at right, an expensive process. Also, darkness and bad weather cause constant interruptions in the reception of the sun's regular energy broadcast. Major industrial applications of solar power are therefore a long way off, but it is in successful use on a smaller scale. Compact solar batteries work well in space satellites, and a multitude of consumer gadgets powered solely by the sun is now on the market (pages 184-185).

MAKING SALT WITH SUNSHINE
Vast salt pans of the Leslie Salt Company of
San Francisco precipitate four inches of salt
crystals a year from sea water by evaporation.
An ancient process, salt drying is now less eco-
nomical than mining solid salt, but evaporators
still produce annually a million tons in the U.S.

A FIERCE FRENCH FURNACE
Technicians adjust some of the 3,500 small mirrors on the solar furnace at Mont-Louis in the
French Pyrenees. Concentrating sunlight, the
furnace focuses heat on a small area, producing temperatures of 5,400°F., which makes
it a valuable instrument for high-heat research.

A Flock of Solar
Gadgets, Some Fads,
Some Functional

Solar energy has had considerable publicity as a fuel of the future because of its application at the consumer level. Few of the exotic fuels that may one day run our power plants will ever be useful on as personalized a scale as the solar cigar lighter at right. After all, sunlight is free —a fact that has inspired a host of consumer gimmicks all over the world. These include solar-powered radios, fans, automobiles, boats, refrigerators, fresh-water stills, heaters for water and even whole houses *(below)*. Though the faddist element is unmistakable, many of these inventions adapt good scientific principles to highly practical uses. One radio, for instance, operates with a power system like that in the Telstar satellite. Sunlight activates the passage of electrons between two special alloys, generating electricity. A refrigerator uses the sun's heat to liquefy ammonia, which then revaporizes into a gas, drawing heat from the refrigerator interior. The solar house shown below makes use of the fact that glass admits sunlight which, on striking an opaque surface, produces heat, as in a greenhouse. When properly engineered this system can heat a home in midwinter to temperatures of 70° F. and higher.

Eagerness to capitalize on the free fuel of solar energy has also led to some foolhardy ventures. In 1946 the Indian government franchised two factories to make a solar cooker for use by India's 300 million peasant-farmers. After one year of production, total sales amounted to 50 cookers. Apparently no one realized that the farmer normally eats his main meal at night and that his wife has no wish to stand over a stove in the sun since midday temperatures in India can be 100°F.

A MATCHLESS LIGHT
Solar enthusiast Harry Thomason of Washington, D.C., gets a solar light. A miniature of the solar furnace on page 183, the device concentrates sunlight with a concave, parabolic mirror, focusing the rays on the end of the cigar. Time required to light up: about 30 seconds.

A CONFERENCE OF SOLAR COOKS
An international gathering of solar-energy experts shows off a variety of solar cookers. From Lebanon *(top left)*, India *(top center)*, Japan *(bottom right)* and the U.S., these devices develop temperatures up to 350° F., hot enough to boil a quart of water in 15 minutes. They can broil, fry or pressure-cook, depending on the cooking apparatus set up at the focusing point.

A HEAVENLY HOUSEWARMING
Sunbursts flash from the glass-paneled roof of a solar house, invention of Harry Thomason, shown above. Sections of window glass backed with black corrugated sheet metal and angled to catch the sun act as heat collectors. A small electric heater pinch-hits on sunless days, but the inventor claims that over-all fuel savings can recoup installation costs in a short time.

Looking for the Ultimate Fuel in Fusion

The coil-ribbed monster shown here is a C-Stellarator, a name meaning "star generator." It is part of an all-out U.S. effort to control the power of thermonuclear fusion, the process which occurs in the hydrogen bomb and in the sun and stars.

Simply, fusion is what happens when two atomic nuclei join to form one. As happens with deuterium (heavy hydrogen) atoms, used in many fusion experiments, the fusing nuclei release enormous amounts of energy. To achieve fusion, however, the deuterium must be heated up to 180 million degrees for a full second.

This poses a tough question: how to contain a substance so hot it would instantly disintegrate any of the known substances? The approach scientists are working on now is to weave an invisible magnetic cocoon to contain the fusing deuterium atoms. So far, devices good for one fiftieth of a second have been built.

If and when the formidable problem is solved, the deuterium in sea water could provide us with a billion times the energy now left in all our coal and oil reserves.

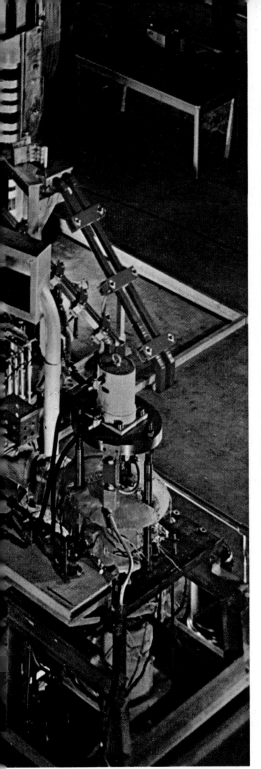

AIMING FOR A FIRST IN FUSION
Part of a $35-million government project to master fusion, the C-Stellarator at Princeton, New Jersey, is one of the largest fusion devices in the world. Inside it flows a stream of free deuterium ions, which scientists hope they can make hot and pure enough for fusion. At lower right is a pump which maintains the required ultrahigh vacuum in the Stellarator's interior.

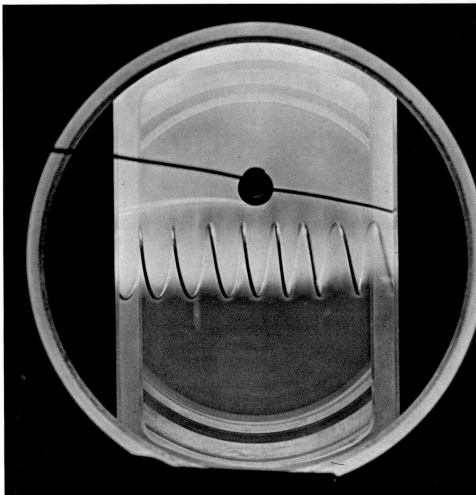

BLUE BLAZE OF PLASMA
In this demonstration of one of the C-Stellarator principles, a stream of free electrons and atomic nuclei, called a plasma, is held inside a magnetic field, created by an electrified wire. The blue areas outside the wire coil indicate that not all the particles are confined by the magnetic field, an instability taken care of in the C-Stellarator by two magnetic fields *(below)*.

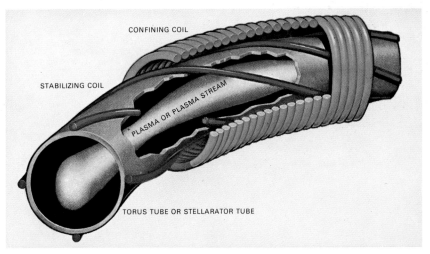

CONFINING COIL

STABILIZING COIL

PLASMA OR PLASMA STREAM

TORUS TUBE OR STELLARATOR TUBE

SPINNING A MAGNETIC COCOON
This cutaway drawing reveals two different types of wire winding which keep the plasma centered in the C-Stellarator's doughnut-shaped "torus" tube. The blue coil provides a basic confining magnetic field for the plasma; the red provide a supplementary field that prevents atomic particles in the lining of the torus from mixing with and contaminating the plasma.

187

The Far-out Laser: Souping Up a Light Beam

Latest and most precocious in the parade of new energy sources is the laser beam, a very special kind of light for which science is finding an astonishing number of uses. What makes laser light so unusual is the fact that all the light waves in the beam are coherent, or exactly in phase with one another *(below, opposite)*. As a result, all the light waves are so nearly parallel that they can travel for miles in a straight line without spreading apart significantly. By contrast, a regular flashlight beam diffuses after a few yards because its light waves are of so many different frequencies that they interfere with one another and scatter themselves.

The coherence of a laser beam has suggested its use as a carrier of enormous pulses of power that would not diminish over great distances. The idea is to translate electric power into laser light and then reverse the process at the receiving end. On earth, where fog or rain would interfere with transmission, lasers would have to be beamed through evacuated pipelines to prevent power loss. Such pipelines would have to be perfectly straight to accommodate the arrowlike laser beam; direction changes would require mirrors to send the beams around corners.

Laser light is promising in another way: it has supershort wavelengths. Unlike radio waves, measured in hundreds of yards, and television waves, measured in feet, laser wavelengths are measured in tenths of millionths of an inch. This opens the possibility of using the laser as a communications transmitter capable of carrying a great volume of messages on a very narrow band of frequencies. It also has a crucial military advantage. To avoid enemy interception, signals may one day be sent to satellites millions of miles in space on a laser beam thinner than a human hair.

A CHANGE FOR THE BETTER
An important discovery in the search for ways to vary the frequencies of laser beams was that an ammonium dihydrogen phosphate crystal *(below)* will double the frequency of a ruby laser beam, changing its color from red to ultraviolet light, which the film "sees" as blue *(below)*. The laser beams have been sent through smoke to make their characteristic colors more visible.

MAKING A COURSE RING TRUE
A weird instrument, the "ring laser," *(right)* gives hope of achieving absolute accuracy in guidance systems in ships and space vehicles. Two laser beams, glowing as they travel around a square in opposite directions, have equal frequencies. Changes in a vessel's position would cause tiny variations in these frequencies, which could trigger devices to correct the vessel's course.

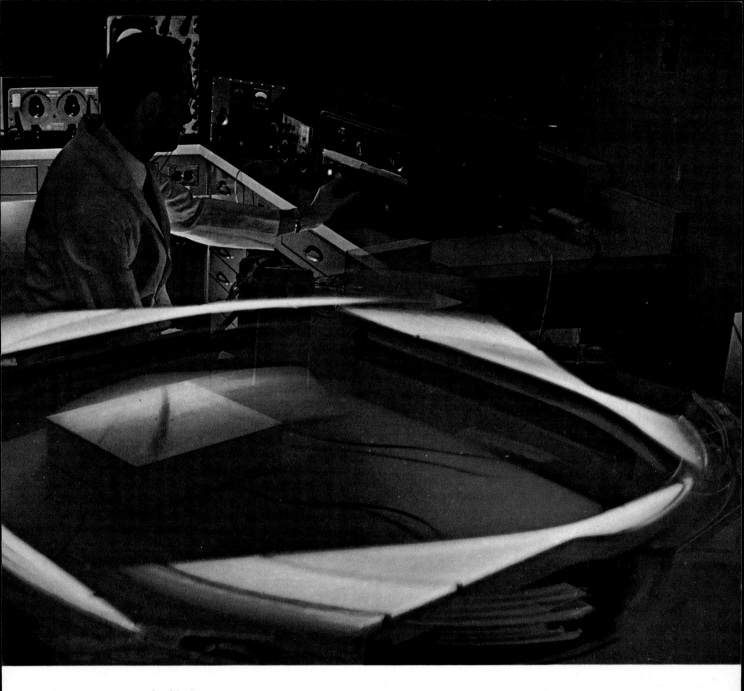

ORGANIZING CHAOS

In this diagram the coherent laser light from a ruby rod is contrasted with the incoherent light of the sun. Light, beamed into the ruby from a spiral-shaped photo flash tube, hits chromium atoms in the rod, exciting their electrons to higher energy levels. In returning to normal, the electrons give off their own light in waves all the same length. Some of this light is reflected back and forth between the mirror-surfaced ends of the ruby, exciting more electrons and creating more light. Finally, a shutter is released at one end of the rod and a giant pulse of parallel light bursts out as a coherent laser beam.

INCOHERENT SUNLIGHT

RUBY CRYSTAL ROD

COHERENT LASER BEAM

PHOTO FLASH TUBE

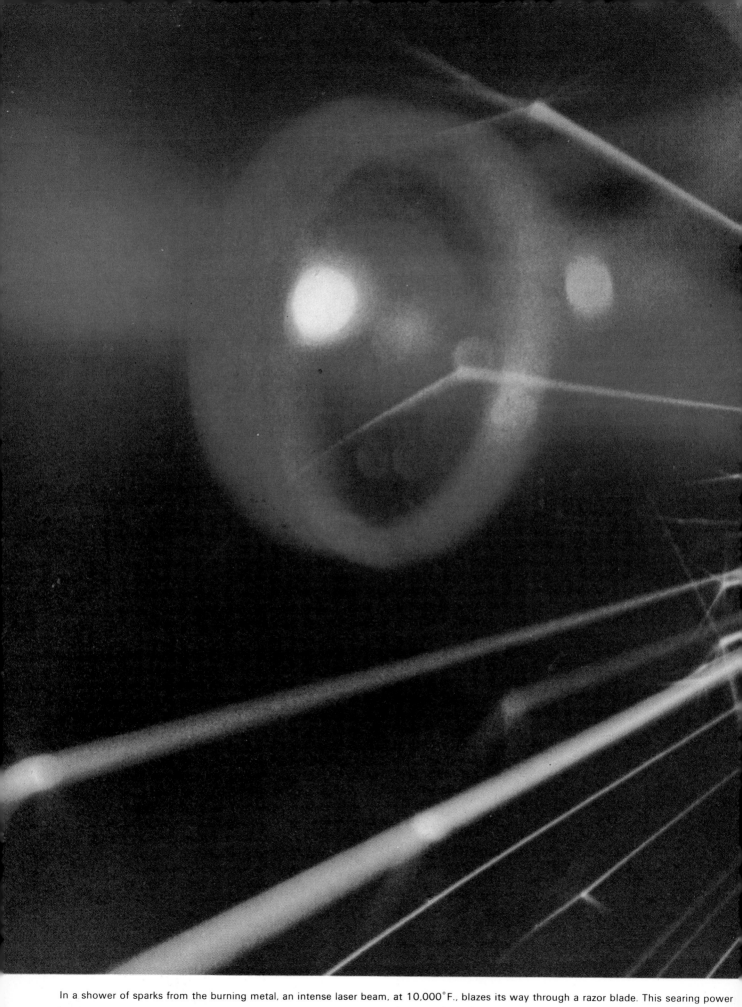

In a shower of sparks from the burning metal, an intense laser beam, at 10,000°F., blazes its way through a razor blade. This searing power

can be controlled with exquisite precision; lasers have proved useful tools in eye surgery and for micro-welding tiny wires in electronic gear.

Energy Reserves: Stockpiles of Power for the Future

TABULATED here are the estimated reserves of man's chief energy sources: coal, oil and natural gas (the fossil fuels), water power and nuclear fuels (uranium and thorium oxides). The major countries and fuel-producing areas of the world are listed. However the figures are necessarily incomplete: all countries do not use the same criteria in estimating reserves and some do not release up-to-date figures; in addition, reserves in many areas have not been fully explored and new deposits are sure to be discovered.

While it is safe to assume that the fossil fuel deposits will last at least another century and a half, there is no doubt that the fuels of the future are the nuclear fuels, with their enormous efficiency: one pound of uranium, for example, can perform as much work as about three million pounds of coal.

HOW THE WORLD'S ENERGY WEALTH IS DISTRIBUTED

COUNTRIES	COALS (MILLIONS OF TONS)	OIL (MILLIONS OF TONS)	NATURAL GAS (BILLIONS OF CUBIC FEET)	WATER POWER (MILLION KILOWATT-HOURS PER YEAR)	URANIUM OR THORIUM OXIDES (IN TONS)
ALGERIA	110	986	140,000	351	UNKNOWN
ARGENTINA	454	415	7,960	1,206	UNKNOWN
AUSTRALIA	109,834	63	8,000	7,033	26,400
BRAZIL	1,872	114,100	877	27,905	220,000
CANADA	84,100	72,167	45,682	129,626	750,000
CHILE	5,555	21	3,530	4,127	UNKNOWN
COMMUNIST CHINA	1,011,700	4,340	UNKNOWN	8,000	UNKNOWN
FRANCE	14,015	29	8,500	51,695	13,142
WEST GERMANY	292,900	101	8,500	16,760	330
INDIA	59,852	234	1,500	17,000	639,604
INDONESIA	2,748	1,286	2,500	752	NONE
IRAN	UNKNOWN	6,259	109,500	361	UNKNOWN
IRAQ	NONE	3,358	20,000	NONE	UNKNOWN
ITALY	890	43	5,500	44,043	3,300
JAPAN	20,981	5	500	79,044	1,894
KUWAIT	NONE	10,003	34,500	NONE	UNKNOWN
NIGERIA	527	507	4,000	142	UNKNOWN
NORWAY	1,980	NONE	NONE	48,188	UNKNOWN
PAKISTAN	506	4	20,300	1,861	NONE
POLAND	88,180	24	UNKNOWN	921	UNKNOWN
SAUDI ARABIA	NONE	10,674	35,000	NONE	UNKNOWN
REPUBLIC OF SOUTH AFRICA	74,936	NONE	NONE	55	247,027
SWEDEN	99	968	NONE	45,053	1,210,000
U.A.R.	NONE	200	13,000	1,819	UNKNOWN
UNITED KINGDOM	188,096	1	25,000	4,535	NEGLIGIBLE
U.S.	2,600,000	318,484	292,908	197,938	341,000
U.S.S.R.	5,900,000	34,500	150,000	90,905	800,000
VENEZUELA	3,381	2,429	31,700	1,391	NONE
YUGOSLAVIA	21,643	36	3,500	9,830	UNKNOWN
OTHER	80,506	19,031	222,342	165,459	65,065
TOTAL	10,564,865	600,268	1,194,799	956,000	4,317,762

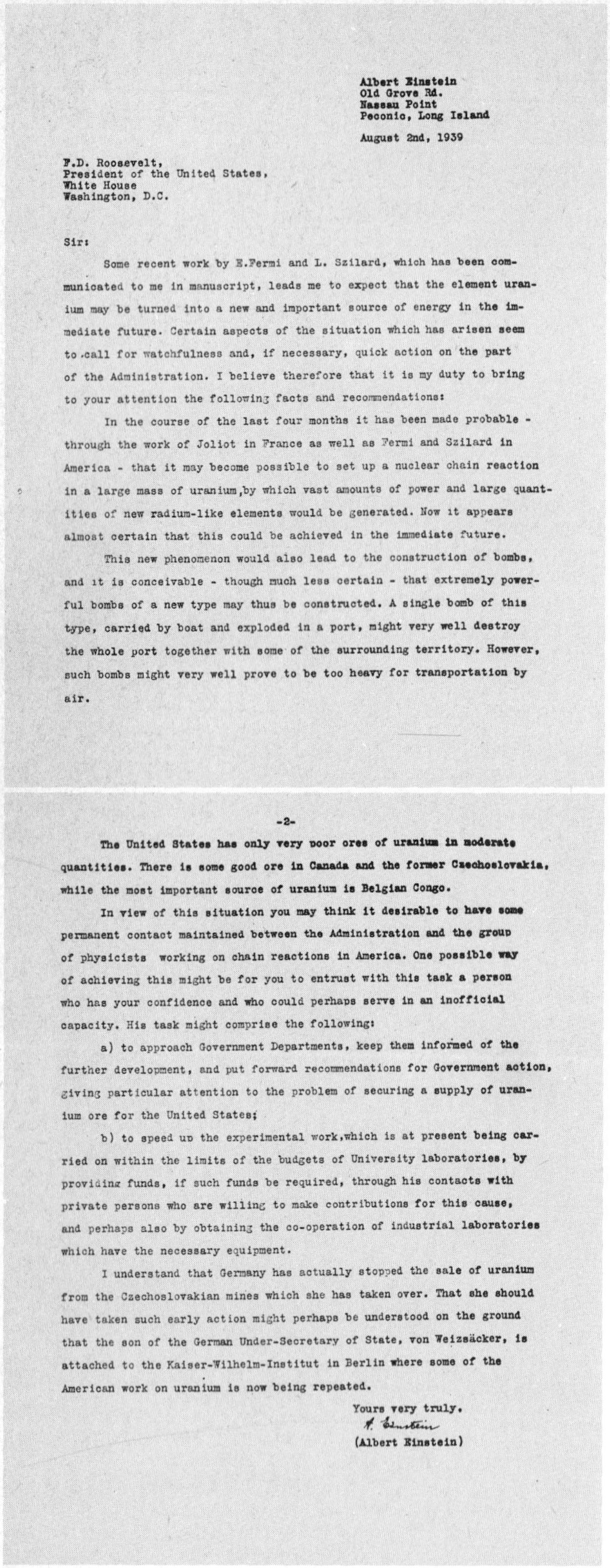

Albert Einstein
Old Grove Rd.
Nassau Point
Peconic, Long Island

August 2nd, 1939

F.D. Roosevelt,
President of the United States,
White House
Washington, D.C.

Sir:

Some recent work by E.Fermi and L. Szilard, which has been communicated to me in manuscript, leads me to expect that the element uranium may be turned into a new and important source of energy in the immediate future. Certain aspects of the situation which has arisen seem
to call for watchfulness and, if necessary, quick action on the part
of the Administration. I believe therefore that it is my duty to bring
to your attention the following facts and recommendations:

In the course of the last four months it has been made probable -
through the work of Joliot in France as well as Fermi and Szilard in
America - that it may become possible to set up a nuclear chain reaction
in a large mass of uranium,by which vast amounts of power and large quantities of new radium-like elements would be generated. Now it appears
almost certain that this could be achieved in the immediate future.

This new phenomenon would also lead to the construction of bombs,
and it is conceivable - though much less certain - that extremely powerful bombs of a new type may thus be constructed. A single bomb of this
type, carried by boat and exploded in a port, might very well destroy
the whole port together with some of the surrounding territory. However,
such bombs might very well prove to be too heavy for transportation by
air.

-2-

The United States has only very poor ores of uranium in moderate
quantities. There is some good ore in Canada and the former Czechoslovakia,
while the most important source of uranium is Belgian Congo.

In view of this situation you may think it desirable to have some
permanent contact maintained between the Administration and the group
of physicists working on chain reactions in America. One possible way
of achieving this might be for you to entrust with this task a person
who has your confidence and who could perhaps serve in an inofficial
capacity. His task might comprise the following:

a) to approach Government Departments, keep them informed of the
further development, and put forward recommendations for Government action,
giving particular attention to the problem of securing a supply of uranium ore for the United States;

b) to speed up the experimental work,which is at present being carried on within the limits of the budgets of University laboratories, by
providing funds, if such funds be required, through his contacts with
private persons who are willing to make contributions for this cause,
and perhaps also by obtaining the co-operation of industrial laboratories
which have the necessary equipment.

I understand that Germany has actually stopped the sale of uranium
from the Czechoslovakian mines which she has taken over. That she should
have taken such early action might perhaps be understood on the ground
that the son of the German Under-Secretary of State, von Weizsäcker, is
attached to the Kaiser-Wilhelm-Institut in Berlin where some of the
American work on uranium is now being repeated.

Yours very truly,

(Albert Einstein)

LETTER THAT ALERTED A NATION
This famous letter from Dr. Albert Einstein to President Roosevelt has
been credited with initiating work on the atom bomb. A group of scientists working in the United States became alarmed by the implications of
atomic research going on in Germany, and convinced Einstein that he
should lend his name to this plea. A few months later, money was appro-
priated for the project which built the first self-sustaining nuclear reactor.

A History of the Development of Atomic Energy

NO ACHIEVEMENT of this century has had such dramatic implications as the wresting of energy from
the nucleus of the atom. Since the discovery of radioactivity in 1896, the accumulation of experimental and theoretical knowledge about the atom has
engaged the passionate attention of a brilliant roll
call of scientists. Under the spur of wartime emer-
gency, an accelerated program of nuclear research,
led by the men shown opposite, produced the atom
bomb. Steps leading to that event and the progress
made since are listed in the chronology that follows.

1896 French physicist Henri Becquerel discovers radioactivity
when his photographic plates are fogged by rays from uranium.
1898 With the encouragement of Becquerel, physicists Marie
and Pierre Curie in Paris undertake a project which culminates
in the discovery of a new element—radium.
1902 British physicist Ernest Rutherford and chemist Frederick
Soddy explain radioactive decay in which elements like radium
turn into different elements, yielding energy in the process.
1905 Albert Einstein, a patent clerk in Berne, shows the equivalence of mass and energy in the equation $E = mc^2$, as part of his
Special Theory of Relativity. This equation predicts that vast
amounts of energy are locked in matter.
1910 Soddy proposes the existence of isotopes—forms of elements which have the same chemical properties but different
atomic weights.
1911 Rutherford, using alpha particles, probes into the interior
of the atom, discovering its heavy nucleus.
1913 Francis Aston, an English chemist, conclusively demonstrates the existence of isotopes. ● Danish physicist Niels
Bohr puts forward his theory of the atom, based on Rutherford's
findings and on German physicist Max Planck's quantum theory.
1919 Rutherford demonstrates the disintegration of nitrogen
into oxygen and hydrogen upon bombardment with alpha particles. This is the first nuclear reaction observed by man.
1928 In the first steps toward a fundamental understanding of
nuclear forces, Americans Edward Condon and Ronald Gurney
and Russian-born George Gamow, in a separate investigation,
explain how alpha particles are emitted from the nucleus.
1931 Deuterium, a heavy isotope of hydrogen later to be used in
the first H-bomb, is discovered by American chemist Harold Urey.
1932 English physicist John Cockcroft and Irish physicist Ernest Walton collaborate in transforming the lithium nucleus into
helium nuclei, using artificially accelerated protons in a primitive "atom-smasher." This is the first experimental verification
of Einstein's equation $E = mc^2$. ● The neutron, atomic building block and eventual key to nuclear fission, is discovered by
British physicist James Chadwick.
1933 Irène and Frédéric Joliot-Curie, French physicists, show
that some normally stable atoms undergo nuclear reactions when
bombarded by alpha particles, and change to short-lived unstable isotopes. This is the first artificially induced radioactivity.
1938 Hans Bethe in the United States theorizes that the sun's
energy comes from the fusion reaction, a process in which two
lightweight nuclei fuse and release great quantities of energy.

ARTHUR H. COMPTON
A Nobel Prize-winning physicist, Compton was administrator of a project to make plutonium in large quantities for use in the atomic bomb.

ENRICO FERMI
Another Nobel Prize winner, Fermi left Mussolini's Italy in 1938, was scientific director of the team which built the first nuclear reactor.

LESLIE R. GROVES
As a major general, the former West Pointer was chief of the "Manhattan Engineer District," the secret wartime project that built the A-bomb.

ERNEST O. LAWRENCE
Head of the University of California's famous Radiation Laboratory, Lawrence won the Nobel Prize for inventing the invaluable cyclotron.

J. ROBERT OPPENHEIMER
From 1943 to 1945 Oppenheimer directed the Los Alamos Scientific Laboratories, where most of the designing of the atom bomb was done.

GLENN T. SEABORG
Seaborg won a Nobel Prize for making such synthetic elements as plutonium. He became head of the Atomic Energy Commission in 1961.

This is the reaction which now produces an H-bomb explosion.
1939 Otto Hahn and Fritz Strassmann in Berlin bombard uranium with neutrons and find the lighter element barium as a product of the reaction, but are unable to account for barium's presence. ● German refugees Otto Frisch and Lise Meitner explain Hahn and Strassmann's experiment to be fission—the splitting apart of a heavy nucleus into lighter pieces, such as barium nuclei, with the release of vast amounts of energy. ● Frédéric Joliot-Curie shows that fission of one uranium atom by one neutron produces two or three free neutrons. This suggests the possibility of a chain reaction, in which the new neutrons continue and amplify the reaction begun by the original bombardment. ● Bohr predicts that uranium 235 is the substance that fissions when bombarded, but U-235 is very rare. ● Albert Einstein, in the U.S. at the Institute for Advanced Study, warns President Roosevelt of the military dangers of atomic energy *(opposite)*.
1940 Chemists at the University of California, headed by Glenn Seaborg and Edwin McMillan, discover plutonium—a radioactive product of U-238 bombardment, and a satisfactory substitute for rare U-235. ● Gaseous-diffusion method of separating uranium isotopes is developed at Columbia University.
1942 Under the direction of Enrico Fermi the first atomic reactor is built, and on December 2, 1942, at 3:25 p.m., the first successful sustained chain reaction is started, in a project initiated and coordinated by Arthur H. Compton. ● A U.S. military atomic program, code-named the Manhattan Project, is formed under Major General Leslie R. Groves. ● At Oak Ridge, Tennessee, the mass spectrometer is put to use in the production of pure U-235, under the direction of Ernest O. Lawrence. ● Construction begins at Los Alamos, New Mexico, of the atom bomb

laboratory, under the direction of J. Robert Oppenheimer.
1943 Reactors are constructed at Hanford, Washington, for the production of plutonium.
1945 The first atomic explosion is set off at Alamogordo, New Mexico, on Monday, July 16. ● The first atom bomb blasts Hiroshima Friday, August 6th. Nagasaki is hit Monday, August 9th.
1949 The U.S.S.R. explodes an atom bomb.
1950 President Harry S. Truman announces on January 31 that he has authorized the Atomic Energy Commission (AEC) to go ahead and develop an H-bomb.
1952 The first British atom bomb is exploded on October 3, at Monte Bello Island off Australia. ● The first U.S. H-bomb test blast occurs near Eniwetok Atoll in the Pacific, on November 1.
1953 In August the U.S.S.R. explodes an H-bomb.
1954 U.S.S. *Nautilus*, first atomic submarine is launched.
1956 The first atomic reactor for the production of electricity goes to work at Calder Hall, England.
1957 The Shippingport reactor, first U.S. atomic electric power plant, begins operation.
1959 The first testing of a small atomic reactor—Kiwi-A—for use in powering rockets takes place in Nevada testing grounds.
1960 France explodes an atom bomb in tests in the Sahara.
1961 The U.S.S.R. sets off the largest H-bomb blast ever: 55 to 60 megatons on the arctic island Novaya Zemlya. ● The U.S. begins Project Ploughshare, a series of experimental large-scale nuclear explosions for peaceful purposes such as making canals.
1962 The U.S. explodes an H-bomb from a Thor rocket, creating a zone of man-made radiation. ● Maiden voyage of the United States' N.S. (Nuclear Ship) *Savannah*, first atomic-powered merchant vessel.

FURTHER READING

General

Ayres, E., and Scarlott, C., *Energy Sources, the Wealth of the World.* McGraw-Hill, 1952.

*Beiser, Arthur, *The World of Physics.* McGraw-Hill, 1960.

*Brown, Harrison, James Bonner and John Weir, *The Next Hundred Years.* Viking Press, 1957.

Gamow, George, *Matter, Earth and Sky.* Prentice-Hall, 1958.

*Gamow, George, *One Two Three . . . Infinity.* Viking Press, 1947; rev. 1961.

Shepherd, Walter, *A New Survey of Science.* Harcourt, Brace, 1950.

*Taylor, Lloyd W., and Tucker, Forrest G., *Physics, the Pioneer Science* (2 vols.). Dover, 1959.

*Thirring, Hans, *Energy for Man.* Indiana University Press, 1958.

History

*Cajori, Florian, *A History of Physics.* Dover, 1962.

Clark, Ronald W., *The Birth of the Bomb.* Horizon, 1961.

*d'Abro, A., *The Rise of the New Physics* (2 vols.). Dover, 1951.

Dampier, William, *A History of Science.* Macmillan, 1949.

Groves, Leslie R., *Now It Can Be Told.* Harper & Row, 1962.

*Jaffe, Bernard, *Crucibles: The Story of Chemistry.* Fawcett, 1957.

Lapp, Ralph E., *Roads to Discovery.* Harper, 1960.

Lemon, Harvey B., *From Galileo to the Nuclear Age.* University of Chicago Press, 1961.

*Mason, Stephen F., *A History of the Sciences.* Collier, 1962. (Originally published as *Main Currents of Scientific Thought.* Henry Schuman, 1953.)

*Van Melsen, Andrew G., *From Atomos to Atom.* Harper, 1960.

Biography

Bryan, George S., *Edison, the Man and His Work.* Alfred A. Knopf, 1926.

Crowther, James G., *Men of Science.* W. W. Norton, 1936.

*Editors of FORTUNE, *Great American Scientists.* Prentice-Hall, 1961.

Editors of *Scientific American*, *Lives in Science.* Simon and Schuster, 1957.

Frank, Philipp, *Einstein: His Life and Times.* Alfred A. Knopf, 1953.

Josephson, Matthew, *Edison.* McGraw-Hill, 1959.

*Lodge, Oliver, *Pioneers of Science.* Dover, 1960.

*Michelmore, Peter, *Einstein: Profile of the Man.* Dodd, Mead, 1962.

*Schilpp, Paul A., ed., *Albert Einstein: Philosopher-Scientist.* Library of Living Philosophers, 1949.

Special Fields

Adler, Irving, *Inside the Nucleus.* John Day, 1963.

*Barnett, Lincoln, *The Universe and Dr. Einstein.* New American Library, 1952; William Sloane, 1957; Time Inc., 1962.

Bullard, Fred M., *Volcanoes.* University of Texas Press, 1961.

Curry, Duncan, and Newman, Bertram R., *The Challenge of Fusion.* D. Van Nostrand, 1960.

Dyson, James L., *The World of Ice.* Alfred A. Knopf, 1962.

*Einstein, Albert, *Essays in Science.* Philosophical Library, 1934.

*Einstein, Albert, *Relativity: the Special and General Theory.* Crown, 1931.

Flora, Snowden D., *Tornadoes of the United States.* University of Oklahoma Press, 1953; rev. 1958.

Gamow, George, *A Planet Called Earth.* Viking Press, 1963.

*Gamow, George, *Biography of the Earth.* Viking Press, 1959.

Gardner, Martin, *Relativity for the Million.* Macmillan, 1962.

*Kiepenheuer, Karl, *The Sun.* University of Michigan Press, 1959.

Menzel, Donald H., *Our Sun.* Harvard University Press, 1959.

Viemeister, Peter E., *The Lightning Book.* Doubleday, 1961.

*Available in paperback edition.

ACKNOWLEDGMENTS

The editors of this book are especially indebted to Dr. Charles K. Bockelman, Associate Professor of Physics at Yale University who served as general consultant, and to Dr. Leonard Eisenbud, Professor of Physics at New York State University, and Dr. Robert E. Schofield, Associate Professor of History of Science at Case Institute of Technology. The following persons and institutions also helped in the preparation of the book: Dr. Paul Aebersold, Duncan Clark and Elton Lord, Atomic Energy Commission, Washington; John Burt, International Atomic Energy Agency, United Nations; Dale Cook, AEC, California; B. Farley, Consolidated Edison of New York; J. R. Farmakes, Argonne National Laboratory; Dr. Robert Fuller, Professor of Physics, Columbia University; Jim Galbreath, AEC, Albuquerque; Dr. Harry B. Gray, Associate Professor of Chemistry, Columbia University; D. Harris and E. Stokeley, Oak Ridge National Laboratory; Michael Hoynes, The Babcock and Wilcox Co.; Charles Kennan and Hans Passburg, Yankee Atomics, Rowe, Massachusetts; C. L. Kennedy, Atomic Energy of Canada Ltd.; Cecil V. King, American Gas and Chemicals, Inc.; Dr. Ralph E. Lapp, Quadri Science, Inc.; Gene Marshall, Garden of the Gods Club, Colorado Springs; Dr. Edward C. Maxie, Professor of Pomology, University of California; Peter Michelmore; Joseph D. Morton, David J. Crowley and Brad J. Stroup, General Electric News Bureau; Tom K. Phares, Charles Carroll, Gilbert H. Furgurson and Charles M. Garvey, Westinghouse Electric Corporation; Andrew T. Purcell, American Petroleum Institute; Arthur J. Ramsdell, Department of Economic and Social Affairs, United Nations; William Regan, Los Alamos Scientific Laboratory; T. Richardson, AEC, New York; Dr. Warren Ross, U.S. Department of Agriculture; A. C. Thompson, Drake Well Museum; United Kingdom Atomic Energy Authority; Betty White, Northwestern University; R. R. Wright Jr., American Petroleum Institute; Charles Yulish, Atomic Industrial Forum. The quotation on page 144 from Peter Michelmore's *Einstein* is used with the permission of Dodd, Mead and Co.

INDEX

Numerals in italics indicate a photograph or painting of the subject mentioned.

PICTURE CREDITS

The sources for the illustrations appear below. Pictures are separated left to right by commas, top to bottom by dashes.

Cover: Edmund B. Gerard

CHAPTER 1: 8—Peter White. 10, 11, 13—Push Pin Studios. 14, 15—Drawings by Otto van Eersel—drawings by Stefan Martin. 17—Emil Schulthess and Walter Huber from DU from Black Star. 18, 19—Humble Oil and Refining Co. 20, 21—Emil Schulthess from Black Star, Andreas Feininger. 22, 23—Leonard McCombe. 24, 25—Chuck Abbot from Rapho Guillumette, John Titchen from Photo Library Inc. 26, 27—Bert from Pix Inc.

CHAPTER 2: 28—Elizabeth Wilcox. 31, 32—The Bettmann Archive. 33—Drawings by Lowell Hess. 34—New York Public Library. 35—Drawings by Anthony Saris. 37—Drawings by Edward Sorel. 39—From *Les Merveilles de la Science* by Louis Figuier courtesy Columbia University Library. 40—The Bettmann Archive. 41—Robert Emmett Bright except drawings by Otto van Eersel. 42—The Royal Institution. 43—New York Public Library—The Bettmann Archive, drawings by Otto van Eersel. 44, 45—Radio Times Hulton Picture Library, drawings by Otto van Eersel—The Science Museum, London. 46—Courtesy Burndy Library, Brown Brothers, drawings by Otto van Eersel—Erich Lessing from Magnum, Photo *Deutsches Museum*, München, drawing by Otto van Eersel. 47—From *Les Merveilles de la Science* by Louis Figuier courtesy Columbia University Library, Culver Pictures, drawings top right and bottom by Otto van Eersel. 48—Derek Bayes courtesy The Royal Institution, courtesy Burndy Library. 49—Eric Schaal.

CHAPTER 3: 50—Battelle Memorial Institute. 52—Drawings by Otto van Eersel. 53—Drawings by George V. Kelvin. 54, 55, 56—Drawings by Byron Goto. 57—Drawings by Otto van Eersel. 58—New York Public Library. 59—Drawings by Lowell Hess. 61 through 69—Push Pin Studios.

CHAPTER 4: 70—Tom Hutchins from Black Star. 73—Drawing by Anthony Saris—drawings by Otto van Eersel. 74, 75—Drawing by Lowell Hess, Vanity Fair Supplement. 76—Drawings by Otto van Eersel. 77—Drawings by George V. Kelvin. 79—Nina Leen. 80, 81—Nina Leen, drawing by Otto van Eersel. 82—Nina Leen—drawing by Otto van Eersel. 83, 84—Nina Leen. 85—Nina Leen—drawing by Otto van Eersel. 86, 87—Nina Leen—drawing by Otto van Eersel. 88, 89—Nina Leen, drawings by Otto van Eersel. 90, 91—Drawing by Otto van Eersel, Nina Leen.

CHAPTER 5: 92—Dimitri Rebikoff from Photo Researchers Inc. 94, 95—Drawings by George V. Kelvin. 96, 97—Drawings by Byron Goto. 98—Drawings by George V. Kelvin. 99—Drawings by Otto van Eersel. 100—New York Public Library. 101—Courtesy Simone Gossner. 103—Andreas Feininger. 104, 105—Drake Well Museum except top right Standard Oil Co., N.J. 106, 107—Culver Pictures, Warshaw Collection—Warshaw Collection—Drake Well Museum. 108—Ivan Massar from Black Star. 109—Drawings by George V. Kelvin. 110, 111—Brown Brothers, Dalmas from Pix Inc. 112, 113—Atsuki Mori. 114, 115—Drawing by George V. Kelvin.

CHAPTER 6: 116—Harry T. Peters Collection, Museum of the City of New York. 118—New York Public Library. 119, 120—Courtesy Burndy Library. 121—From the collection of Eric Schaal—courtesy Burndy Library. 122, 123—Drawings by Otto van Eersel. 125—*Foto Porcellan Fabrik*, Langenthal. 126—Berenice Abbott. 127—Albert Fenn. 128, 129—Lighting and Transients Research Institution, Fritz Goro—Post-Dispatch Pictures from Black Star. 130, 131—William McClellan, U.S. Bureau of Reclamation. 132—Eric Schaal except top left and bottom right Phil Brodatz. 133—Eric Schaal, Phil Brodatz—Eric Schaal—Phil Brodatz. 134—Phil Brodatz except top left Eric Schaal. 135—Lee Boltin.

CHAPTER 7: 136—Wide World. 138—Drawings by Otto van Eersel. 139—Drawings by George V. Kelvin. 140, 141, 142—Drawings by Otto van Eersel. 143—Drawings by Adolph E. Brotman. 144, 145—Drawings by Fred Hausman. 147—Courtesy Union Carbide. 148—Courtesy Argonne National Laboratory—drawing by Dan Todd. 149—Courtesy Lookout Mountain Air Force Base. 150, 151—Courtesy U.S. Atomic Energy Commission, drawing by Lowell Hess. 152, 153—U.S. Atomic Energy Commission except bottom University of California. 154, 155—Ketchum McLeod and Grove, Atomic Energy of Canada Ltd.—S. M. Machlin, United Kingdom Atomic Energy Authority. 156, 157—Fritz Goro except drawings by Lowell Hess. 158—Arnold Newman. 159—Los Alamos Scientific Laboratories. 160—Jerry Cooke. 161—N. R. Farbman. 162, 163—General Electric Co.—Los Alamos Scientific Laboratories, U.S. Coast Guard Official Photo. 164—Courtesy U.S. Department of Agriculture. 165—A. Y. Owen.

CHAPTER 8: 166—Fritz Goro. 168—Drawings by Otto van Eersel. 170, 171, 172—Drawings by Adolph E. Brotman. 174, 175—Drawings by George V. Kelvin. 177—Ralph Morse. 178—*Photo aerienne* HEURTIER RENNES—Jean Marquis. 179—Don Almquist, Eliot Elisofon—Don Almquist, Eliot Elisofon. 180, 181—Carlo Bavagnoli. 182, 183—Fairchild Aerial Surveys, Jean Marquis. 184—J. R. Eyerman. 185—Ted Russell. 186, 187—Allis-Chalmers Manufacturing Co., Avco Everett Research Laboratories—drawing by Dan Todd. 188, 189—Sperry Gyroscope Co.—Ford Motor Co., drawing by Dan Todd. 190, 191—Fritz Goro. 194—Franklin D. Roosevelt Library, Hyde Park, New York. 195—Albert Fenn from Pix Inc., Brown Brothers, Marie Hansen—Walter Daran for TIME, Alfred Eisenstaedt from Pix Inc., Walter Bennett for TIME.

A
STONEHENGE
BOOK

XXXXXX